Spanish Film Policies and Gender

This book provides a comprehensive cultural and historical account of the key film policies put into place by the Spanish state between 1980 and 2010 through a gendered lens, framing these policies within the wider context of European film legislation.

Departing from the belief that there is no such thing as an objective and value-neutral approach to policy analysis because our society is organised around gender, this volume builds upon Pierre Bourdieu's theory of field to propose that film policies do not emerge in a vacuum because they respond to different demands from those agents involved in the field of the Spanish cinema. By so doing, it critically assesses how these policies have come into being, by whom, in response to what interests, how they have shaped the Spanish film industry, and how far and in what ways they have tackled gender inequality in the Spanish film industry.

This book will be of great interest to scholars and students of Spanish cinema, gender studies, film industry studies, film policy, and feminist film studies.

Jara Fernández Meneses is a lecturer in film studies at the University of Southampton, UK, where she teaches international film industry and film policy studies at undergraduate, postgraduate (taught) and PhD levels. Her research focuses on film policy, film industry and contemporary European cinema. Within this framework, she has published several articles in peer-reviewed journals and several chapters in edited books. She conducts her current research in two international research groups: TECMERIN (UC3M) and DeVisiones (UAM).

Routledge Focus on Media and Cultural Studies

Community Media and Identity in Ireland
Jack Rosenberry

Cultural Chauvinism
Intercultural Communication and the Politics of Superiority
Minabere Ibelema

Crowdfunding and Independence in Film and Music
Blanka Brzozowska and Patryk Galuszka

Building Communities of Trust
Creative Work for Social Change
Ann E. Feldman

Secrecy in Public Relations, Mediation and News Cultures
The Shadow World of the Media Sphere
Anne Cronin

Spanish Horror Film and Television in the 21st Century
Vicente Rodríguez Ortega and Rubén Romero Santos

Gender-Based Violence and Digital Media in South Africa
Millie Phiri

The Politics of Media Scarcity
Greg Elmer and Stephen J. Neville

Spanish Film Policies and Gender
Jara Fernández Meneses

Spanish Film Policies and Gender

Jara Fernández Meneses

LONDON AND NEW YORK

First published 2024
by Routledge
4 Park Square, Milton Park, Abingdon, Oxon OX14 4RN

and by Routledge
605 Third Avenue, New York, NY 10158

Routledge is an imprint of the Taylor & Francis Group, an informa business

© 2024 Jara Fernández Meneses

The right of Jara Fernández Meneses to be identified as author of this work has been asserted in accordance with sections 77 and 78 of the Copyright, Designs and Patents Act 1988.

All rights reserved. No part of this book may be reprinted or reproduced or utilised in any form or by any electronic, mechanical, or other means, now known or hereafter invented, including photocopying and recording, or in any information storage or retrieval system, without permission in writing from the publishers.

Trademark notice: Product or corporate names may be trademarks or registered trademarks, and are used only for identification and explanation without intent to infringe.

British Library Cataloguing-in-Publication Data
A catalogue record for this book is available from the British Library

Library of Congress Cataloging-in-Publication Data
Names: Meneses, Jara Fernández, author.
Title: Spanish film policies and gender / Jara Fernández Meneses.
Description: Abingdon, Oxon ; New York, NY : Routledge, 2024. | Includes bibliographical references and index.
Identifiers: LCCN 2023056662 (print) | LCCN 2023056663 (ebook) | ISBN 9781032439648 (hardback) | ISBN 9781003373087 (ebook)
Subjects: LCSH: Motion pictures and state--Spain. | Motion pictures--Law and legislation--Spain. | Motion picture industry--Spain--History. | Motion pictures--Production and direction--Spain. | Women in the motion picture industry--Spain.
Classification: LCC PN1995.9.P6 M46 2024 (print) | LCC PN1995.9.P6 (ebook) | DDC 791.4302/30946--dc23/eng/20231220
LC record available at https://lccn.loc.gov/2023056662
LC ebook record available at https://lccn.loc.gov/2023056663

ISBN: 978-1-032-43964-8 (hbk)
ISBN: 978-1-032-44618-9 (pbk)
ISBN: 978-1-003-37308-7 (ebk)

DOI: 10.4324/9781003373087

Typeset in Times New Roman
by KnowledgeWorks Global Ltd.

To my parents, Antonio and Patricia. *Os quiero. Gracias por todo.*

To my *tío* Ubaldo, who did not get to see this book published. *Te quiero.*

Contents

List of Figures	*viii*
Acknowledgements	*x*
Introduction	1
1 Contemporary Spanish Film Policies	10
2 The 1980s: The Making of a New Democratic Cinema	26
3 The 1990s: Hoping for a Better Future	59
4 The 2000s: Towards a Feminist Film Law?	94
Conclusion	131
Index	*136*

Figures

2.1	The presence of women in the above-the-line roles in the 1980s	40
2.2	The presence of women in the Film Editing department in the 1980s	42
2.3	The presence of women in the Production Management department in the 1980s	43
2.4	The presence of women in the Second Unit or Assistant Director department in the 1980s	44
2.5	The presence of women in the Art department in the 1980s	45
2.6	The presence of women in the Sound department in the 1980s	46
2.7	The presence of women in the Camera and Electrical department in the 1980s	47
2.8	The presence of women in the Costume and Wardrobe department in the 1980s	48
2.9	The presence of women in the Makeup and Hairdressing department in the 1980s	49
2.10	The presence of women in the Editorial department in the 1980s	50
2.11	The presence of women in the Script and Continuity department in the 1980s	51
2.12	The presence of women in the Music department in the 1980s	52
3.1	The Semprún Decree's main changes in the subsidies for film production	65
3.2	The presence of women working in the above-the-line roles in the 1990s	70
3.3	The presence of women in the Film Editing department in the 1990s	75
3.4	The presence of women in the Production Management department in the 1990s	76

3.5	The presence of women in the Second Unit or Assistant Director department in the 1990s	77
3.6	The presence of women in the Art department in the 1990s	78
3.7	The presence of women in the Sound department in the 1990s	79
3.8	The presence of women in the Camera and Electrical department in the 1990s	80
3.9	The presence of women in the Costume and Wardrobe department in the 1990s	81
3.10	The presence of women in the Makeup and Hairdressing department in the 1990s	82
3.11	The presence of women in the Editorial department in the 1990s	83
3.12	The presence of women in the Script and Continuity department in the 1990s	84
3.13	The presence of women in the Music department in the 1990s	85
3.14	The presence of women in the Cinematography department in the 1990s	86
4.1	The presence of women in the above-the-line roles in the 2000s	107
4.2	The presence of women in the Film Editing department in the 2000s	112
4.3	The presence of women in the Production Management department in the 2000s	113
4.4	The presence of women in the Second Unit or Assistant Director department in the 2000s	114
4.5	The presence of women in the Art department in the 2000s	115
4.6	The presence of women in the Sound department in the 2000s	116
4.7	The presence of women in the Camera and Electrical department in the 2000s	117
4.8	The presence of women in the Costume and Wardrobe department in the 2000s	118
4.9	The presence of women in the Makeup and Hairdressing department in the 2000s	119
4.10	The presence of women in the Editorial department in the 2000s	120
4.11	The presence of women in the Script and Continuity department in the 2000s	121
4.12	The presence of women in the Music department in the 2000s	122
4.13	The presence of women in the Cinematography department in the 2000s	123

Acknowledgements

This book would have not been possible without Suzanne Richardson, Commissioning Editor, Media, Cultural and Communications Studies at Routledge Taylor & Francis Group, who believed in this book since I showed her my proposal and who has encouraged and helped me throughout all the writing and editing process. I am greatly indebted to her. I am also very grateful to Stuti Goel, Editorial Assistant at Routledge Taylor & Francis Group, for all her kind help and guidance. I am also grateful to the anonymous reviewers for their constructive comments and suggestions.

Many thanks to Diego Blázquez Martin, Gonzalo de Pedro, Mónica Martin, Juan Andrés Segura García, Manuel Asín, Inés González, Diego Martínez, Leila Rodríguez and Concepción Cascajosa Virino for their help. To Carmen Calvo, Fernando Méndez Leite, Miguel Marías, Susana de la Sierra, Inés París and Fernando Lara for finding the time to talk to me and giving me essential insights on how the film laws assessed in this book came into being.

Professor Valeria Camporesi, Professor Nuria Triana-Toribio and Professor Sally Faulkner have taught me a lot about film studies and they have always believed in me. I am also honoured to call them my friends. I owe them much. Professor Hilary Owen helped me greatly in drafting this book proposal. I benefited enormously from her feedback.

My colleagues at the Film Department at the University of Southampton, where I moved in to take a new position as a Film Lecturer while writing this book, have helped me a lot to settle in. They made me feel very welcome from day one. I thank them all for their support and collegiality.

Special thanks go to my dad, Antonio Fernández Segura, who made the graphics for this book. To my dear friends in Madrid for always being there for me, regardless of the distance. You will always be my chosen family. To my nephew Ian and my goddaughter Paula. To Elsa and Pilar. To Ione. To Tere. To my friends in Southampton for making me feel like home. Thank you. To my partner, Nacho, I love you.

Finally, to all the film and media feminist scholars who came before me and showed me the way. Thank you.

This book is written as part of the research project +I+D+i "Cine y televisión en España en la era digital (2008–2022): nuevos agentes y espacios de intercambio en el panorama audiovisual", Proyecto financiado por la Agencia Estatal de Investigación (PID2022-140102NB-I00/AEI/10.13039/501100011033)

Introduction

Aims and objectives

Film policies have been essential to support the Spanish film industry since its inception due to its weak nature. Firstly, like most of the European film industries, the Spanish film industry suffers from the competence of Hollywood films and the major presence of the American majors' branches in the distribution sector. Secondly, the Spanish production sector is heavily reliant on public funding – this dependence has nonetheless been decreasing consistently since the 1980s to the present day with the involvement of the public and private television companies in the 2000s and the streaming platforms from 2015 onwards in film production, but public funding is still fundamental for the production of independent cinema in Spain. However, we need to bear in mind that the involvement of both televisions and streaming platforms in film production did not grow out of their good willing: it was imposed by law. Consequently, the study of the film policies is fundamental to understanding how the Spanish film industry is regulated and how it operates.

In a similar fashion, when it comes to gender inequality, the Spanish film industry is not running behind the international film industry (Liddy 2020, 1–18). In 2022 – last year with available data – 37% of film professionals were women in the Spanish film industry, against 63% of men. Looking closer to these numbers, we can observe how these roles are gendered because they are organised following traditional stereotypes of what type of work is deemed to be more suitable for women in the film industry.[1] Women have a major presence in the following departments: costume and wardrobe (80% women–20% men), makeup and hairdressing (73% women–27% men), artistic direction (63% women–37% men) and production management (55% women–45% men) (Cuenca Suárez 2023, 7–9). When it comes to either above-the-line roles or below-the-line technical roles, the presence of women decreases substantially: cinematography has 81% men and 19% women, scriptwriting has 28% women and 72% men, and direction has 24% women and 76% men.[2] How can this structural gender inequality be explained? I do not claim to have a definite answer, neither that I can fairly assess the multiple factors that explain it in this monograph. However, I argue that the film policies enacted between 1980 and 2010 are a key factor in explaining the sustaining gender inequality that structures the Spanish film industry, be it because film legislation does not address gender inequality or because when it has done it – as late as 2007 through the Law 55/2007 – the outcomes have not been as expected, as we will see in Chapter 4. Further research can delve deeper into the myriad of reasons that account for the gender imbalance that characterises the Spanish film industry.

This book is grounded in the idea that androcentric bias should be purged from film policy analysis, understanding androcentrism as the belief:

> that assumptions, concepts, beliefs, arguments, theories, methods, laws, policies, and institutions may all be 'gendered' [even those] that are officially 'gender-blind', 'gender-neutral' or 'equal opportunity' if [they] make it more difficult for women than for men to achieve the same outcome by following the same procedures.
>
> (Hawkesworth 1994, 105)

Consequently, this book departs from the belief that there is no such thing as an objective and value-neutral approach to policy analysis because our society is organised around gender, as it will be explained in detail in Chapter 1. This is the first book that provides a comprehensive historical and cultural account of the key film policies put into place by the Spanish state between 1980 and 2010 through a gendered lens by critically assessing how these policies have come into being, by whom, in response to what interests, and whether they have advanced gender equality in the Spanish film industry and, if so, how far and in what ways. The lack of scholarship on this subject demonstrates that women's film studies is still a field in which plenty of work needs to be done.

As Patrice Petro has argued:

> the project of reconstituting film history from a feminist perspective is not merely a matter of making visible the invisible. It also involves submitting regimes of visibility to a general critique of objectivity and subjectivity in the writing of film history and rethinking critical methods and theoretical procedures in contemporary film theory.
>
> (Pietro 2002, 32)

Following Petro, this book makes visible the invisible by bringing into light those women who had been working in above- and below-the-line roles between 1980 and 2010. These terms are used in this book as follows: above-the-line refers to those professions deemed to be the senior creative roles – director, executive producer/producer and scriptwriter. "Deemed to be" is used intentionally here; as many scholars before me, I do not agree with the traditional division of labour in the film industry which argues that artistic decisions are only made at the top of the hierarchical pyramid. Regarding below-the-line roles, the term refers to craft/technical labour. The informed reader will find well-known names such as the directors Pilar Miró, Josefina Molina or Isabel Coixet. However, he/she also will find the names of those lesser known directors, producers and scriptwriters who do not usually make it to the canon of Spanish cinema but who have indeed played a fundamental part in creating and developing what has come to be known as contemporary Spanish cinema. Regarding the roles below-the-line, I must acknowledge here the limitations of this research, limitations that will be detailed in the next section and that are closely related to the scarcity and inconsistency of the data available by the Spanish Film Institute (ICAA), the public funding body in charge of the film policies in Spain, about the artistic and technical crews that work in each Spanish film produced. Due to this scarcity and inconsistency, I have had to rely on the International Movie Data Base (IMDB), where the limitations and dispersion of data are even bigger. Therefore, for the sake of clarity and consistency in how data has been processed and how information has been presented, the reader will find percentages of the women working in below-the-line roles, but I have not been able to provide a systematic naming of these women. This endeavour is due to further research. This point is closely related with Petro's assertion that assessing film history from a feminist perspective involves questioning traditional regimes of objectivity and subjectivity. By acknowledging its own limitations, this research does not make any claim of historical objectivity or historical truth: I am well aware that the history that I trace and the conclusions that I have drawn are dependent on the data I have had access to. Consequently, both history and conclusions are fragmented, as the data they are based on is, and I have no doubt that they could be challenged and rewritten if/when new data comes available. I hope they will. Finally, this research has been approached from a cultural and an historical perspective, not from a theoretical one, so I have no intentions of subverting current film theory. I leave it to the film theorists, but, as I explain in Chapter 1, I do propose a new theoretical framework from which to approach the study of film policies – Pierre Bourdieu's theory of field – that I hope will open further lines of research.

As with many other studies that assess the role that women have had in cinema historically, this book confronts a range of methodological questions about *how* to research women's film history (Gledhill and Knight 2015, 2). These issues are addressed in the next section.

Methodological issues

As Shelley Cobb and Natalie Wreyford have already argued building upon Ann Oakley (1999), feminist research has traditionally leaned towards qualitative methods, such as interviews, to ensure that the experiences of women and other oppressed social groups are heard. However, when researching specific industrial contexts where there is gender inequality, hearing from members of the minority group only includes the experiences of those who have managed to be part of that labour market, but it does not tell us about the women who are not able to be part of that profession and the scale of their exclusion (Cobb and Wreyford 2017, 107–108). Even more, as Jacqueline Scott further argues, "quantitative approaches are essential to examine the processes of selection and exclusion that reflect and create gender inequalities" (Scott 2010, 223). The strength of quantitative research, Scott claims, is that it allows the understanding of patterns (Scott 2010, 224). Consequently, in order to have a broader view on how structural gender inequality operates, we need to resort to quantitative data; as Cobb and Wreyford have succinctly put it: "through quantitative methods the missing women, whilst still not heard, can at least be made visible by their astonishing absence" (Cobb and Wreyford 2017, 108).[3] As the reader will see, this book makes a systematic use of statistics to make visible the gender imbalance that has dominated the Spanish film industry between 1980 and 2010.

However, numbers never tell the complete story. Since the main interests of this book are to critically assess (1) whether Spanish film policies have contributed to gender equality in the film industry and (2) how Spanish film policies have come into being, a cultural studies approach is also used in this book. Consequently, I also rely on traditional materials of film history – archival research – and on qualitative methods – interviews with key agents in the field of Spanish cinema – in order to reach a broader understanding of how Spanish film policies have been created and how far and in what ways they have tackled gender inequality in the Spanish film industry.

Regarding archival research, this book uses the following sources:

- Close readings of the film laws.
- Reports from the European Audiovisual Observatory on gender equality.
- To gather information about the main struggles in the field of Spanish cinema between 1980 and 2010, the following primary sources have been used: daily newspapers, *El País*, *El Mundo* and *ABC*; both non-specialised and specialised film magazines, *Fotogramas*, *Cinemanía* and *Cahiers du Cinéma. España*; and, finally, the trade journal *Cineinforme*. These are the sites where the ongoing debates about the problems that the Spanish film industry faces take place in Spain. Therefore, they are primary sources to locate the demands raised by the key agents within the field of Spanish cinema and to determine which agents and institutions are engaged in the struggle to advance gender equality in the Spanish film industry.
- Reports from the ICAA. The ICAA issues yearly reports on the performance of the Spanish film industry and the films produced that qualify as Spanish each year. These reports are used to gather data on how many films have been produced yearly and who has directed them.

- IMDB.
- Reports from the Spanish Women's Filmmakers and Audiovisual Professionals Association, CIMA, created in 2006, that address gender inequality in the Spanish film industry.

This book also relies on the following interviews with policymakers and key agents in the field in order to provide first-hand testimonies on how the policies have been shaped and how they have contributed to the advancements of women in the Spanish film industry, General Directors of the ICAA and Ministers of Culture (1980–2010): Fernando Méndez Leite (1986–1988), Miguel Marías (1988–1990), Fernando Lara (2004–2009) and Carmen Calvo (Minister of Culture, 2004–2007). When it is not possible to arrange an interview, print interviews have been used, such as in the cases of Pilar Miró (General Director of ICAA, 1982–1985, deceased in 1997) and Jorge Semprún (Minister of Culture, 1988–1991, deceased in 2011). I have also interviewed Inés París, Head of CIMA between 2006 and 2012.

Unfortunately, the Spanish film industry does not have a film union such as the British Association of Cine-Technicians from where to extract data on the "movie workers" (Bell 2021, 2). Therefore, the process of gathering data on the presence of women in the Spanish film industry between 1980 and 2010 has been done as follows: firstly, I checked how many films were produced yearly and who directed them in the ICAA yearly reports (called *Anuarios del cine español*). Since these reports only contain systematic information on the directors but not on the producer and scriptwriter, neither on the below-the-line roles, I had to restore them to IMDB. Again, IMDB has only stable information on producers and scriptwriters throughout the decades, but not on the roles below-the-line. Therefore, the only categories that remain stable between 1980 and 2010 are Film Editing, Production Management, Second Unit or Assistant Director, Art Department, Sound Department, Camera and Electrical Department, Costume and Wardrobe, Makeup and Hairdressing, Editorial Department, Script and Continuity, Music Department and Cinematography. This is the reason why my focus has been on these categories, having to leave outside my analysis such important professions as Casting Director or Location Manager, on which data was too scattered throughout the decades for me to be able to draw any meaningful conclusions. I am aware of these exclusions.

The reader will also find that the figures are organised around how many films produced yearly have women working in below-the-line roles instead of the number of women working in each category. This is again a decision made because of the scarcity and inconsistency of the data available. As pointed out above, each category in the below-the-line roles contains incomplete information and, therefore, I did not want to add to the exclusions already present in this book by only counting the women who appear in IMDB knowing that there were many not listed in each category. I found fairer to count the films that had women working in each category to give a picture of the structural inequalities in the Spanish film industry. Again, I am the only one responsible for such exclusions.

As many feminist scholars before me, I am also concerned about intersectionality (Crenshaw 1989) and how the complex set of cross-cutting influences such as class, race, sexuality, ableism, age and other differences shape the construction and representation of identities, behaviour, and social relations and modify the experience of gender inequality. However, I have not incorporated other forms of inequality in my analysis for two main reasons: firstly, because there is very limited data on the multiple, intersecting and complex patterns of inequalities that cross class, race, sexuality, ableism, age and other differences that can support statistical analysis[4]; secondly, because this book's focus is on gender inequalities across different time periods and at different levels – above and below – the-line roles in the Spanish film industry throughout three decades. For these reasons, following Herminia Ibarra, this book focuses on the commonalities, rather than the differences, of women working in the Spanish film industry to argue that women are numerical minorities within both above- and below-the-line roles and that they are subjected to negative stereotypes and attributions concerning work-related competencies (Ibarra 1993, 65). However, an intersectional analysis of the inequalities in the Spanish film industry is essential because it will illustrate the ways different bases of discrimination and inequality interact. I leave this endeavour for further research.

Structure

This book is organised around three watershed pieces of legislation that mark turning points in the history of Spanish film policies since the advent of democracy in 1982 up to the last piece of legislation enacted in 2007. For the sake of clarity, the book follows a chronological timeline structured around the three decades the timeline covers.

Chapter 1: Contemporary Spanish Film Policies. This chapter starts by explaining how this book uses Pierre Bourdieu's theory of field to study film policies. This book then argues that the social and political context in which film policies emerge should be considered as a field – this is to say, that the film policies do not emerge in a vacuum because they respond to different demands from those agents involved in the field of the Spanish cinema: the policymakers in charge of the film policies and the film professionals, who gather in different associations that lobby to have their interests consecrated by the different film laws. Consequently, to have a whole understanding of how film policies operate, it is necessary to locate and interrogate the demands raised by the agents in the field, to identify who has raised them and what are the interests underlying them and, finally, to analyse whether these demands have been enshrined in law or not. From there, this chapter moves on to map out how the field of Spanish cinema has been constituted, how it operates, and

Introduction 7

who the key agents are within it. Finally, this chapter highlights why it is key to apply gendered lens to the study of film policies in order to unveil the fact that film policies are, as with many other aspects of our society, inflected by gender.

Chapter 2: The 1980s. Women Making Film Policies. This chapter focuses on the R.D. 3304/1983,[5] popularly known as the Miró Law, enacted under the first Socialist government led by the Socialist Party (PSOE; 1982–1986), when democracy was definitely established in Spain after the transition period (1975–1982). The Law was named after Pilar Miró, a cinephile female auteur in charge of the film policies in her position as Head of the ICAA between 1982 and 1985; this law ruled the Spanish film industry throughout the 1980s. The three key issues this chapter assesses are: firstly, which were the main competing interests in the field of Spanish cinema during the period when the country was creating a new cinema that had to convey its new democratic values and to what of those interests the Law enacted by Miró responded to; secondly, how far and in what ways Miró own status as a cinephile shaped her tastes and how these tastes were enshrined in the Law; finally, what effects did the Miró Law had over the film industry and, particularly, over the women working in the film industry.

Chapter 3: The 1990s. Hoping for a Better Future. In 1992, Spain achieved three milestones that secured its status as a fully modernised democratic nation on the global stage: the Barcelona Olympics, the Seville Expo '92 and Madrid's tenure as European City of Culture. In a similar fashion, a new generation of younger filmmakers entered the industry, with an unprecedented rise of women directors – with 158 first-time directors debuting feature-length films, 31 of whom were women. It has to be noted that since the beginning of the Transition period in 1975 up to the 1990s, very few women had directed films in Spain, such as Cecilia Bartolomé, Josefina Molina and Pilar Miró. The 1990s also saw the most important shifts in the Spanish film industry, due to its progressive globalisation and the birth of private television channels in 1990. This chapter, therefore, starts by mapping out what these changes were; secondly, it assesses how far and in what ways the R.D. 1282/1989,[6] popularly known as the Semprún Decree, enacted under Jorge Semprún's position as Minister of Culture (1988–1991) and Miguel Marías as Head of the ICAA(1988–1990), was essential in shaping those changes; finally, it traces whether the promise of a renewed generation entering the film industry in the early 1990s led to the establishment of solid careers for women or, to the contrary, it only advanced male careers.

Chapter 4: The 2000s. Towards a Feminist Film Law? The 2000s saw the first film law that included affirmative action measures directed towards the inclusion of women in the film industry, when the Socialist Party regained power in 2004 and passed the Law 55/2007 with Fernando Lara as Head of the ICAA (2004–2009) under Carmen Calvo's term as Minister of Culture (2004–2007)[7]. This chapter, therefore, undertakes a critical assessment of how this pioneering law came into being and how far the Law reconfigured the Spanish film industry in terms of tackling gender inequality, since gender equality is far from being achieved in the Spanish film industry. Can we, consequently, talk about a feminist film law?

By following this structure, this study aims to provide a critical historical overview of how Spanish film policies have developed throughout three decades and how they have tackled both the demands raised by the key agents in the field of Spanish cinema and the structural inequality of the Spanish film industry – either by a blatant inaction during the 1980s and 1990s or by well-intended measures whose positive effects are yet to be seen.

Notes

1 See Hesmondhalgh and Baker (2015, 23–36) for a comprehensive account of how segregation by sex operates in the cultural industries.
2 These numbers include both the above- and the below-the-line roles. Sara Cuenca includes the following in her study: wardrobe, makeup and hairdressing, special effects, production management, editing, artistic direction, cinematography, music, sound, production, scriptwriting and direction.
3 Quantitative methods also allow the researcher to counteract postfeminist discourses on how gender inequality is based on individual women's desires, choices and behaviours are the key reasons for remaining gender inequalities. For a comprehensive account of the discussion on quantitative versus qualitative methods in feminist film studies see Cobb and Wreyford 2017.
4 Neither the reports issued by the ICAA and CIMA nor the studies made by the Women's Institute, the public body dependent on the Ministry for Equality, set in 1983 that deal with gender inequality in Spain, acknowledge differences in class, race, sexuality, ableism, age or any other differences when addressing gender inequality in both the Spanish film industry and in Spanish society. The same happens with the reports issued by the European Audiovisual Observatory that deal with gender inequalities in the European film industry.
5 Real Decreto 3304/1983 de 28 de diciembre, sobre protección a la cinematografía.
6 Real Decreto 1282/1989, de 28 de agosto, de Ayudas a la Cinematografía.
7 Ley 55/2007, de 28 de diciembre, del Cine.

References

Bell, Melanie. 2021. *Movie Workers. The Women Who Made British Cinema*. Champaign, IL, USA: University of Illinois Press.
Cobb, Shelley and Wreyford, Natalie. 2017. "Data and responsibility: Towards a feminist methodology for producing historical data on women in the contemporary UK film industry". *Feminist Media Histories*, 3(3): 107–132.
Crenshaw, Kimberle. 1989. "Demarginalizing the intersection of race and sex: A black feminist critique of antidiscrimination doctrine, feminist theory and antiracist politics". *University of Chicago Legal Forum*, 1989(1): 39–167. https://scholarship.law.columbia.edu/faculty_scholarship/3007
Cuenca Suárez, Sara. 2023. *Informe Anual CIMA: la representación de las mujeres del sector cinematográfico del largometraje español*. Madrid: CIMA.

Gledhill, Christine and Knight, Julia. 2015. "Introduction". In *Doing Women's Film History: Reframing Cinemas, Past and Future*. (Julia Knight and Christine Gledhill eds.), 1–12. Champaign, IL, USA: University of Illinois Press.

Hawkesworth, Mary. 1994. "Policy studies within a feminist frame". *Policy Sciences*, 27(2/3): 97–118.

Hesmondhalgh, David and Baker, Sarah. 2015. "Sex, gender and work segregation in the cultural industries". *The Sociological Review*, 63: 23–36. https://doi.org/10.1111/1467-954X.12238.

Ibarra, Herminia. 1993. "Personal networks of women and minorities in management: A conceptual framework". *The Academy of Management Review*, 18(1): 57–87.

Liddy, Susan. 2020. "The Gendered Landscape in the International Film Industry: Continuity and Change". In *Women in the International Film Industry. Policy, Practice and Power*. (Susan Liddy ed.), 1–18. London, UK: Palgrave Macmillan.

Oakley Ann. 1999. "Paradigm wars: Some thoughts on a personal and public trajectory." *International Journal of Social Research Methodology* 2(3): 247–254.

Pietro, Patric. 2002. *Aftershocks of the New: Feminism and Film History*. New Brunswick, NJ, USA: Rutgers University Press.

Scott, Jacqueline. 2010. "Quantitative methods and gender inequalities", *International Journal of Social Research Methodology* 13(3): 223–236.

1 Contemporary Spanish Film Policies

Introduction

In order to critically address how film policies were created in Spain between 1980 and 2010 and how far and in what ways these policies have contributed to advance gender equality in the Spanish film industry, this book is informed, first, by Pierre Bourdieu's theory of field and habitus as specifically stated in *Distinction. A Social Critique of the Judgements of Taste* ([1984] 2010) and *The Rules of Art* ([1996] 2012). This book argues that the social and political context in which film policies emerge should be considered as a field; this is to say, that film policies do not emerge in a vacuum because they respond to different demands from those agents involved in the field of Spanish cinema: the policymakers in charge of the film policies and the film professionals, who gather in different associations that lobby to have their interests consecrated by the different film policies. This book, therefore, locates and interrogates the main demands raised by the agents in the field of Spanish cinema; secondly, it identifies whether those demands have been enshrined in the laws and how they have informed the laws. Finally, it provides an understanding of how the key policymakers have acquired their ideas about cinema and how those ideas have been reflected in the policies they have supported and developed.

Secondly, this book is grounded in the idea that feminism is a political movement committed to eradicate inequality between men and women, not without acknowledging the rich tradition of feminism and the multiple debates inside the movement (see Grant 1993 and Whelehan 1995, to name a few) as well as recognising that some feminists have argued for difference and complementarity rather than equality (Wilson 1986, 8). This book contends that there is no such thing as an objective and value-neutral policy approach because, as Beverly A. McPhail argues, "most policy analysis models (…) approach policy in a gender-neutral manner. This fact belies the many ways our society is organised around gender" (McPhail 2003, 39). Consequently, this book departs from the fundamental notion that androcentric bias should be purged from film policy analysis, as has been explained in Introduction.

A feminist policy analysis' key objective, therefore, is to analyse policy for its effect upon women with the goal of bringing to light the ways structural inequality and gender bias operate – particularly for this book, how structural inequality operates in the Spanish film industry and how far and in what ways film policies have tackled such inequality. In this sense, I follow Mary Lou Kendrigan recommendation that the definition of equality should be expanded (1991); bearing in mind that structural gender inequality exists in the Spanish film industry, policies that advocate for positive discrimination are required in order to grant the ground for women to achieve truly equality; therefore, instead of film policies that seek equal treatment – those that have been applied in the field of Spanish cinema up to the Law 55/2007 of 2007 – policies that advance the presence of women because they are women and therefore structurally discriminated in the film industry are necessary to level the field. Only by acknowledging such structural discrimination in the Spanish film industry, we can accomplish the study of film legislation through a gender lens.

The timeframe that concerns me starts in 1980 for two main reasons. Firstly, the victory of the Socialist Party (PSOE) in the general election of 1982 not only marks the moment when democracy was definitively established in Spain after the Transition (1975–1982), but it is also the time when the state began to implement a systematic cultural policy aimed at establishing a coherent legislative project that would protect the Spanish film industry. It was also the moment when Spanish film policies, following the French model, endorsed the notion that cinema had to be considered, above all, a cultural good that could not be left to the rules of the free market. Secondly, Spain joined the European Economic Community (EEC) in 1986 and the European Union (EU) in 1993. Spanish film policies therefore cannot be understood outside the European context. As it has been widely noted, the nation states across Europe protect and promote their indigenous film industries because cinema is deemed to be a cultural good. That is to say, a substantial way through which national identities are created. This notion, shaped against the domination of Hollywood films within the European markets that began after the First World War, is what ultimately justifies the protectionist film policies deployed by the European countries throughout the 20th and 21st centuries and by the supranational European funding mechanisms since 1988 (Guback 1969 and 1985, de Gracia 1989, Sorlin 1991, Dyer and Vincendeau 1992, Lev 1993, Hollows 1995, Finney 1996, Moran 1996, Nowell-Smith and Ricci 1998, Vincendeau 1998, Forbes and Street 2000, Mazdon 2000, Fowler 2002, Jäckel 2003, Elsaesser 2005, Bergfelder 2005, Rivi 2007, Wood 2007). Framing Spanish film policies within the broader European context is also determining to understand how far and in what ways Spain has implemented measures to foster gender equality in the film industry since Sweden was as for 2016, the only other European country with a mandatory policy to achieve gender equality in the film industry (EWA 2016, 72).

The studies that have dealt with the Spanish film industry and film policy so far have focused on the analysis of the structure and performance of the film industry and have just addressed the different pieces of legislation as part of the context in which the Spanish film industry is inscribed (Gómez B. de Castro 1989, Hopewell 1991, Álvarez Monzoncillo 1993, Besas 1995, Fernández Blanco 1998, Cuevas 1999, Jordan 2000, Monterde 2002 and 2006, Ansola 2003a/b/c, 2004 and 2006, Cerdán and Pena 2006, Padrós Reig and Muñoz Fernández 2008, Riambau and Torreiro 2008, Yáñez 2010).

There are nonetheless two pioneering studies that have accomplished an in-depth analysis of the film policies that depart from the usual approach to the study of Spanish film laws. That is to say, that do not conceive film legislation as a part of the background where the historical development of Spanish cinema takes place (Losilla 1989, Caparrós Lera 1992 and 2005, Monterde 1993, Gubern et al, [1995] 2010, Rodríguez and Gómez 2000, Díez Puertas 2003, to name but a few). Neither do they deal with censorship, one of the most studied aspects of Spanish film policies (Gubern and Font 1975, Gubern 1981, González Ballesteros 1981, Gil 2009, among others). These two studies are *La industria del cine en España: legislación y aspectos económicos 1896–1970* by Santiago Pozo Arenas, (1984) and *Historia de la política de fomento del cine español* by Antonio Vallés Copeiro del Villar, [1992] 2000). Pozo Arenas analyses the film legislation enacted between 1896 and 1970 in order to understand the films produced over that period. His main argument is that, since cinema is first and foremost an industry, it is impossible to fully understand it without taking into account the industrial, legislative and economic context in which it is produced. Vallés Copeiro del Villar focuses on the different measures the Spanish state has established to protect and promote the national film industry from 1986 up to 2000 and how these policies have affected the production, distribution and exhibition of Spanish films in the national market. Valuable though these works are, Pozo Arenas and Vallés Copeiro del Villar have not taken into account the broader cultural and social context that explains the development of the laws. To be more precise, both scholars analyse the political and economic context in which the laws were enacted and account for the film industry's economic problems that the laws were trying to solve. However, both scholars fail to explain why different film policies were applied throughout the years because their studies focus mainly on whether the laws had a positive or negative impact on the film industry, rather than analysing the demands that the laws were trying to meet. Neither Pozo Arenas, nor Vallés Copeiro del Villar bring to light the interests of those behind the laws. In other words, their studies seem to contend that the enactment of the laws ultimately responded to political decisions aimed at resolving the Spanish film industry's financial difficulties exclusively.

As for the scholars who have assessed the presence of women in the Spanish film industry, the focus has been on writing the stories of those female directors in film and television who have been made invisible by (usually male) scholarship who had written the canon of Spanish cinema: this has been the purpose of the works of Susan Martín-Márquez (1999), María Camí-Vela (2005), Trinidad Núñez Domínguez, Josefa María Silva Ortega and Teresa Vera Balanza (2012), Barbara Zecchi (2014), Concepción Cascajosa Virino (2015), María Concepción Martínez Tejedor (2016), Annette Scholz & Marta Álvarez (2018) and Sonia García-López (2021). These studies have been essential to bring to light the power imbalance and structural inequality that have always existed in the Spanish film and television industry and to reassess the importance of women in the creation and development of Spanish cinema and television. However, these studies reproduce traditional European paradigms of film historiography: that of the auteur who builds the national canon, making visible those female film creators who had been traditionally invisible. This book, nonetheless, aligns with the research paradigm that focuses on the institutional and economic conditions of cinema to address not only the conditions of those women working in above-the-line roles but of those who constitute, to use Melanie Bell's terminology, the "movie workers" (Bell 2021) – those women working in below-the-line roles. In so doing, this book aims to offer a wider picture on how gender inequality operates in the Spanish film industry.[1]

By addressing the film policies enacted between 1980 and 2010 through a gendered lens and by framing them within the wider context of European film policies, this book provides a systematic explanation of the Spanish film policies carried out since the beginning of democracy up to the present day *vis-à-vis* European regulations that have shaped them. Spanish film policies have always been studied as either part of Spanish cinema's historical background or as the instrument used to try to solve the economic problems of the Spanish film industry. However, Spanish film policies have never been considered in relation to the social demands that the policies were trying to meet and the interests and aesthetic preferences of those behind them. Neither have Spanish film policies been analysed closely in relation to the broader debates on European cultural policy, to which it is undoubtedly indebted. Above all, Spanish film policies have not systematically been studied valuing how far and in what ways they have contributed to foster gender equality in the Spanish film industry. This book aims to fill this lack of scholarship.

Bourdieu's theory of field

Bourdieu conceptualises modern society as an array of relative but structurally homologous fields of production, circulation, and consumption of various forms of cultural and material resources (for example, the fields of politics, economics, religion, cultural production, etc.) that are governed by their own rules of the game and offer their own particular economy of exchange and reward. As defined in *The Rules of Art*, field is the network of objective relations (of domination or subordination, of complementarity or antagonism) in which the agents are struggling to reach the positions that would allow them to obtain the kind of capital (namely, power) that is at stake in the field. The dynamic nature of the field implies that the subjects involved in it have the capacity to act upon its structure according to their interests. This ability is what turns them into agents. The structure of the field, therefore, is constituted by the positions agents occupy in it, the positions that the agents would perceive as worthy and would be able to occupy, and the strategies that the agents use in the struggle for occupying the positions they want. The dynamic nature of the field also implies that any change in an agent's position necessarily involves a change in the field's structure (Bourdieu [1996] 2012, 231).

Inherent to the theory of field is the notions of habitus. The concept of habitus was developed by Bourdieu throughout his career. In *Distinction*, he gives the clearest definition of habitus as "the dispositions of an agent or class of agents" (Bourdieu [1984] 2010, 94); that is, "the schemes of perception, appreciation and action" (Bourdieu [1984] 2010, 95) which allow agents "to produce classifiable practices and works, and the capacity to differentiate and appreciate these practice and products" (Bourdieu [1984] 2010, 166). Since "the schemes of the habitus [...] owe their specific efficacy to the fact that they function below the level of consciousness and language", they work as "the most fundamental principles of construction and evaluation of the social world" (Bourdieu [1984] 2010, 468). That is to say, the particular habitus of the agents or groups of agents with which they enter the field has a threefold effect. First, it will provide them with their "sense of place" (Bourdieu [1984] 2010, 469) within the field. Second, it will determine the positions that they would perceive as worthy and attainable. Finally, it will dictate the agents' ability to engage with and succeed in both the material and symbolic struggles they will have to carry out to reach the necessary capital to dominate a particular field.[2]

By relying in Bourdieu's theory of field, this book broadens the critical parameters that have underpinned the discussion on Spanish film policies, since, as explained before, studies in this field have been mainly concerned with the description of film policies and the impact they have had on the Spanish film industry, leaving aside in their analysis the sociological context in which policies have been created. Hence, they provide a fragmentary explanation of the political and social conditions that have produced the film policies in Spain.

The field of Spanish cinema

As I have argued already, in order to understand how and why the film policies have been created, we need to consider the political and social context in which the policies have been enacted as a field. This is so because the struggles with which these agents engage in order to have their demands consecrated by the laws explain the different film policies enacted throughout 1980 and 2010. For this reason, it is only by accounting for the changes in the positions that the main agents occupy within the field that we can critically address the diverse film policies established between 1980 and 2010.

As Bourdieu explains, in order to understand "the internal structure of the field" (Bourdieu [1996] 2012, 216) we need to account for "the structural properties linked to the positions [that the agents] occupy in the field" (Bourdieu [1996] 2012, 186). These properties, nonetheless, are "not generally evident except through the generic characteristics such as memberships of groups or institutions" (Bourdieu [1984] 2010, 5–6). Thus, the first task is to identify the agents within the field and the positions they occupy therein. As I have mentioned before, the main agents in the field of Spanish cinema are the policymakers in charge of the film policies and the film professionals who lobby for having their demands enshrined by law. While it is true that only the policymakers have the power to legislate cinema, the film professionals occupy positions within the field that give them the necessary power to take part in the struggle to establish what film policies are more suitable depending on their own interests.

The policymakers in charge of the film policies are clearly identifiable, since they either belong to the left-wing Socialist Party (PSOE) or the conservative Popular Party (PP), the two main parties that governed Spain between 1982 and 2010. However, it would be reductive to assert that their political affiliation is the only reason for the film policies they have enacted and promoted. It is true, nonetheless, that there are two evident differences concerning how both parties have approached the management of culture and cinema. First, when the PSOE has been in power, the Ministry of Culture has been a single entity (1982–1996 and 2004–2011), revealing the importance that culture had for the PSOE. On the other hand, the PP has always subsumed it under the Ministry of Education and Culture (1996–2000) or the Ministry of Education, Culture and Sports (2000–2004). Second, the heads of the Ministry of Culture under the PSOE have tended to be intellectuals (Jorge Semprún [1988–1991]), writers (César Antonio Molina [2007–2008]), filmmakers (Ángeles González Sinde [2009–2011]), or lawyers (Javier Solana [1982–1986], Jordi Solé Tura [1991–1993], Carmen Alborch [1993–1996] and Carmen Calvo [2004–2007]), whereas the PP has always put in charge of the management of culture agents with a more unified and technical profile: Esperanza Aguirre (1996–1999), Mariano Rajoy (1999–2000) and Pilar del Castillo (2000–2004), are all lawyers.

When it comes to the agents in charge of the film policies, there is no clear distinction. Since 1985, the ICAA has been headed by different agents who started their careers as film professionals, film critics or lawyers before becoming policymakers. Under the PSOE government, Pilar Miró (1983–1985) was a female film auteur; Fernando Méndez Leite (1986–1988), a film critic, filmmaker and television director, and Head of the National Film School (EOC) since 1994; Miguel Marías (1988–1990), a film critic and former Head of the Spanish Cinematheque; Enrique Balmaseda (1990–1992 and 1994–1996) a lawyer with expertise in European audiovisual media; Juan Miguel Lamet (1992–1994), producer and screenwriter; Fernando Lara (2004–2009), film critic, and, alongside Méndez Leite, a collaborator in the specialised film programme of the national Spanish television, (TVE), *La Noche del Cine Español*, and the director of the Valladolid International Film Festival between 1984 and 2004; finally, Ignasi Guardans (2009–2010) was, like Balmaseda, a lawyer with expertise in European audiovisual media. Under the PP, the ICAA was headed only by the film producer José María Otero. There is nonetheless a key difference that can be inferred from the different profiles of the ICAA's directors. In the same fashion that the PSOE valued culture as much as to have it managed by a single ministry, it put agents in control of the film policies who, it can be argued, had a cultural profile, like the Ministers of Culture. To be more precise, five of out of the seven Heads of the ICAA have had previous professions that engaged with the most cultural aspects of cinema, ranging from criticism, festival management and education to filmic heritage preservation and diffusion. On the other hand, the PP opted for a film professional with connections to the economic aspect of filmmaking.

In order to reach a better understanding of how those agents have come to support different film policies, and taking the above into account, it is necessary to explore the ways in which the policymakers' habitus has shaped their preferences for certain notions of cinema over others. Habitus is understood here as the ways these agents have socialised, the connections they have made, their aesthetic preferences and their acquisitions of ideas about cinema. According to the policymakers' habitus, they can be distinguished into two different, although not completely homogenous, groups. On the one hand, what the film historian José Enrique Monterde has labelled as the dissident film agents, those left-wing producers, directors and film critics who, since the mid-1950s, were opposing Francoist cinema (Monterde [1995] 2010, 278–293). These agents conceive that cinema has to serve, above all, as a vehicle for culture, as it will be explained in detail in the next chapter. On the other hand, those policymakers who believe that cinema has to be valued as a profitable industry as well. The different positions that these two groups have been occupying as Head of the ICAA have ultimately determined the film laws enacted between 1980 and 2010.

As noted previously, film professionals also participate in the discussion about what film policies are better. Beyond their own professional and corporate interests, their habitus, as in the case of the policymakers, also plays an important role on the type of films they support. Consequently, among the film professionals the division outlined above between the dissident film agents and those who support market-driven films also stands. However, film professionals have tended to gather into professional associations in order to defend their corporate interests rather than because they shared a particular habitus. The producers' associations have had more impact over the government's film policies: while during the 1980s producers' joined associations depending on whether they were struggling to have culturally- or market-driven films protected by the state – UPCE and AIPCE respectively – both associations merged in 1991 into FAPAE, that became the major producers' lobby from that moment onwards. The producers' association has been successively headed by Pedro Pérez (1993–1997 and 2003–2013), Gerardo Herrero (1997–1999) and Eduardo Campoy (1999–2003). The major struggle facing the FAPAE during the 1990s and the 2000s was against the private television companies that appeared in Spain in 1990. Since 1998, these companies gathered in UTECA which represented the private television companies Telecinco, Antena 3 and Sogecable. Cuatro and La Sexta joined UTECA in 2005 and 2006, respectively (Yáñez 2009, 39). Thus, the changes in the positions of the film professionals within the field greatly influenced the outcome of the laws enacted by the policymakers.

To conclude, Bourdieu's theory of field is the most appropriate theoretical framework to analyse film policies because it allows me to go beyond the mere description of the different film policies and the impact they have had over the film industry by critically assessing the political, social and economic context under which film policies emerge. Conceptualising such context as a dynamic field gives an in-depth explanation of how the process of creating film policies do actually work. Furthermore, Bourdieu's notion of habitus contributes to a wider understanding of how the different interests, aesthetic preferences and connections of those involved in the creation of the film policies have shaped them. Consequently, Bourdieu's theory of field allows me to give a more comprehensive account of the historical development of the film policies carried out by the subsequent Spanish governments between 1980 and 2010. However, Bourdieu's theory of cultural production is not enough to assess film policies from gendered lens. The following section will explain how to accomplish it and why it does matter.

Why studying film policies through gender lens matters

Feminist film theory was born within the "second wave" feminism of the late 1960s, which is characterised by Imelda Whelehan – and I am simplifying her description here widely for the sake of the argument's clarity – as the second peak of the feminist movement that recognised that, despite the movement's "first wave" success in enfranchising women with the political and legal system, the system itself propended towards institutionalised gender – and other – inequalities. Therefore, it was necessary to interrogate women's social and material conditions of existence in order to transform the social and economic status of women and the ideological discourses that sustained such status as well as to challenge the dominant ideological representations of femineity (Whelehan 1995, 3–5). According to Sue Thornham, feminist film theory was born when the American journal *Women and Film* was launched in 1972 (Thornham 1999, 9). It is not this chapter's aim to summarise feminist film theory's history and main debates – that has been done much better elsewhere (Kuhn 1982, Kaplan 1983, Thornham 1997 and 1999, Muvely and Backman Rogers 2015 and Hole, Jelaca, Kaplan and Petro 2017, to name but a few), but to locate this book within feminist film theory's main lines of research. Following Thornham, from the beginning, as stated in the editorial of *Women and Film,* the concern of feminist film theory has been to fight against the three oppressions that women face in cinema:

> women are oppressed within the film industry (they are 'receptionists, secretaries, odd job girls, prop girls' etc.); they are oppressed by being packaged as images (sex objects, victims or vampires); and lastly they are oppressed within film theory, by male critics who celebrate auteurs like Sirk or Hitchcock for their complexity or irony or for in some way rising above their material – often the humble 'woman's picture' or 'weepie' (...) Its desired outcome will be threefold: a transformation in film-making practice, an end to oppressive ideology and stereotyping, and the creation of a feminist critical aesthetics.
>
> (Thornham 1999, 9–10)

Consequently, the study of the film industry, its structure and its power imbalance has always been a key issue for feminist film theory.

The study of the film industry in a broader sense has been labelled as "political economy of film" as decoded by Janet Wasko ([1999] 2004) and Tom O'Regan (2008). The political economy conceives cinema as an economic institution rather than exclusively as a textual and aesthetic system. Within the political economy of film, cultural policy studies constitute a field in itself. As O'Regan notes in an article of 1992, Tony Bennet, Stuart Cunningham, Ian Hunter, Colin Mercer, Jennifer Craik, Toby Miller and other scholars associated with the Griffith University in Brisbane, especially since the founding of its Institute for Cultural Policy Studies (ICPS) in 1987, have called for the consideration of cultural policy as an object of study in its own right (1992, 411). O'Regan defines the focus for cultural policy studies as:

> [t]hose things which are called policy in political and bureaucratic terms – and these things, together with their agents and agencies, would constitute strategic targets for cultural policy studies.
>
> (O'Regan 1992, 412)

An important, albeit less recognised, field of research within cultural policy studies is film policy research. Albert Moran, also associated to the ICPS, is one of the most prominent scholars who has been systematically mapping and contributing to this field of research, as it can be seen in his pioneering edited volume *Film Policy. International, National and Regional Perspectives* (1996). Moran describes film policy as follows:

> [film policy] applies across a series of areas and institutions including production, distribution and exhibition, film education, film as visual art, and censorship. It may be prompted by an immediate practical need to analyse the effectiveness of existing policies, or it may be [...] more concerned with gaining broader understanding of the historical and social context that produced particular policies.
>
> (Moran 1998, 365)

This book aims to merge these two fields of research – feminist film theory and political economy of film with special emphasis on film policy research – in order to provide a comprehensive explanation on how far and in what ways the film laws enacted between 1980 and 2010 have tackled the Spanish film industry's structural gender inequality. As Susan Liddy brilliantly explains in the "Introduction" for her edited collection *Women in the International Film Industry: Policy, Practice, Power*, while there is some excellent scholarly work on gender inequality in Hollywood and the Swedish film industry – and also on the British film industry thanks to the work of Melanie Bell, Shelley Cobb, Linda Ruth Williams and Natalie Wreyford, amongst others, I may add – there is still plenty of work to do regarding other parts of the world (2020: 1); in fact, Liddy's collection itself does not include a chapter on gender inequality in the Spanish film industry. This book aims to fill such gap in scholarship. Moreover, as the research in Liddy's collection have shown, the international film industry is gendered. Consequently, it is paramount to assess how gender inequality operates and what governments are doing to solve it, because it is an international and lasting problem. This book aims to contribute to such discussion by providing a critical cultural history on how far and in what ways film policies have tackled gender inequality in Spain – one of the European Big 5 film industries – between 1980 and 2010 and what effects these policies have had over the film industry.

As it has been widely explored, gender inequality is not exclusive to the film industry, but it marks all the cultural and creative industries (CCI) (Conor, Gill and Taylor, 2015). As Rosalind Gill has already convincingly argued, it is necessary to point to the distinctiveness of how sexism and gender inequality operate in the CCI in the current post-feminist, neoliberal and individualistic moment, in which all the battles are supposed to have been won and, therefore gender inequality renders typically invisible and unspoken – or, at best, extremely difficult to voice because sexism is seen as something from the past that has been actually overcome (Gill 2014, 511; McRobbie 2004, 255).[3] Consequently, drawing on Joan Acker's notion of "gender regime", understood as "the ways that gender is part of organisational processes at a particular time, in a particular organisation" (Acker 2006, 8), this book considers the Spanish film industry as a "gender regime" and it focuses on how it operates by looking at the regulations that govern it – the film policies.[4] And it carries such analysis using a feminist policy analysis.

As Beverly A. McPhail has argued:

> a feminist policy analysis is an action-oriented model with the explicit goal of ending the sexist oppression of women. Thus, the policy is explicitly analysed for its effect upon women with the goal of shifting power differences in society, working towards the empowerment of women. A feminist policy analysis model acknowledges that there is no such thing as an objective and value-neutral policy approach.
>
> (McPhail 2003, 45)

To conclude, by relying on Bourdieu's theory of field and Acker's notion of "gender regime", this book uses feminist policy analysis to provide a new insight of an overlooked area in film policy research: how far and in what ways the Spanish film policies enacted between 1980 and 2010 have contributed to gender equality in the Spanish film industry. This approach seeks to provide a comprehensive cultural history of how these policies came into being in a gendered field, who enacted them, in response to what interests and demands from the key agents in the field and whether these policies have changed women's power imbalance within the film industry, or, to the contrary have maintained the traditional gendered roles that have been dominating the contemporary Spanish film industry. In so doing, this book aims to broaden the discussion not only on how gender inequality operates in the Spanish film industry, but also on how film policy can be analysed from a feminist perspective in order to understand the reasons why Spanish film policies have contributed to maintain the structural inequalities of the Spanish film industry between 1980 and 2010.

Notes

1 This institutional approach has also been used by in Fátima Arranz's pioneering book *Cine y género en España. Una investigación empírica* (2010) and by Elena Oroz and Mar Binimelis to analyse the presence of women directors in Spanish independent cinema in their 2020 article "Who counts? The presence of women directors in Spanish independent cinema through a data analysis of film circulation (2013–2018)".
2 Bourdieu's theory of field has been used to study contemporary Spanish cultural practices and contemporary Spanish cinema in the pioneering work of Paul Julian Smith (2000, 2003, 2006a/b, 2007, 2009, 2012). Similarly to Smith, Antonio Lázaro-Reboll and Andrew Willis in their edited volume *Spanish Popular Cinema* (2004) and Lázaro-Reboll in his *Spanish Horror Film* (2012) account for "the field of Spanish popular cinema" and "the field of Spanish horror" respectively in order to analyse the discursive structures through which Spanish popular cinema and Spanish horror films are produced, circulated and consumed. In so doing, they go beyond the dominant histories on Spanish cinema - or beyond the usual historical accounts of the development

of a particular genre by scholarship on Spanish cinema - to place the emphasis on examining the ways in which the cultural value of Spanish popular and horror cinema has been created. They accomplish this task by looking not only at the films and the filmmakers themselves but also at the institutions, cultural agents and paths of circulation that have shaped both popular genres. In her landmark study *Fans, Cinéfilos y Cinéfagos. Una aproximación a las culturas y los gustos cinematográficos* (2011), the Spanish media scholar Cristina Pujol Ozonas builds on Bourdieu's theory of cultural production, among others, to analyse the cultural, ideological and political implications of the tastes and discourses of Spanish cinephiles.

3 Gill defines sexism as "an agile, dynamic, changing and diverse set of malleable representations, discourses and practices of power" (2014, 517).

4 Deborah Jones and Judith K. Pringle have already applied Acker's concept of gender regime to their study of the New Zealand's film industry and how gender inequality operates amongst below-the-line films workers (Jones and Pringle 2015, 37–49)

References

Acker, Joan. 2006. "The gender regime of Swedish banks". *Scandinavian Journal of Management*, 22: 195–209

Álvarez-Monzoncillo, José María Álvarez (coord.). 1993. *La industria cinematográfica en España (1989–1991)*. Madrid: Ministerio de Cultura/ICAA.

Ansola, Txomin. 2003a. "La producción de cine en España durante la década de los noventa: una aproximación". *Área Abierta*, 6: 1–14.

Ansola, Txomin. 2003b. "La industria cinematográfica española en los tiempos del Partido Popular (1996–2002): viejos problemas, viejas recetas". *Archivos de la Filmoteca*, 45: 60–73.

Ansola, Txomin. 2003c. "Muchas sombras y pocas luces. La comercialización de las películas españolas durante la década de los noventa". *Zer. Revista de Estudios de Comunicación*, 14: 153–173.

Arranz, Fátima. 2010. *Cine y género en España. Una investigación empírica*. Madrid: Cátedra.

Bell, Melanie. 2021. *Movie Workers. The Women Who Made British Cinema*. Illinois: University of Illinois Press.

Bergfelder, Tim. 2005. "National, transnational or supranational cinema? Rethinking european film studies". *Media, Culture, Society*, 27(3): 315–331.

Besas, Peter. 1995. "The Financial Structure of Spanish Cinema". In *Refiguring Spain. Cinema, Media, Representation*, edited by Marsha Kinder, 241–259. Durham and London: Duke University Press.

Bourdieu, Pierre. 1984. *Distinction. A Social Critique of the Judgments of Taste*. London and New York: Routledge Classics.

Bourdieu, Pierre. 1986. "The Forms of Capital". In *Handbook of Theory and Research for the Sociology in Education*, edited by John Richardson, 241–258. New York, Westport and London: Greenwood Press.

Bourdieu, Pierre. 1993. *The Field of Cultural Production*. Cambridge: Polity Press.

Bourdieu, Pierre. 1996. *The Rules of Art*. Cambridge: Polity Press.

Camí-Vela, Maria. 2005. *Mujeres detrás de la cámara. Entrevistas con cineastas españolas 1990–2004*. Madrid: Ocho y Medio.

Caparrós Lera, José María. 1992. *El cine español de la democracia. De la muerte de Franco al "cambio" socialista*. Barcelona: Anthropos.

Caparrós Lera, José María. 2005. *La Pantalla Popular. El cine español durante el Gobierno de la derecha, 1996–2003*. Madrid: AKAL.
Cascajosa Virino, Concepción (ed.). 2015. *A New Gaze: Women Creators of Film and Television in Democratic Spain*. Newcastle-upon-Tyne: Cambridge Scholars Publisher.
Cerdán, Josexto y Pena, Javier. 2006. "Variaciones sobre la incertidumbre (1984–2000)". In *La nueva memoria: Historia(s) del Cine Español (1939–2000)*, edited by José Luis Castro de Paz, Julio Pérez Perucha and Santos Zunzunegui, 254–331. Vía Láctea Editorial.
Cobb, Shelley and Williams, Linda Ruth. 2020. "Histories of now: lisentening to women in British film". *Women's History Review*, 29(5): 890–902.
Cuevas, Antonio. 1999. *Economía cinematográfica: la producción y el comercio de películas*. Madrid: Imanógrafo.
de Gracia, Victoria. 1989. "Mass culture and sovereignty: The American challenge to European cinemas, 1920–1960". *The Journal of Modern History*, 61:(1) 53–87.
Díez Puertas, Emeterio. 2003. *Historia social del cine en España*. Madrid: Editorial Fundamentos.
Dyer, Richard and Vincendeau, Ginette (eds.). 1992. *Popular European Cinema*. London and New York: Routledge.
Elsaesser, Thomas. 2005. *European Cinema. Face to Face with Hollywood*. Amsterdam: Amsterdam University Press.
European Women's Audiovisual Network (EWA). 2016). *Where are the Women Directors in European Films? Gender Equality Report on Female Directors*. Strasbourg: EWA.
Fernández Blanco, Victor. 1998. *El cine y su público en España: un análisis económico*. Fundacion Autor, Sociedad General de Autores y Escritores.
Finney, Angus. 1996. *The State of European Cinema: A New Dose of Reality*. London: Cassell.
Forbes, Jill and Street, Sarah. 2000. *European Cinema. An Introduction*. New York: Palgrave Macmillan.
Fowler, Catherine (ed.). 2002. *European Cinema Reader*. London and New York: Routledge.
García López, Sonia. 2021. "Miradas invisibles: mujeres en la Escuela Oficial de Cinematografía (1947–1976)". *Journal of Spanish Cultural Studies*, Vol. 22, n°3: 311–322.
Gill, Rosalind. 2014. "Unspeakable Inequalities: Post feminism, entrepreneurial subjectivity, and the repudiation of sexism among cultural workers". *Social Politics*, 509–528.
Gómez Bermúdez de Castro, Ramiro. 1989. *La producción cinematográfica española. De la Transición a la Democracia (1976–1986)*. Bilbao: Ediciones Mensajero.
Grant, Judith. 1993. *Fundamental Feminism: Contesting the Core Concepts of Feminism Theory*. New York: Routledge.
González Ballesteros, Teodoro. 1981. *Aspectos jurídicos de la censura cinematográfica española*. Madrid: Universidad Complutense de Madrid.
Gil, Alberto. 2009. *La censura cinematográfica en España*. Madrid: Ediciones B.S.A.
Guback, Thomas. 1969. *The International Film Industry: Western Europe and America Since 1945*. Bloomington: Indiana University Press.
Guback, Thomas. 1985. "Hollywood's International Market". In *The American Film Industry*, edited by Tino Balio, 463–486. Wisconsin: The University of Wisconsin Press.

Gubern, Román. 1981. *La censura. Función política y ordenamiento jurídico bajo el franquismo (1936–1975)*. Barcelona: Editorial Península.
Gubern, Román and Font, Doménec. 1975. *Un cine para el cadalso. Cuarenta años de censura cinematográfica en España*. Barcelona: Euros.
Gubern, Román et al. [1995] 2010. *Historia del cine español*, Madrid: Cátedra.
Hawkesworth, Mary. 1994. "Policy Studies within a Feminist Frame". *Policy Sciences*, 27(2/3), *Feminism and Public Policy*: 97–118.
Hollows, Joanne. 1995. "Mass Culture and Political Economy". In *Approaches to Popular Film*, edited by Joanne Hollows and Mark Jancovich, 15–37. Manchester: Manchester University Press.
Hole, Kristin, Jelaca, Dijana, Kaplan, Elizabeth Ann and Petro, Patrice (eds.). 2017. *The Routledge Companion to Cinema and Gender*. London and New York: Routledge.
Hopewell, John. 1991. "Art and a Lack of Money: The Crises of the Spanish Film Industry, 1977–1990". *Quarterly Review of Film Studies*, 13(4) 113–122.
Jäckel, Anne. 2003. *European Film Industries*. London: BFI.
Jordan, Barry. 2000. "The Spanish Film Industry in the 1980s and 1990s". In *Contemporary Spanish Cultural Studies*, edited by Barry Jordan and Rikki Morgan-Tamosunas, 179–192. London: Arnold.
Jones, Deborah and Pringle, Judith K. 2015. "Unmanageable inequalities: sexism in the film industry". In *"Gender and Creative Labour"*, edited by Bridget Conor, Rosalind Gill and Stephanie Taylor, 37–49. *Sociological Review Monograph Series*, 63:S1.
Kendrigan, Mary Lou (ed.). 1991. *Gender differences: their impact on public policy*. New York: Greenwood Press.
Kaplan, Elizabeth. Ann. 1983. *Women and Film: Both Sides of the Camera*. New York and London: Methuen.
Kuhn, Annette. 1982. *Women's Pictures: Feminism and Cinema*. London: Routledge & Kegan Paul.
Lázaro-Reboll, Antonio. 2012. *Spanish Horror Film*, Edinburgh: Edinburgh University Press.
Lázaro-Reboll, Antonio and Willis, Andrew (eds.). 2004. *Spanish Popular Cinema*. Manchester: Manchester University Press.
Lev, Peter. 1993. *The Euro-American Cinema*. Austin: University of Texas Press.
Losilla, Carlos. 1989. "Legislación, industria y escritura". In *Escritos sobre el cine español (1937–1987)*, edited by Vicente Benet, 33–43. Valencia: Filmoteca Valenciana.
Liddy, Susan. 2020. "The Gendered Landscape in the International Film Industry: Continuity and Change". In *Women in the International Film Industry. Policy, Practice and Power*, edited by Susan Liddy, 1–18. Palgrave Macmillan.
Martín-Márquez, Susan. 1999. *Feminist Discourse and Spanish Cinema: Sight Unseen*. Oxford: Oxford University Press.
Martínez Tejedor. 2016. *Directoras pioneras del cine español: de los años veinte a los años setenta*. Madrid: Fundación First Team.
Mazdon, Lucy. 2000. *Encore Hollywood: Remaking French Cinema*. London: BFI.
McPhail, Beverly A. 2003. "A feminist policy analysis framework". *The Social Policy Journal*, 2(2–3): 39–61.
McRobbie, Angela. 2004. "Post-feminism and popular culture". *Feminist Media Studies*, 4(3): 255–264.
Monterde, José Enrique. 1993. *Veinte años de cine español (1973–1992). Un cine bajo la paradoja*. Barcelona: Paidos.

Monterde, José Enrique. 2002. "Panorama desde el siglo XXI. La industria cinematográfica de los años noventa". In *Semillas de futuro: cine español 1990–2001*, edited by Carlos F Heredero, and Antonio Santamarina, 88–127. Madrid: Sociedad Estatal Nuevo Milenio.

Monterde, José Enrique. 2006. "Cuando el destino nos alcance. Contextos del último cine español". In *Miradas para un nuevo milenio. Fragmentos para una historia futura del cine español*, edited by Hilario J Rodríguez, 53–56. 36 Festival de Cine de Alcalá de Henares.

Moran, Albert (ed.). 1996. *Film Policy. International, National and Regional Perspectives*. London and New York: Routledge.

Moran, Albert. 1998. "Film Policy: Hollywood and Beyond". In *The Oxford Guide to Film Studies*, edited by John Hill and Church Pamela Gibson, 365–370. Oxford: Oxford University Press.

Nowell-Smith, Geoffrey and Ricci, Steve (eds.). 1998. *Hollywood and Europe. Economics, Culture, National Identity: 1945–1995*. London: BFI.

Muvley, Laura and Blackman Rogers, Anna (eds.). 2015. *Feminisms. Diversity, Difference and Multiciplity in Contemporary Film Cultures*. Amsterdam: Amsterdam University Press.

Núñez Domínguez, Trinidad, Silva Ortega, Josefa María and Vera Balanza, Teresa (coords.). 2012. *Directoras del cine español. Ayer, hoy y mañana mostrando talentos*. Sevilla: Universidad de Sevilla.

O'Reagan, Tom. 2008. "The Political Economy of Film". In *SAGE Handbook of Film Studies*, edited by James Donald and Michael Renov, 244–262. The London: SAGE.

Oroz, Elena & Binimelis, Mar. 2020. "Who counts? The presence of women directors in Spanish independent cinema through a data analysis of film circulation (2013–2018)". *Communication & Society*, 33(3): 101–118.

Padrós-Reig, Carlos y Muñoz-Fernández, Marc. 2008. "Efectos económicos de la normativa de protección y fomento de la cinematografía en España". In *Estudios sobre Derecho y Economía del Cine*, edited by Carlos Padrós-Reig and Jordi López-Sintas, 43–79. Barcelona: Atelier.

Pozo Arenas, Santiago. 1984. *La industria del cine en España: legislación y aspectos económicos*. Barcelona: Publicacions i Edicions de la Universitat de Barcelona.

Pujol Ozonas, Cristina. 2011. *Fans, Cinéfilos y Cinéfagos. Una aproximación a las culturas y los gustos cinematográficos*. Barcelona: Editoria UOC.

Rodríguez, Eduardo and Gómez, Concha. 2000. "El cine de la democracia (1978–1999)". In *Un siglo de cine español*, edited by Román Gubern, 191–245. Madrid: Cuadernos de la Academia, Academia de las Artes y las Ciencias Cinematográficas.

Riambau, Esteve and Torreiro, Casimiro. 2008. *Productores en el cine español. Estado, dependencias y mercado*. Madrid: Cátedra/Filmoteca Española.

Rivi, Luisa. 2007. *European Cinema After 1989: Cultural Identity and Transnational Production*. New York: Palgrave McMillan.

Scholz, Annette and Álvarez, Marta (eds.). 2018. *Cineastas emergentes: mujeres en el cine del siglo XXI*. Madrid: Iberoamericana Editorial.

Smith, Paul Julian. 2000. *The Moderns: Time, Space and Subjectivity in Contemporary Spanish Culture*. Oxford: Oxford University Press.

Smith, Paul Julian. 2003. *Contemporary Spanish Culture: TV, Fashion, Art and Film*, Cambridge: Polity Press.

Smith, Paul Julian. 2006a. *Television in Spain: From Franco to Almodóvar*. London: Tamesis Books.

Smith, Paul Julian. 2006b. *Spanish Visual Culture: Cinema, Television, Internet*. Manchester: Manchester University Press.
Smith, Paul Julian. 2007. "Introduction: New Approaches to Spanish Television". *Journal of Spanish Cultural Studies*, 8:1: 1–4.
Smith, Paul Julian. 2009. *Spanish Screen Fiction. Between Cinema and Television*. Liverpool: The University of Liverpool Press.
Smith, Paul Julian. 2012. *Spanish Practices: Literature, Cinema, Television*. London: Legenda Movie Image.
Sorlin, Pierre. 1991. *European Cinemas, European Societies, 1939–1990*. London and New York: Routledge.
Thornham, Sue. 1997. *Passionate Detachments: An Introduction to Feminist Film Theory*. London: Arnold
Thornham, Sue (ed.). 1999. *Feminist Film Theory: A Reader*. Edinburgh: Edinburgh University Press.
Vallés Copeiro del Villar, Antonio. [1992]2000. *Historia de la política del fomento del cine español*. Valencia: Filmoteca de la Generalitat Valenciana.
Vincendeau, Ginette. 1998. "Issues on European Cinema". In *The Oxford Guide to Film Studies*, edited by John Hill and Pamela Gibson, 440–448. New York: Oxford University Press.
Whelehan, Imelda. 1995. *Modern feminism thought: from second wave to "postfeminism"*. Edinburgh: Edinburgh University Press.
Wilson, Elisabeth. 1986. *Hidden Agendas: Theory, Politics,and Experience in the Women's Movement*. London: Tavistock Publications.
Wood, Mary P. 2007. *Contemporary European Cinema*, London: Hodder Arnold.
Zecchi, Barbara. 2014. *Desenfocadas: cineastas españolas y discursos de género*. Vilassar de Dalt; Icaria.
Wasko, Janet. [1999] 2004. "The Political Economy of Film". In *A Companion to Film Theory*, edited by Toby Miller and Robert Stam, 221–233. Oxford: Blackwell Publishing.
Wreyford, Natalie. 2018. *Gender Inequality in Screenwriting Work*. Springer International Publishing AG.
Yáñez, Jara. 2010. *La artimética de la creación. Entrevistas con productores del cine español contemporáneo*. 39 Festival de Cine de Alcalá de Henares-Comunidad de Madrid.

2 The 1980s[1]
The Making of a New Democratic Cinema

Introduction

The Miró Law has been one of the most studied pieces of legislation by Spanish film scholars throughout the decades because it was passed at a crucial moment of Spanish history: the end of the Transition period (1975–1982) and at the birth of a new democratic Spain when the PSOE won the elections in 1982.[2] As Nuria Triana-Toribio argues, by the time this modern Spain was being built legally and socially, the new cinema that could depict and convey the democratic values had to be defined as well; the Miró Law was the main instrument through which the PSOE aimed to produce this new democratic cinema (Triana-Toribio 2003, 109–111). Likewise, the Law's relevance also lies in the fact that funding policies it established became the major support for the production of films during the years it was in force (1984–1989) (Gómez B. de Castro 1988, 248 and Ansola 2004, 117). This chapter aims are twofold: firstly, to propose a different reading of the Law's main objectives and effects that depart from the tropes already established by the scholarship on the subject. Secondly, to assess how far and in what ways the presence of a female policymaker behind the shaping of the Law fostered feminist film policies.

Initially, this chapter addresses the key arguments and debates around the Law that scholars have established and to propose that the Law should be reframed within Pierre Bourdieu's theory of field to reach a better understanding of the Law's aims. This is so because this chapter contends that the Miró Law is the result of the victory of the dissident film agents over the field of Spanish cinema in the 1980s. As Manuel Palacio affirms, cinema became one of the major cultural spaces of resistance to the dictatorship from the mid-1950s onwards. Taking part in the dissident film culture of the specialised film magazines and the cine-club movement became one of the major means through which the Spanish left-wing movement exercised its opposition to the dictatorship (Palacio 2011, 23). Consequently, it is necessary to understand how the field of Spanish cinema operated in the 1980s and how the dissident film agents came to be a group that reached the positions of power to have the film policies they wanted consecrated by the Law.

DOI: 10.4324/9781003373087-3

This chapter also contends that the Miró Law should be framed within the European modes of cultural production; this is to say, this chapter argues that the Law was enacted following the principles of the new film policies that the European countries began to carry out from the 1970s onwards because the Law aimed to create a Spanish cinema that could be in dialogue with other European cinemas. As Jill Forbes and Sarah Street explain, from the 1970s onwards, "state intervention in cinema [in Europe] became overtly cultural rather than implicitly industrial and films were subsidised in the same way, although less generously, as other forms of art such as theatre or opera" (Forbes and Street 2000, 21). This mode of state intervention in cinema has been labelled by Thomas Elseasser as "the cultural mode of production" (Elseasser 2005, 69). Thus, to better understand the Miró Law's objectives, it is necessary to account for how the PSOE embraced this "cultural mode of production", explaining the role that culture had for the PSOE and the paradigm of cultural policy under which the Miró Law was conceived.

This chapter claims that, according to Bourdieu's notion of habitus, in order to fully comprehend the film policies that the Miró Law promoted, Pilar Miró's aesthetic preferences and her ideas about the role that films have to fulfill in society, have to be brought to light. Likewise, it is necessary to assess how far and in what ways she being a female policymaker shaped her film policies. Due to her education and socialisation, Miró has to be considered a cinephile, understanding cinephilia as Antoine de Baecque and Thierry Frémaux first defined it in their article "La cinéphilie ou l'invention d'une culture", which traces the history of the French cinephilia.[3] According to Baecque and Frémaux, cinephilia, in its very basic meaning, is the love of cinema. In a broader sense, it is a system of cultural organisation composed by rites of watching films, speaking about them and then disseminating discourses about cinema. Baecque and Frémaux highlight differences between two generations of cinephiles: the first one, located between the 1950s and the 1960s around the critics of *Cahiers du Cinéma*, idolised the films made by auteurs through the practice of film criticism (1995, 133–142).[4] Miró belonged to the first generation of cinephiles or, in Cristina Pujol Ozona's categorisation of the Spanish context, the classic cinephilia, as it will be explained later (Ozona 2011, 127–146).

The field of Spanish cinema in the 1980s: The Miró Law and the new democratic cinema

As it has been amply studied, the Miró Law was enacted when the Spanish production sector was in deep crisis. Censorship had been abolished in 1977 and the film market was liberalised for the first time in forty years, allowing distributors to import as many foreign films as they wanted.[5] As a result, the home market was flooded with foreign films previously banned, especially

Hollywood films which appealed to national audiences more than national production. Subsequently, there was a decrease of 30 million spectators and losses of 1,092 million pesetas (6,500,000€/£5,700,000) for Spanish produced films between 1978 and 1979. Furthermore, film production dropped from 107 films made in 1978 to 89 films in 1979 (Ansola 2004, 104). Similarly, the end of censorship led to a massive production of S-rated films in the late 1970s: those low-budget genre films (mainly soft pornography, sex comedies and horror films) labelled as subproducts by many Spanish film studies scholars (Gómez B. de Castro 1988, Heredero 1991 and 1998, Monterde 1993, Riambau [1995] 2010) because of their low-quality aesthetic values.[6] As Triana-Toribio points out, the main aim of the Law was to end this S-rated production because, thematically and aesthetically, it "represented the last vestiges of the Francoist cinema apparatus" (Triana-Toribio 2003, 116). The S-rating was replaced by a new X-rating for those films considered to portray excessive sex or violence. The new X-rated production was no longer entitled to receive any state funding; thus, the number of films that were entitled to receive it was severely limited (Gómez B. de Castro 1988, Losilla 1989, Hopewell 1991, Monterde 1993, Riambau [1995] 2010, Triana-Toribio 2003). Miró herself explained the aims of the Law in the following terms:

> To put an end to a situation in which one-third of the national productions were S-rated films, another third false co-productions exclusively made to obtain dubbing licenses, and only the remaining third good films, the following measures were taken. The good films were promoted, and all co-productions closely observed; the creation of special X-rated movie theatres made the S rating unnecessary. In addition, the distribution of Spanish films was promoted by increased publicity at international film festivals and a greater frequency of Spanish film weeks abroad.
>
> (Miró 1990, 44)

In order to promote those "good films" a new advance subsidy, which was never previously considered by Spanish film legislation, and which was inspired by the French *avances sur recettes* system, was introduced. The subsidy was to be paid in advance to producers and directors by resorting to the Film Protection Fund. This advance subsidy, only to be refunded if the subsequent box-office returns allowed it, was specially designed to encourage the production of quality films, films directed by novel directors, those specially aimed at children and experimental films (R.D. 3304/1983/Preámbulo). It has to be noted that not a single measure to promote the presence of women in the film industry was taken. The Miró Law maintained the automatic subsidy of 15% of box-office returns to which any non-X-rated Spanish film was entitled to during the first four years of its commercialisation.[7] Besides the advance subsidy and the automatic subsidy, the Law also granted 25% (of box-office returns) more for those films considered to be of special quality and another

25% for films budgeted at more than 55 million pesetas (330,000€/£277,000). As those subsidies were cumulative, a film could be financed up to 65% entirely with public funds. Since the fact that selective funding was directed to the production of quality films has been the Law's most controversial aspect for scholars who have addressed it, this chapter provides a different reading of what was understood by quality films in the 1980s and why the Law placed emphasis on the production of those types of films.

Overall, the Miró Law has been considered something of a failure by most of the Spanish film studies scholars due to the negative impact it had both on the Spanish film industry and over the visual and narrative style of the films it funded. Regarding the impact the Law had on the Spanish film industry, the main criticism has been that the Law not only failed in triggering the recovery of the Spanish film industry (Besas 1985, 230–231, Hopewell 1991, 117) but it also exacerbated its traditional problems: its undercapitalisation and its atomisation (Gómez B. de Castro 1988, 248, Hopewell 1991, 116, Vallés [1992] 2000, 14–15, Fernández Blanco 1998, 13, Trenzado Romero 1999, 173 and Ansola 2004, 114). Firstly, rather than increasing, film production dropped from 99 films in 1980 to only 38 films in 1989. Secondly, the advance subsidy made private investment virtually disappear since many production companies were created purely so that they could have access to it. Hopewell has argued that the advance subsidy "released Spanish directors [and producers] from countervailing market pressures, which would derive from investing substantial sums of their money in a project. Filmmakers could make the films they wanted to make while ignoring their marketability" (1991, 119). Consequently, the attempt to create an independent industrial sector that could carry out a continued production activity failed, since the traditional role of producer changed to that of director–producer (Gómez B. de Castro 1989, 126–138, Monterde 1993. 105, Riambau [1995] 2010, 404). Since in order to obtain the advance subsidy, the artistic criterium prevailed over the film's potential marketability, directors no longer needed professional producers, because they came to act as their own producers (Ansola 2004, 115).

Scholars have also pointed out two other negative consequences derived from the implementation of the advance subsidy. Firstly, as subsidies were cumulative, profits were assured at the financing stage and not at the box office (Monterde 1993, 105 and Besas 1995, 241).[8] For instance, *Tasio* (Montxo Armendariz, 1984), produced by Elías Querejeta, was awarded 50 million pesetas (300,000€/£252,000) as an advance subsidy. It was also awarded another 25 million (150,000€/£125,000) by the Basque government and it gained a further 30 million (180,000€/£150,000) by pre-selling the broadcasting rights to the Spanish National Television (TVE). With a budget of 100 million (600,000€/£500,000), the film gained 5 million (30,000€/£25,000) even before being released (Ansola 2004, 116). Secondly, most of the subsidised films did not perform well at the box-office and, therefore, were unable to refund the advance subsidy to the Film Protection Fund. *El caballero del dragón*

(Fernando Colomo, 1985) is a case in point. It was awarded 132 million pesetas (800,000€/£672,000), but it made only 71 million (425,000€/£357,000) at the box-office (Riambau [1995] 2010, 435).

In respect of whether the Law shaped the narrative and visual style of Spanish films, the major criticism made in subsequent studies is that, since the advance subsidy was awarded by a Sub-committee for Technical Valorisation which evaluated the projects and allocated the money on the basis of the quality of the applications, the filmmakers conceived their projects purely to satisfy the sub-committee's tastes rather than to satisfy the tastes of mainstream audiences.[9] Therefore, a standardised production based on the quality cinema criterium emerged (Hopewell 1986, Zunzunegui 1988, Losilla 1989, Heredero 1991 and 1998, Monterde 1993, Riambau [1995] 2010, Trenzado Romero 1999, Ansola 2004). According to these scholars, the Law fostered an auteurist art-cinema, aimed at being successfully exported to Europe and at competing in prestigious international film festivals. This standardised production took the form of literary adaptations and costume dramas set either in the Civil War or the post-war period, primarily characterised by their high production values, their standardised visual and narrative style and their polished look. These films were fundamentally designed to both retrieve the historical past altered by Francoism and to reassess the Spanish progressive cultural heritage silenced by the dictatorship.

Los santos inocentes (Mario Camus, 1984) is one of the most cited films as paradigmatic of the production fostered by the Miró Law, even though the film was produced before the Law was actually passed. Triana-Toribio argues that *Los santos inocentes* is the best example of the good films promoted by the law since it became canonical almost as soon as it was released, it was "a box office success, it was widely seen outside Spain, and it received critical prestige and prestigious awards" (Triana-Toribio 2003, 122). Therefore, the film worked perfectly as an "international calling card" that, for Triana-Toribio, is one of the most important roles that good films had to fulfil (Triana-Toribio 2003, 113). Finally, the film is a literary adaptation of a short novel by the oppositional writer Miguel Delibes, a fact that not only brings "the legitimising power of 'high art'" to the film but also makes it "a celebration of a kind of Spanish cultural heritage that debunks or deflates Francoist myths of achievement" (Triana-Toribio 2003, 123).

One could question whether the Law led in fact to a standardised production, since the advance subsidy was awarded to such disparate films as *Tasio, El caballero del dragon, Se infiel y no mires con quién* (Fernando Trueba, 1985), *La vieja música* (Mario Camus, 1985), *Bandera negra* (Pedro Olea, 1986), *El Lute: camina o revienta* (Vicente Aranda 1987), *El pecador impecable* (Augusto Martínez Torres, 1987) or *Tu novia está loca* (Enrique Urbizu, 1988), to name but a few (Bermúdez de Castro 1989, 251–253 and 266–267).[10] Not to mention that Almodóvar's *Matador* (1986) and *La ley del deseo* (1987) also benefited from the Law's funding policies with advance subsidies of 35 and 38 million pesetas respectively (210,300€/£185,000 and 228,000€/£200,000) (Bermúdez de Castro 1989, 252 and 266). These examples prove that the quality criterion encompassed a wider range of films than exclusively literary adaptations and costume dramas. In fact, these films could easily fit within any of the following genres: biopics – *Tasio* and *El Lute*; fantasy or science-fiction – *El caballero del dragón*; comedy – *Se infiel y no mires con quién*, *El pecador impecable* and *Tu novia está loca*; drama – *La vieja música* – or thrillers – *Bandera negra*. Clearly, the Miró Law did not promote only auteurist art-cinema, it also funded genre films. Thus, the Law, rather than simply eradicating genre films, fostered different genres that could act as substitutes for subproducts. Furthermore, it is also questionable that films such as *Se infiel y no mires con quién*, *El pecador impecable* or *Tu novia está loca* were meant to be distributed in Europe, since their specific cultural references and local allusions are only intelligible to an indigenous audience. Similarly, it is also debatable that *El caballero del dragón* or *El Lute*, to mention just two examples, were intended to participate in prestigious international film festivals rather than to be consumed by national audiences.

Although it appears that the Miró Law did not become the expected instrument through which the Spanish production sector could finally overcome the crisis it was facing in the late 1970s and early 1980s, as explained above, the Law was enacted following the cultural mode of production mentioned before. It is therefore necessary to address how the PSOE's cultural policy endorsed this paradigm. As Manuel Trenzado Romero has suggested, the PSOE's cultural policy should be framed within the democratic paradigm (1999, 144). José Vidal-Beneyto defines the democratic paradigm as the cultural policy carried out by the European countries from the 1950s onwards that sought to democratise the production and consumption of cultural goods which had been traditionally in the hands of the upper classes as a result of patronage. In the light of this new paradigm, the creation of culture was no longer decided only by the upper classes, but instead *by* the people *for* the people, since it was the people, through their political representatives, who chose which cultural producers were to be helped and protected by the state (Vidal-Beneyto 1981, 126–127). The PSOE's manifesto for the general elections of 1979 explicitly stated that the PSOE had as a main objective in its cultural policy to achieve a truly cultural democracy based on the active participation of both the individuals and collectives in the creation, production and enjoyment of the cultural goods (Programa Electoral del Partido Socialista 1979, 24).

The democratic paradigm was embraced later on by Jack Lang when he was appointed Ministry of Culture by François Mitterrand in 1981. Lang's key concept during his time in office (1981–1986 and 1988–1993) was "*l'état culturel*" (the cultural State). Incorporated within this idea, Lang's policies were directed towards an unprecedented increase in cultural funding. The Ministry's budget was doubled in 1982 and gradually increased to represent nearly 1% of the state budget. The idea was to widen the Ministry's scope of activities and to guarantee a steady state support for the production, protection, promotion and consumption of cultural goods. Regarding the film industry, "Lang believed fervently that it was the state's responsibility to facilitate the filmmakers' task" (Hayward 1993, 381–382). Lang's cultural policies became the model for Javier Solana's own cultural policies during his time as Minister of Culture between 1982 and 1986. Following this paradigm, the PSOE defined culture in its manifesto of 1982 as a basic right for all citizens and one of the key means to achieve a fairer, freer and more solidary society (Programa Electoral del Partido Socialista 1982, 25). Therefore, in 1982 the PSOE directed its focus at the cultural arena and assumed as its principal task the creation of the necessary conditions to assure the production, protection, promotion and consumption of cultural goods and to guarantee a free and equal access to them (Rubio Aróstegui 2003, 111). Ultimately, the PSOE's main aim was to create the conditions that would guarantee the birth of a new democratic culture for Spanish people who had faced forty years of cultural isolation, state-controlled cultural practices, censorship and massive exile of artists and intellectuals. Regarding the film policy, according to a 1982 internal report of the PSOE on film policy, it was stated that cinema could not be defined exclusively as a commercial good, but as a cultural good (Llinás 1987, 16–26). That is to say, cinema was conceived as a means through which culture could be disseminated among Spanish people and as a major means through which Spanish people could participate in the production and consumption of cultural goods. With this in mind, it could be argued that the aim of the Miró Law went beyond merely solving the problems of the Spanish film industry. The ultimate objective was to promote a cinema with cultural values which contributed to the creation of a fairer and freer society and the quality cinema was the key instrument to achieve this goal.

As Triana-Toribio argues, the imminent entry of Spain in the EEC made Miró to promote a cinema that could be in dialogue with other European cinemas, not only because the EEC was seen as the perfect arena in which Spanish cinema could legitimate and explain to the world the new democratic Spain (Triana-Toribio 2003, 113), but also because Miró believed that through the promotion of a quality cinema she was setting the conditions that would allow Spanish cinema to compete in the forthcoming European free market. As Miró stated "we had to prepare ourselves to enter into the EEC and to be able to operate within a global market" (Miró in Galán 2006, 212). Clearly, Miró aimed to position Spanish cinema within the same European strategy that was trying to counteract the competition of what Tino Balio has labelled the Hollywood "ultra-high- budget film" of the 1980s, which he identifies as "action-filled blockbusters" led by top stars such as Sylvester Stallone and Arnold Schwarzenegger (1996, 24–25). Against these films, a major production cycle in Europe took the form of heritage cinema, as it can be seen in the British and French films of the 1980s and 1990s. Andrew Higson has described it as films that "operate primarily as middle-class quality products, somewhere between the art-house and the mainstream [...] These films tend to be valued for their cultural significance rather than their box-office takings" (Higson 1996, 233). Guy Austin has characterised the French heritage cinema of the 1980s and 1990s, which he identifies with the "quality costume drama", as "classic in form, historical or literary in inspiration. [It] tends to place a premium on high production values, often relying on [...] famous stars in order to ensure a larger audience" (1996, 142). Arguably, the literary adaptations and costume dramas promoted by the Miró Law should be considered as the Spanish version of the European heritage production trend, which should be framed within the shifting conception of quality cinema that took place in Europe from the 1980s on. As Mary P. Wood remarks in her book *Contemporary European Cinema*, from the 1980s onwards, "the notion of quality cinema in Europe shifted from the auteurist art-cinema tradition of the 1960s to the development of high-budget films directed by well-known auteurs but firmly directed at a mainstream audience" (Wood 2007, 44).

Similarly, it has been argued that these costume dramas and literary adaptations served both to "retrieve the historical past [that was] hijacked and refashioned by Francoism" (Jordan and Morgan-Tamosunas 1998, 15) and to celebrate "a certain cultural heritage" (Triana-Toribio 2003, 113). Acknowledging both purposes, it seems possible that Spanish heritage film was primarily aimed at popularising highbrow Spanish culture. Hence, the obsession for adapting writers such as Benito Pérez Galdós, Leopoldo Alas Clarín, Ramón del Vallé-Inclán, Camilo José Cela or Miguel Delibes. Miró herself took Lope de Vega's *El perro del hortelano* original verse to the screen in 1996, which ultimately became a very successful film. Accordingly, it was believed that by producing films that embraced highbrow cultural values – the heritage film – Spanish audiences would not only acquire the necessary critical tools that would allow them to get over the subproducts – and therefore the Francoist cinema – but they would also actively participate in the consumption of cultural goods.

The idea that cinema had to function as a vehicle of culture, however, was not solely an idea of the PSOE. In fact, it had been a long-demanded claim among the dissident film agents that had been opposing Francoist cinema since the Salamanca Conference of 1955.[11] The outcome of the conference was that Spanish films had to show the reality of Spanish people for what it was necessary to establish a clear distinction between commercial cinema and a cinema of artistic qualities, which would require special protection from the state (Conclusiones, Epígrafe V. Problemas económicos in García-Escudero et. al, 1995, 84).[12] Therefore, since the PSOE belonged to the same cultural tradition of the dissident film agents, it could only guarantee the creation of a truly democratic cinema, which was defined by Salvador Clotas, the PSOE's Culture Secretary between 1982 and 1986, as a "quality and independent cinema with global projection" (Clotas in Pozo Arenas, Diciembre 1982, 13), by supporting and promoting a cinema that functioned as a vehicle for culture.

Throughout the 1970s, the dissident film agents gradually reached positions of power within the field; for instance, in 1970, film critics Fernando Lara and Diego Galán joined *Triunfo* (1962–1982), founded in 1946 as a weekly film magazine but turned into a cultural magazine in 1962 (Lara et. al 1975). Juan Pecourt places *Triunfo* within those cultural magazines that from the mid-1960s onwards become a serious threat to the dictatorship's symbolic order because they were nurtured by the prestige that the intellectuals who opposed the dictatorship had amongst the students and other social groups who were unhappy with Franco's regime (Pecourt 2008, 103). Hence, the dissident film agents managed to reach the necessary cultural capital, that is, the necessary intellectual prestige, to broaden their influence beyond the scope of specialised film magazines; consequently, they were able to contribute to the symbolic process through which the intellectuals were fighting against the dictatorship. According to the dissident film agents, cinema had to participate actively in the democratisation of Spanish society, as Lara affirmed in a text of 1975.[13] Lara wondered how Spanish cinema could become a cultural instrument that could contribute to the democratisation of Spain. He argued that it was essential to provide the necessary support to those dissident auteurs such as Juan Antonio Bardem, Luis García Berlanga, Carlos Saura, Basilio Martín Patino, José Luis Borau, Víctor Erice or Manuel Gutiérrez Aragón, because they were the ones contributing to the creation of a critic culture. These auteurs opposed to what he labelled commercial cinema – the popular genres. Thus, auteur dissident cinema was the only one which has the potential to transform Spanish reality (Lara et. al 1975, 219–243). In the late 1970s, the dissident film agents had theirs demands further institutionalised when the PSOE publicly endorsed them in the First Democratic Conference on Spanish Cinema of 1978, where the PSOE stated that cinema could not be conceived exclusively as a commercial good, but as a cultural one. Consequently, state protection should be directed towards cinema understood as a vehicle of culture (Reproduced in *Contracampo*, abril 1979, 21–22). The PSOE embraced the main claim of the dissident film agents whereby the type of cinema that deserved to be especially protected by the state was the cinema with artistic qualities, while the commercial production had to be left outside of that protection because it did not serve as a vehicle of culture. This is probably one of the reasons why the conference triggered the breakup of the main producer's association, AIPCE, headed by José Frade, producer of the highest grossing Spanish film of the 1970s, *No desearás al vecino del quinto* (Ramón Fernández, 1970). From 1978 onwards, Frade was identified by the dissident film agents as one of the greatest enemies of Spanish cinema. Firstly, because he was considered to be the paradigmatic producer of commercial cinema. Secondly, because he became one of the major opponents of the PSOE's film policy and its defence of cinema as a vehicle for culture. A new association was then born, the UPCE, which gathered those producers who were ideologically closer to the PSOE, such as Elías Querejeta, Luis Megino, Alfredo Matas or Juan Miguel Lamet (who was the spokesman of the PSOE along with Miró at the conference) among others. The links that the UPCE had with the PSOE allowed the dissident film agents to acquire the necessary positions of power within the field that enabled them to underpin their demands in the early 1980s and have them consecrated once the PSOE came to power in 1982.

As it has been explained at the beginning of this chapter, the end of the censorship in 1977 and the liberalisation of the film market flooded the national film market with Hollywood films. For the dissident film agents, the Hollywood "ultra-high-budget film" of the 1980s lacked any cultural value. The dissident producer Querejeta asserted that it was absolutely disgraceful that Spanish policymakers had handed over the Spanish market to Hollywood films, which were nothing but cultural misery (Querejeta in *Fotogramas*, diciembre 1981, 29). Since the dissident film agents believed that cinema had to function as a vehicle of culture and it had to contribute to the democratisation of Spanish society, the idea that Spanish cinema could not survive in a free market and thus it needed to be protected by the state against the competition of Hollywood films became an article of faith beyond discussion. As Lara stated in 1983, for Spanish cinema to survive, it needed an industrial protectionist and cultural nationalistic film policy (Lara in *Diario 16*, 8/01/1983, 25). Lara demanded that the government had to carry out a film policy that protected quality cinema (Lara in *Fotogramas*, mayo 1983:53). In order to reach the desired quality for national cinema, as Lara continued, it was necessary to increase the budget available for Spanish films because with low-budget films it was impossible to be competitive both in national and international markets (Lara in *Fotogramas*, mayo 1983, 53). For Matas, the only thing that the Spanish state had to do to counteract the competition of Hollywood films was to translate and apply the French film law and to implement the *avance sur reccettes* funding system (Matas in *Fotogramas*, diciembre 1981, 29).

The appointment of Miró as General Director of Cinematography should therefore be considered as a statement made by the PSOE, and particularly by Spain's president, Felipe González, who personally decided on the appointment (Galán 2006, 180), to ensure that the dissident film agents would have their demands validated by the PSOE's film policy. Miró had been a symbol of the dissident films agents because she had faced a military court under the UCD government due to her film *El crimen de Cuenca* (1979), based on a true story that had occurred in Spain in 1912. The film was prohibited because of its realistic portrayal of the tortures practiced by the state police force established by Franco (*Guardia Civil*). The Decree of 1977, which theoretically prohibited censorship, allowed the administration to denounce any film considered to constitute a felony. In April 1980 Miró was formally indicted for defamation against the *Guardia Civil*. She was finally released in December 1980 and the film finally premiered in 1981, being the highest grossing film of the year (Torreiro [1995a] 2010, 370). The Miró *affaire* proved the difficulties that Spanish cinema still had to address Spanish reality in a committed way under the UCD government. In order to reach a better understanding of what Miró understood by quality cinema, this following section argues that, beyond her status as a symbol, she was also a classic cinephile.

Pilar Miró and the classic cinephilia: Shaping a policy maker

Miró (1940–1997) belonged to the same generation as, and had strong bonds with, key members of the dissident film agents, such as Lara, Galán, Lamet, Querejeta, Erice and Megino, each of whom were born between the mid-1930s and the mid-1940s, therefore reaching adulthood in the early and mid-1960s. As mentioned before, Pujol Ozonas, drawing on Baecque's history of French cinephilia, has defined this generation as the classic cinephilia (1950–1960). As Pujol Ozonas explains, the Spanish classic cinephiles were heavily influenced by the French cinephiles of the 1950s and their defence of the film as a personal statement by the auteur exposed in the film magazine *Cahiers du Cinéma* (Pujol Ozonas 2011, 127–146). However, the political context of the Francoist dictatorship made the Spanish cinephiles develop two particular characteristics. Firstly, cinema acquired a symbolic status as a way of escaping from the oppressive cultural, social and political reality of the 1940s when this generation had grown up. As Miró herself affirmed in 1998, referring to her childhood, when six or seven years old, she was always at the cinema, because she wanted to live over and over the different stories screened in the cinema and not having to go back home (Miró in Galán 1998, 9). Secondly, being a cinephile in the 1960s was inseparable from political activism. These cinephiles had the conviction that they had the moral obligation to fight against the Francoist ideology through the defence of a committed cinema. In Galán's own words: to defend political committed cinema was another way to fight against Francoism (Galán 2006, 61).

Miró got in contact with the directors of the New Spanish Cinema of the 1960s (NCE) and with the cinephile culture of the dissident film agents when she enrolled in the official film school in 1963 (EOC). As Casimiro Torreiro explains, the EOC, former IIEC, was established in 1947 and revamped as the EOC in 1962 by José María García Escudero.[14] The school became one of the main instruments through which the NCE was created. Between 1963 and 1967, 48 former students of the EOC made their debut, among them were Miguel Picazo, Francisco Regueiro, Pedro Olea, Camus, Borau, Erice and Patino, all of whom were members of the NCE (Torreiro [1995b] 2010, 308–320). Miró was contemporary to the only two female directors who graduated in the EOC in 1969: Josefina Molina (born in 1936) and Cecilia Bartolome (born in1940) – Miró graduated in scriptwriting one year before, in 1968. She had been working in the Spanish National Television (TVE) since 1960, being the first female television director in Spain.[15]

Moreover, as Jesús Angulo points out, during the 1950s and 1960s, Patino and Picazo actively engaged with cine-clubs; Borau and Erice practiced film criticism (Angulo 2003, 50). Miró herself contributed as a film critic for *Mundo Joven* in the 1960s and 1970s (Galán 2006, 79). These filmmakers engaged not only with the production of films but also with the aforementioned rites of watching films, speaking about them and then diffusing the discourse, the three characteristics that define cinephilia. Furthermore, Carlos Heredero argues that in the mid-1960s, the EOC was also a site of political activism and one of the main places where the dissident film culture could be exercised through both the shared screening of films that were prohibited by censorship and the shared production of films that would not be made as a result of censorship (Heredero 2007, 21).

According to Palacio (2006, 109–118) and Pujol Ozonas (2011, 136–137), the NCE became the cinema that the Spanish classic cinephiles considered to be worthy enough because it was the first Spanish film movement that had opposed the popular Francoist cinema, regardless of the contradiction that it was a cinema produced under and due to the Francoist government support, as Sally Faulkner has explained (Faulkner 2006, 16–17). As Pujol Ozonas continues, stylistically and thematically, the classic cinephilia considered that the NCE was a cinema that tackled Spanish reality in a committed way that was far from the evasive manners utilised by the popular genres. This happened even in spite of all the limitations of censorship. For John Hopewell, censorship made the NCE filmmakers develop what he has named an oblique style; this oblique style, according to him, was the main sign of auteurism of the NCE's filmmakers, particularly as it can be seen in the work of Saura (Hopewell 1986, 63–76). Therefore, the NCE became the model for the classic cinephilia because, as Faulkner has defined it, it was "the politically dissident work of a group of auteurs" (Faulkner 2006, 19).

In the particular case of Miró, her cinephilia was manifested in her romantic notion that making films was above all a means of personal expression (Miró in Hernández Les, mayo 1982, 10). This notion, as well as the difficulties she faced to produce *Gary Cooper que estás en los cielos* (1980) – for which she had to mortgage her own house and set up her own production company, Pilar Miró P.C – added to the problems she later had with the producer Matas to carry out her fourth film *Hablamos esta noche* (1982). These problems, taken collectively, are what informed her belief that producers were always the ones who impeded the ability of filmmakers to express themselves (Galán 2006, 204). For Miró, cinema had to be more than a simple business and therefore she strongly opposed those producers who she considered were producing movies only to make profit, as she stated in 1983 (Miró in Pozo Arenas, febrero 1983, 15). Therefore, when she became General Director of Cinematography, her main aim was to ensure that the financial conditions that allowed filmmakers to express themselves, regardless of the marketability of the films they would make (Miró in Pozo Arenas, febrero 1983, 15). In particular, as it has been previously mentioned, since the NCE became the model for the classic cinephiles, Miró put in place the financial conditions that allowed the former filmmakers of the NCE to make films again. She also ensured the same conditions for the two main producers of NCE, Querejeta and Lamet, who she considered were the kind of producers who were truly interested in cinema and not only in business.

Miró's aim to bring an end to the subproducts explained at the beginning of this chapter can be now framed differently. Certainly, like the other classic cinephiles, she identified the subproducts with Francoist cinema. However, she wanted to provide Spanish audiences with the films she loved because she believed that if Spanish audiences had different films to choose from beyond the subproducts, they will naturally reject them in favour of the quality cinema she aimed to promote, as she stated in 1983, referring to the forthcoming implantation of the advance subsidy. She believed that all filmmakers and producers should be able to access selective funding and that General Direction of Cinematography (later ICAA) could not select a priori which films could access selective funding and which could not, neither to impede the production of popular cinema. She believed that the General Direction of Cinematography could promote an auteur cinema so people could choose between popular and auteur cinema so the subproducts will naturally disappear because the audiences will support and prefer quality cinema (Miró in Pozo Arenas, febrero 1983, 14). Consequently, she believed that by granting the conditions that would allow the production of a quality cinema, she was contributing to the demise of the subproducts and, therefore, to the development of a more democratic film culture in Spain. Having analysed Miró's habitus to explain her role as a classic cinephile, a key factor in her defence of quality cinema, it is now time to assess how far and in what ways she, as a female policymaker, did indeed foster concrete measures to advance the presence of women in the film industry. This aspect has not been addressed by any of the scholarship who has studied the Law.

The effects of the Miro Law on the film industry

I have previously focused on the advance subsides the Law applied, because this has been the most discussed aspect of the Law, since, as explained before, scholarship has argued that selective funding did not only worsen the traditional problems of the Spanish film industry, but it also fostered a standardised production. Both notions have now been challenged. As for whether Miró aligned with a feminist film policy, there is not a single measure in the Law directed towards fostering the presence of women in the film industry. As it has been explained before, selective funding was specially designed to encourage the production of quality films, films directed by novel directors, those specially aimed at children, experimental films and high-budget films – those films budgeted at more than 55 million pesetas (330,000€/£277,000). Consequently, it cannot be said that the Law, despite being envisaged by a female policymaker, did indeed set concrete measures to promote a more inclusive and gender-balanced film industry. Furthermore, in a personal interview with the author, Fernando Méndez Leite, who substituted Miró as Head of the ICAA (1986–1988) and continued with her policy, stated that, back in the 1980s, gender inequality in the film industry was not even discussed by the film professionals' associations – all male – in the meetings Méndez Leite had with them to design the better policies aimed at protecting and promoting the Spanish film industry. However, he further commented that it was believed at the ICAA that it was necessary to foster the presence of women directors and, consequently, when a project directed by a woman applied for public funding, it was fully supported. However, looking at the numbers below, one could wonder how this support was actually put into place. The Miró Law' emphasis was therefore placed on fostering a quality auteur cinema, promoting novel directors and building a solid film industry that would allow Spanish films to be competitive in both the national market and abroad. According to Méndez Leite, for Miró gender inequality in the film industry was not an issue, and, consequently, she did not consider that any measure to tackle it was necessary (Méndez Leite in Fernandez-Meneses, 2023).

The presence of women in above-the-line roles (direction, scriptwriting and production) was very low throughout the 1980s despite 715 films were produced between 1980 and 1989, as it can be seen in Figure 2.1.

Only eleven women directed films in the 1980s: Molina – the collective soft – pornography film *Cuentos eróticos* (1980), *Función de noche* (1981) and *Esquilache* (1988) – Miró herself – *Gary Cooper que estas en los cielos* (1980), *Hablamos esta noche* (1982), and *Werther* (1986), Bartolomé – the two part documentary on the Transition co-directed alongside his brother *Después de...* (1981), Isabel Mula the two soft-pornographic films *Depravación* (1982) and *Los nuevos curanderos* (1986), Lina Romay co-directed the soft pornographic *Las chicas del tanga* (1983) alongside Jesús Franco, Tanaa Kaleya the soft pornographic film, *Mujeres* (1983), Maria Luisa Bemberg *Camila* (1984), Pilar Távora *Nanas de espinas* (1984), Cristina Andreu the collective *Delirios de amor* (1984) and her debut *Brumal* (1988), Ana Diez *Ander eta Yul* (1988) and Isabel Coixet her first feature film *Demasiado viejo para morir joven* (1988).

Regarding scriptwriters, the following conclusions can be gathered: first, the traditional auteurist paradigm was followed by Spanish female directors, since they all wrote and/or co-wrote the scripts that they directed, except Molina's fragment in *Cuentos eróticos,* wrote by Alicia Hermida, Mula's *Depravación*, wrote by Jose Maria Cunillés, Romay's *Las chicas del tanga*, wrote by Jesús Franco, and Andreu's segment in *Delirios de amor*, wrote by Domingo Sánchez. Consequently, only the popular films were written by a scriptwriter who was not the director. Secondly, only two scriptwriters managed to write more than one film throughout the decade: Lola Salvador, who wrote four films – she was the in-house scriptwriter in Mata's production company: *Bearn, o la sala de muñecas* (1983), *Las bicicletas son para el verano*

The 1980s

YEARS	TOTAL	WOMEN IN ABOVE THE LINE ROLES 1980-1989					
		FILMS DIRECTED BY WOMEN		FILMS WRITEN BY WOMEN		FILMS PRODUCED BY WOMEN	
		Nº	%	Nº	%	Nº	%
1980	99	2	2.02	6	6.06	5	5.05
1981	104	3	2.88	7	6.73	8	7.69
1982	115	2	1.74	9	7.83	7	6.09
1983	72	2	2.78	6	8.33	6	8.33
1984	70	4	5.71	7	10.00	8	11.43
1985	58	0	0.00	6	10.34	5	8.62
1986	59	2	3.39	1	1.69	9	15.25
1987	53	0	0.00	6	11.32	7	13.21
1988	47	3	6.38	7	14.89	6	12.77
1989	38	0	0.00	3	7.89	5	13.16
TOTAL	715	18	2.52	58	8.11	66	9.23

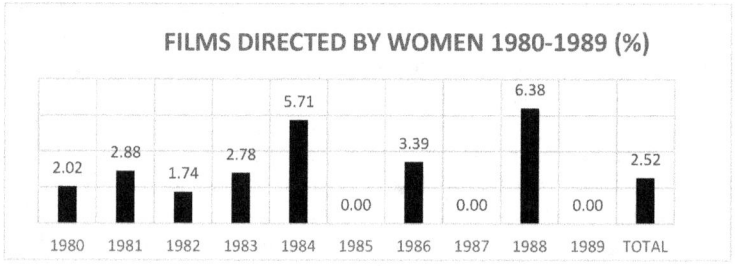

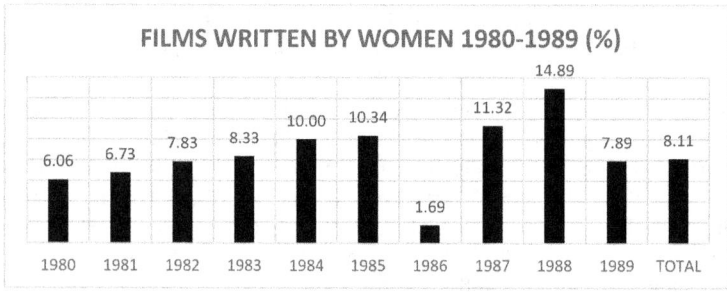

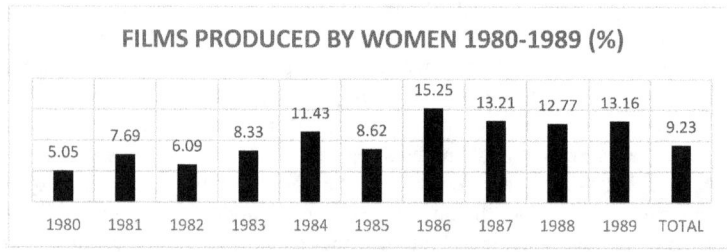

Figure 2.1 The presence of women in the above-the-line roles in the 1980s
Source: Antonio Fernández Segura with data from the ICAA and IMDB.

(1984), *El jardín secreto* (1984) and *Barrios altos* (1987) – and Juliana San José de la Fuente (known as Jackie Kelly), who wrote/co-wrote *La desnuda chica del relax* (1981), *Secta siniestra* (1982) and *Yo amo la danza* (1984).

Finally, when it comes to production, women managed to have more prominent roles and continuous careers than in both direction and scriptwriting: Isabel Mula, who specialised in low/medium-budget genre films and co-productions[16]; Julia Saly, producer of Paul Naschy's low budget horror films[17]; Ana Huete backed auteurist filmmakers such as Fernando Trueba, Oscar Ladoire, Fernando Colomo, Fermín Cabal and Manuel Iborra[18]; Helena Matas, daughter of the producer Matas, was responsible of five high-profile films throughout the decade[19]; finally, the directors Bartolomé and Miró produced their own films – *Después de...* (1981) and *Werther* (1986) respectively, – whereas the scriptwriter Juliana San José de la Fuente produced her own scripts *Secta siniestra* (1982) and *Yo amo la danza* (1984) and Ignacio F. Iquino's *Hombres que rugen* (1984).

In a similar fashion, the roles below-the-line maintained the traditional gendered division of masculinised and feminised roles that we can see in other film industries (see Bell, 2021: 2–18 and Jones and Pringle, 2015: 37–49). As Figures 2.1–2.12 show, women's presence was major in the departments of Makeup and Hairdressing, Costume and Wardrobe, Editorial and Script and Continuity; men dominated the technical departments such as Sound, Camera and Electrical, Cinematography and Music – with not a single woman being in charge of Cinematography in the whole decade. In those departments closer to the above-the-line roles – Film Editing, Production Management: Second Unit, and Assistant Direction and Art Department – the presence of women was extremely low – not even reaching 15% in any of them.

It can be therefore argued that women were not deemed of technical mastery and, as such, were not allowed in technical roles. On the contrary, women were assigned tasks deemed auxiliary which support others in film production, as Melanie Bell has brilliantly pointed out already. However, following Bell, these positions are far from being auxiliary since filmmaking is a collaborative endeavour that requires the whole machinery to be perfectly greased. In this sense, the work carried out by those women in the Makeup and Hairdressing, Costume and Wardrobe, Editorial and Scrip and Continuity departments is equally important for bringing any film to a satisfactory end as it is the work carried out by men in the Sound, Camera and Electrical, Music and Cinematography departments (Bell 2021: 2–18). This division tells us about the structural inequalities of the Spanish film industry, which is organised around gendered roles because women work in the film industry is subjected to gender stereotypes. These assumptions explain women's overrepresentation in Makeup and Hairdressing, Costume and Wardrobe, Editorial and Script and Continuity. These gender stereotypes that determine this gendered division of labour will prevail throughout the decades, as the following chapters will show.

FILMS WITH WOMEN WORKING IN THE FILM EDITING DEPARTMENT			
YEARS	FILMS	Nº	%
1980	99	22	22.22
1981	104	8	7.69
1982	115	15	13.04
1983	72	9	12.50
1984	70	5	7.14
1985	58	8	13.79
1986	59	9	15.25
1987	53	12	22.64
1988	47	8	17.02
1989	38	7	18.42
TOTAL	715	103	14.41

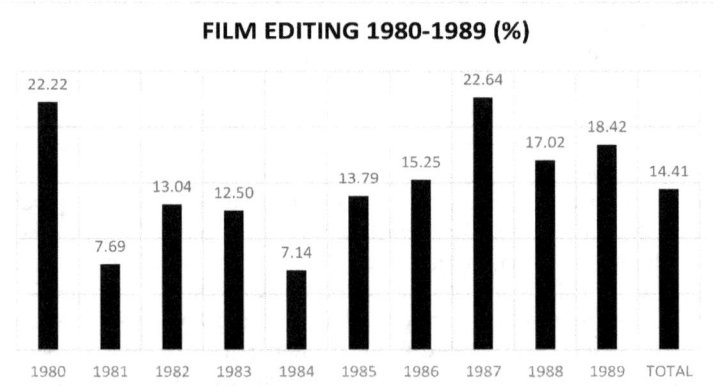

Figure 2.2 The presence of women in the Film Editing department in the 1980s
Source: Antonio Fernández Segura with data from the ICAA and IMDB.

FILMS WITH WOMEN WORKING IN THE PRODUCTION MANAGEMENT DEPARTMENT			
YEARS	FILMS	Nº	%
1980	99	10	10.10
1981	104	8	7.69
1982	115	9	7.83
1983	72	3	4.17
1984	70	9	12.86
1985	58	3	5.17
1986	59	16	27.12
1987	53	7	13.21
1988	47	9	19.15
1989	38	13	34.21
TOTAL	715	87	12.17

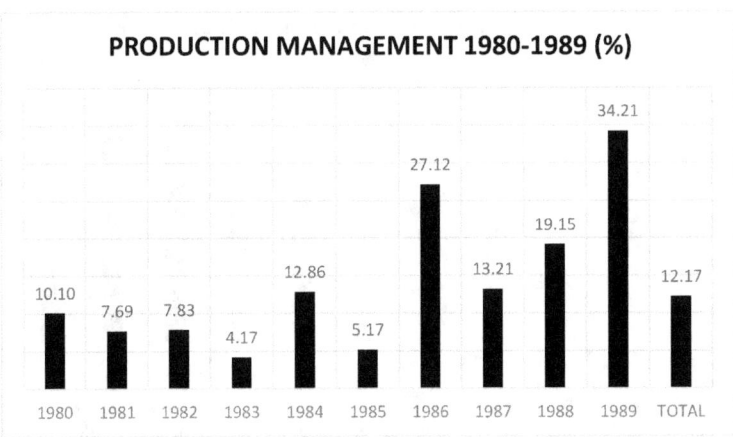

Figure 2.3 The presence of women in the Production Management department in the 1980s

Source: Antonio Fernández Segura with data from the ICAA and IMDB.

FILMS WITH WOMEN WORKING IN THE SECOND UNIT OR ASSISTANT DIRECTOR DEPARTMENT			
YEARS	FILMS	Nº	%
1980	99	4	4.04
1981	104	11	10.58
1982	115	7	6.09
1983	72	8	11.11
1984	70	10	14.29
1985	58	4	6.90
1986	59	11	18.64
1987	53	9	16.98
1988	47	12	25.53
1989	38	10	26.32
TOTAL	715	86	12.03

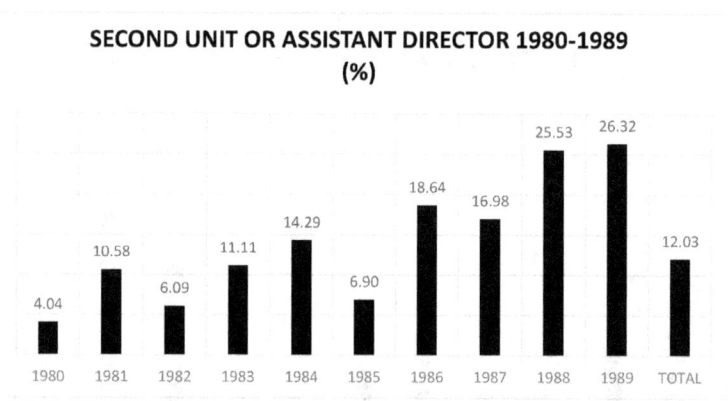

Figure 2.4 The presence of women in the Second Unit or Assistant Director department in the 1980s

Source: Antonio Fernández Segura with data from the ICAA and IMDB.

FILMS WITH WOMEN WORKING IN THE ART DEPARTMENT				
YEARS	FILMS	Nº	%
1980	99	12	12.12
1981	104	9	8.65
1982	115	8	6.96
1983	72	5	6.94
1984	70	4	5.71
1985	58	2	3.45
1986	59	9	15.25
1987	53	10	18.87
1988	47	11	23.40
1989	38	12	31.58
TOTAL	715	82	11.47

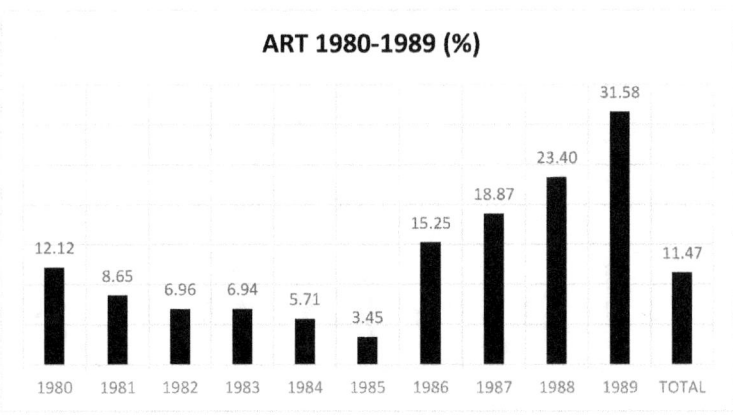

Figure 2.5 The presence of women in the Art department in the 1980s
Source: Antonio Fernández Segura with data from the ICAA and IMDB.

FILMS WITH WOMEN WORKING IN THE SOUND DEPARTMENT			
YEARS	FILMS	Nº	%
1980	99	0	0.00
1981	104	2	1.92
1982	115	1	0.87
1983	72	1	1.39
1984	70	1	1.43
1985	58	1	1.72
1986	59	3	5.08
1987	53	1	1.89
1988	47	0	0.00
1989	38	1	2.63
TOTAL	715	11	1.54

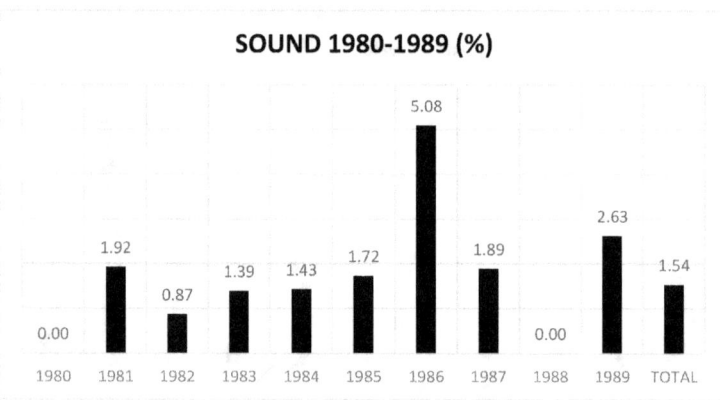

Figure 2.6 The presence of women in the Sound department in the 1980s
Source: Antonio Fernández Segura with data from the ICAA and IMDB.

FILMS WITH WOMEN WORKING IN THE CAMERA AND ELECTRICAL DEPARTMENT			
YEARS	FILMS	Nº	%
1980	99	11	11.11
1981	104	10	9.62
1982	115	5	4.35
1983	72	9	12.50
1984	70	6	8.57
1985	58	5	8.62
1986	59	12	20.34
1987	53	5	9.43
1988	47	8	17.02
1989	38	8	21.05
TOTAL	715	79	11.05

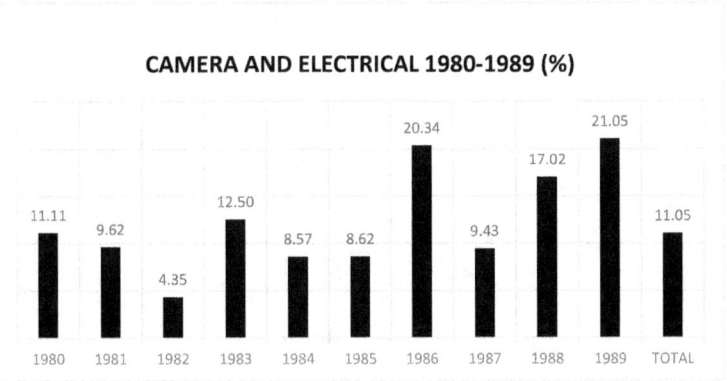

Figure 2.7 The presence of women in the Camera and Electrical department in the 1980s

Source: Antonio Fernández Segura with data from the ICAA and IMDB.

FILMS WITH WOMEN WORKING IN THE COSTUME AND WARDROBE DEPARTMENT			
YEARS	FILMS	Nº	%
1980	99	40	40.40
1981	104	38	36.54
1982	115	41	35.65
1983	72	24	33.33
1984	70	30	42.86
1985	58	22	37.93
1986	59	36	61.02
1987	53	27	50.94
1988	47	29	61.70
1989	38	26	68.42
TOTAL	715	313	43.78

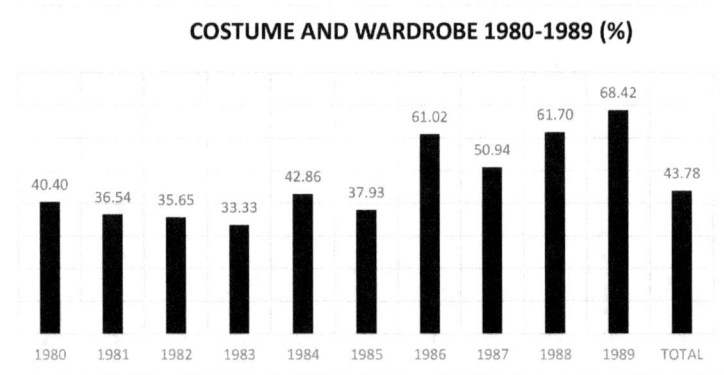

Figure 2.8 The presence of women in the Costume and Wardrobe department in the 1980s

Source: Antonio Fernández Segura with data from the ICAA and IMDB.

FILMS WITH WOMEN WORKING IN THE MAKE UP AND HAIRDRESSING DEPARTMENT			
YEARS	FILMS	Nº	%
1980	99	42	42.42
1981	104	45	43.27
1982	115	41	35.65
1983	72	27	37.50
1984	70	37	52.86
1985	58	24	41.38
1986	59	30	50.85
1987	53	32	60.38
1988	47	28	59.57
1989	38	23	60.53
TOTAL	715	329	46.01

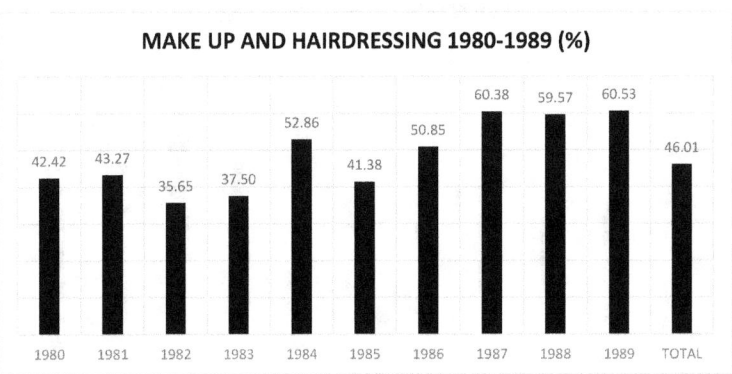

Figure 2.9 The presence of women in the Makeup and Hairdressing department in the 1980s

Source: Antonio Fernández Segura with data from the ICAA and IMDB.

The 1980s

FILMS WITH WOMEN WORKING IN THE EDITORIAL DEPARTMENT			
YEARS	FILMS	Nº	%
1980	99	42	42.42
1981	104	30	28.85
1982	115	27	23.48
1983	72	21	29.17
1984	70	23	32.86
1985	58	16	27.59
1986	59	25	42.37
1987	53	22	41.51
1988	47	23	48.94
1989	38	18	47.37
TOTAL	715	247	34.55

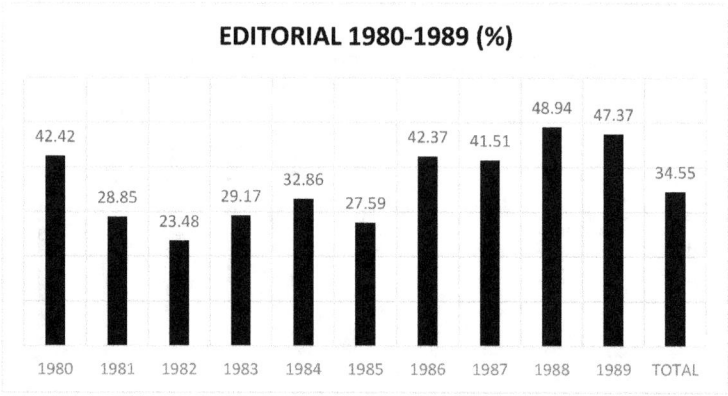

Figure 2.10 The presence of women in the Editorial department in the 1980s
Source: Antonio Fernández Segura with data from the ICAA and IMDB.

FILMS WITH WOMEN WORKING IN THE SCRIPT AND CONTINUITY DEPARTMENT			
YEARS	FILMS	Nº	%
1980	99	31	31.31
1981	104	32	30.77
1982	115	23	20.00
1983	72	14	19.44
1984	70	20	28.57
1985	58	13	22.41
1986	59	31	52.54
1987	53	21	39.62
1988	47	24	51.06
1989	38	14	36.84
TOTAL	715	223	31.19

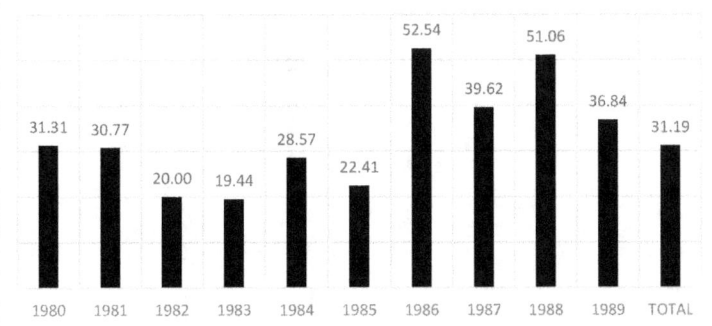

Figure 2.11 The presence of women in the Script and Continuity department in the 1980s

Source: Antonio Fernández Segura with data from the ICAA and IMDB.

FILMS WITH WOMEN WORKING IN THE MUSIC DEPARTMENT			
YEARS	FILMS	Nº	%
1980	99	1	1.01
1981	104	2	1.92
1982	115	0	0.00
1983	72	3	4.17
1984	70	2	2.86
1985	58	1	1.72
1986	59	3	5.08
1987	53	0	0.00
1988	47	1	2.13
1989	38	0	0.00
TOTAL	715	13	1.82

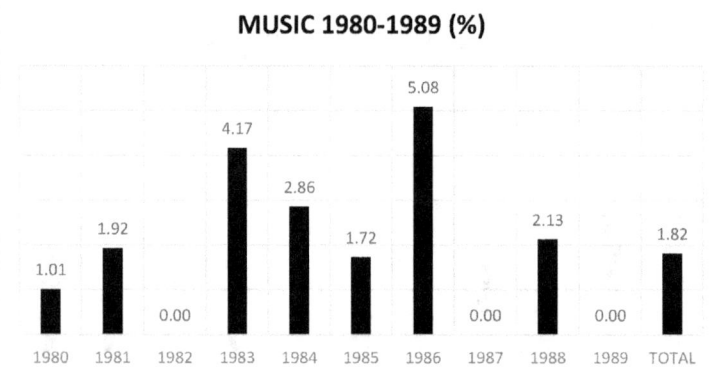

Figure 2.12 The presence of women in the Music department in the 1980s
Source: Antonio Fernández Segura with data from the ICAA and IMDB.

Conclusion

This chapter began addressing the main criticisms raised against the Miró Law by the Spanish film scholarship in order to propose a different reading of the Law and the films it funded. As it has been analysed before, the major criticism made by Hopewell, Zunzunegui, Heredero, Monterde, Riambau and

Losilla regarding the types of films that the Miró Law funding policies led to, is that they generated a polished, unimaginative and standardised production based on the quality cinema criterium. However, taking into account the European paradigm of cultural policy under which the Law was enacted, the role that cinema had for the PSOE as a vehicle for culture, and Miró's aesthetic preferences as a classic cinephile, her film policy placed the role of cinema beyond the mere personal statement of the auteur and beyond the idea that cinema had to serve only artistic purposes – the art for art's sake notion of cinema: Miró wanted to produce a cinema that was primarily aimed at popularising the highbrow Spanish culture in order to provide Spanish audiences with the necessary critical tools that would allow them to move beyond the subproducts and therefore break with the Francoist film culture. It is in this sense in which the heritage cinema to which the Law led can be considered to be totally coherent with the demands of the dissident film agents the Law tried to meet.

As for the Law contributing in any manner to the advance of women in the film industry, it is evident from the discussions that were taking part on the field of Spanish cinema of the period that the under representation of women in the film industry was not an issue, not even for Miró, the key policymaker in charge of the film policies of the 1980s. Arguably, her habitus as a classic cinephile informed her ideas about the role that cinema had to fulfill in society and her support for the NCE's filmmakers and producers, who were mostly all male. Consequently, she fostered the presence of such filmmakers and producers, who embodied her idea of quality cinema, rather than proposing concrete measures to encourage the presence of women in the film industry. It can be argued that the emphasis that the Law placed in directing selective funding to projects directed by novel filmmakers did in fact promoted a major presence of female directors. In 1984, first year the Law was in place, out of 70 films, the two female filmmakers that managed to direct a film were novel directors – Maria Luisa Bemberg with *Camila* and Isabel Mula with *Los nuevos curanderos*. In 1985, 1987 and 1989 not a single film out of a total of 58, 53 and 38 films produced respectively was directed by a woman. In 1986, Cristina Andreu debuted with her fragment in the collective film *Delirios de amor* and in 1988 debuted Ana Diez with *Ander eta Yul* and Isabel Coixet with *Demasiado viejo para morir joven*. Consequently, a gender-blind measure contributed to foster the presence of female directors in the 1980s, even if this presence was minimum. The 1990s saw a boom of women directors, as it will be analysed in the next chapter. However, the Spanish film industry, even with the advanced of democracy, stayed as a gender regime in the 1980s, since one of its structural organisational principles was the gendered division of labour. Consequently, the victory of the left-wing dissident film agents over the field of Spanish cinema did not improve the situation of women working in the film industry. The Spanish film industry remained as a gender regime for the following decades to come, as next chapters will show.

Notes

1 All translations from Spanish quotes made by the author. An older version of this chapter was published in 2020 as an article titled "Rethinking Quality Cinema" in the *International Journal of Cultural Policy*.
2 See Hopewell (1986 and 1991), Besas (1985 and 1995), Zunzunegui (1988), Gómez B. de Castro (1989), Losilla (1989), Heredero (1991 and 1998), Vallés [1992] 2000, Monterde (1993), Riambau ([1995] 2010), Trenzado Romero (1997), Fernández Blanco (1998), Triana-Toribio (2003) and Ansola (2004).
3 The study of the history of the French cinephilia was further analysed by de Baecque in his exhaustive book of 2003 *La cinéphilie: Invention d'un regard, historie d'une culture. 1944–1968*.
4 Elsaesser has further addressed the feeling of disenchantment among the cinephilia in his text "Cinephilia and the Uses of Disenchantment" (2005, 27–43).
5 Through the the Real Decreto 3071/1977, de 11 de noviembre, introduced by the UCD government (1977–1982). The screening quota for Spanish films was nonetheless maintained. Exhibitors had to screen Spanish films for 120 days a year.
6 This S-rated production, particularly the comedies by Mariano Ozores and Pedro Lazaga such as *¡Que vienen los socialistas!* (Mariano Ozores, 1982), have also been labelled as extreme right-wing cinema by scholars such as Casimiro Torreiro ([1995a] 2010, 389–390).
7 This automatic subsidy was first established in 1964 and maintained throughout the subsequent legislation up to the Miró Law.
8 Apart from the advance subsidy, public funding could be also found in the Spanish National Television (TVE) and in the autonomous governments.
9 Some studies have argued that the specific criteria for awarding the advance subsidy was at times arbitrary, and the system tended towards favouritism and corruption (Gómez B. de Castro 1988, 247 and 1989, 123–133 and Vallés [1992] 2000, 227). For Besas, "the criteria for giving subsidies have always been murky, vague enough so that political and private favouritism could be exercised. Nepotism and influence-pulling overshadowed the system and continued to be a key factor in the subsidy system, whether under Franco or under the Socialists" (1995, 246).
10 *Tasio* (50 million pesetas, 300,000€/£263,500), *El caballero del dragón* (132 million pesetas, 790,000€/£695,000), *Se infiel y no mires con quién* (30 million pesetas, 180,000€/£160,000), *La vieja música* (37 million pesetas, 222,000€/195,000£), *Bandera negra* (44 million pesetas, 265,000€/£230,000), *El Lute: camina o revienta* (54 million, 325,000€/£285,000), *El pecador impecable* (40 million, 240,000€/£210,000) or *Tu novia está loca* (23 million, 138,000€/£121,000)
11 See Besas 1985, 77; Hopewell 1986, 63–71; Vallés [1992] 2000, 42–45; Heredero 1993, 80–85; Monterde ([1995] 2010, 280 and 2003, 103–107; Torreiro [1995b] 2010, 295–302; Trenzado Romero 1999, 77–79; Triana-Toribio 2003, 70–109; Faulkner 2006, 8; Palacio 2011, 20–22; Pujol Ozonas 2011, 11–115.
12 Among many other delegates, the conference was attended by left-wing personalities such as Basilio Martín Patino, Juan Antonio Bardem, Ricardo Muñoz Suay, both of them members of the Spanish Communist Party (PCE), and members of the Francoist regime such as José María García Escudero and Fernando Vizcaíno Casas.
13 Titled *El cine español, ante una alternativa democrática*
14 IIEC reads for *Instituto de Investigaciones y Experiencias Cinematográficas*
15 There is plenty of literature on Bartolomé, Molina and Miró: see, among others, Martin-Márquez, Susan (1999), Cerdán and Díaz (2001), Vernon (2011) and Cascajosa Virino (2015).
16 *Apocalipsis caníbal* (1980), *Huida al sur: la desbandada* (1981), *El caso Almería* (1984), *Crimen en familia* (1985), *Apache Kid (Bianco Apache)* (1986), *Así como*

habían sido (1986), *El Lute camina o revienta* (1987) and *El Lute II, mañana seré libre* (1988).
17 *El carnaval de las bestias* (1980), *El retorno del hombre lobo* (1981), *La bestia y la espada mágica* (1983), *Latidos de pánico* (1983), *Operación mantis* (1984) and *El ultimo kamikaze* (1984).
18 *Opera prima* (Fernando Trueba, 1980), *A contratiempo* (Oscar Ladoire, 1981), *Estoy en crisis* (Fernando Colomo, 1982), *La línea del cielo* (Fernando Colomo, 1983), *El caballero del dragón* (Fernando Colomo, 1985), *La vida alegre* (Fernando Colomo, 1987) and *El baile del pato* (Manuel Iborra, 1989).
19 *Las aventuras de Enrique y Ana* (Ramon Fernández, 1981), *Nacional III* (Luis García Berlanga, 1982), *Bearn, o la sala de muñecas* (Jaime Chávarri, 1983), *Las bicicletas son para el verano* (Jaime Chávarri, 1984) and *Barrios altos* (Luis García Berlanga, 1987).

References

Angulo, Jesús. 2003. "Los antecedentes (1951–1962). El cine español de los años cincuenta". In *Los nuevos cines en España., Ilusiones y desencantos*, edited by Carlos F. Heredero and José Enrique Monterde, 29–52. Valencia: IVAC-Filmoteca Valenciana.
Ansola, Txomin. 2004. "El decreto Miró: una propuesta ambiciosa pero fallida para impulsar el cine español de los 80". *Archivos de la Filmoteca* 48: 102–121.
Austin, Guy. 1996. *Contemporary French Cinema: An Introduction*. Manchester: Manchester University Press.
Balio, Tino. 1996. "Adjusting to the New Global Economy. Hollywood in the 1990s". In *Film Policty. International, National and Regional Perspectives*, edited by Albert Moran, 23–38. London and New York: Routledge.
Bell, Melanie. 2021. *Movie Workers. The Women Who Made British Cinema*. Illinois: University of Illinois Press.
Besas, Peter. 1985. *Behind the Spanish Lens: Spanish Cinema under Fascism and Democracy*. Denver: Arden Press.
Besas, Peter. 1995. "The Financial Structure of Spanish Cinema". In *Refiguring Spain. Cinema, Media, Representation*, edited by Marsha Kinder, 241–259. Durham and London: Duke University Press.
Bourdieu, Pierre. 1993. *The Field of Cultural Production*. Cambridge: Polity Press.
Cascajosa Virino, Concepción (ed.). 2015. *A New Gaze: Women Creators of Film and Television in Democratic Spain*. Newcastle: Cambridge Scholars Publishing.
Cerdán, Josetxo and Díaz, Marina (eds.) (2001). *Cecilia Bartolomé: El encanto de la lógica*. Barcelona: La Fàbrica de Cinema Alternatiu/Ocho y medio.
de Baecque, Antoine. 2003. *La cinéphilie. Invention d'un regard, historie d'une culture. 1944–1968*. Paris: Fayard.
de Baecque, Antoine and Frémaux, Thierry. 1995. "La cinéphile ou l'invention d'une culture". *Revue d'historie*, 46: 133–142.
Elsaesser, Thomas. 2005. *European Cinema. Face to Face with Hollywood*. Amsterdam: Amsterdam University Press.
Elsaesser, Thomas. 2005. "Cinephilia or the Uses of Disenchantment". In *Cinephilia. Movies, Love and Memory*, edited by Marijke De Valck and Malte Hagener, 27–44. Amsterdam: Amsterdam University Press.

Faulkner, Sally. 2006. *A Cinema of Contradiction. Spanish Films in the 1960s*. Edinburgh: Edinburgh University Press.
Faulkner, Sally (ed.). 2016. *Middlebrow Cinema: Remapping World Cinema*. London and New Yotk. Routdledge.
Fernández Blanco, Victor. 1998. *El cine y su público en España: un análisis económico*. Fundacion Autor, Sociedad General de Autores y Escritores.
Fernandez-Meneses, Jara. 2023. "Personal interview with Fernando Méndez Leite", 14th April 2023.
Forbes, Jill and Street, Sarah. 2000. *European Cinema. An Introduction*. New York: Palgrave Macmillan.
Galán, Diego. 1975. "El cine 'político' español". In *7 trabajos de base sobre el cine español*, edited by Fernando Lara, 87–108. Valencia: Fernando Torres Editor.
Galán, Diego. 2006. *Pilar Miró. Nadie me enseñó a vivir*. Barcelona: Plaza Janés.
García Escudero, José María et al. 1995. *El cine español desde Salamanca. 1955–1995*. Junta de Castilla y León: Consejería de Educación y Cultura.
Gómez Bermúdez de Castro, Ramiro. 1989. *La producción cinematográfica española. De la Transición a la Democracia (1976–1986)*. Bilbao: Ediciones Mensajero.
Gubern, Roman and Font Domènec. 1975. *Un cine para el cadalso. 40 años de censura cinematográfica en España*. Barcelona: Editorial Euros.
Hayward, Susan. 1993. "State, culture and the cinema: Jack Lang's strategies for the French film industry". *Screen* 34(4) 380–391.
Heredero, Carlos F. 1991. "El cine español de los 80: cineastas en la periferia". In *1975–1990. La moralidad del cine*, edited by Javier Luengos, 96–125. Oviedo: Fundación Municipal de Oviedo.
Heredero, Carlos 1998. "La Ley Miró. Luces y sombras de una política para el cine español". *Nosferatu* 28: 42–51.
Higson, Andrew. 1996. "The Heritage Film and the British Cinema". In *Dissolving Views. Key Writings on British Cinema*, edited by Andrew Higson, 236–249. London and New York: Cassell.
Hopewell, John. 1986. *Out of the Past. Spanish Cinema after Franco*. London: British Film Institute.
Hopewell, John. 1991. "Art and a lack of money: The crises of the Spanish film industry, 1977–1990". *Quarterly Review of Film Studies*, 13:4: 113–122.
Jordan, Barry 1995. "Genre cinema in Spain in the 1970s: The case of comedy", *Revista Canadiense de Estudios Hispánicos* 20(1): 127–141.
Jordan, Barry. 2000. "The Spanish film industry in the 1980s and 1990s". In *Contemporary Spanish Cultural Studies*, edited by Barry Jordan and Rikki Morgan-Tamosunas, 179–192. London: Arnold.
Jordan, Barry and Morgan-Tamosunas, Rikki. 1998. *Contemporary Spanish Cinema*. Machester: Manchester University Press.
Labanyi, Jo. 1997. "Race, gender and disavowal in Spanish cinema of the early franco period: The missionary film and the folkloric musical". *Screen*, 38(3): 215–231.
Lara, Fernando. 1975. "El cine español ante una alternativa democrática". In *7 trabajos de base sobre el cine español*, edited by Fernando Lara et al, 219–244. Valencia: Fernando Torres Editor.
Losilla, Carlos. 1989. "Legislación, industria y escritura". In *Escritos sobre el cine español (1937–1987)*, edited by Vicente Benet, 33–43. Valencia: Filmoteca Valenciana.

Llinás, Fancesc (ed.). 1987. *4 años de cine español 1983–1986*. Madrid: Festival Internacional de Cine de Madrid: 174–193.
Martin-Márquez, Susan. 1999. *Feminist Discourse and Spanish Cinema: Sight Unseen*. Oxford: Oxford University Press.
Miró, Pilar. 1990. "Ten Years of Spanish Cinema". In *Literature, the Arts and Democracy: Spain in the Eighties*, edited by Samuell Amell, 38–45. London: Associated University Press.
Monterde, José Enrique. 1993. *Veinte años de cine español (1973–1992). Un cine bajo la paradoja*. Barcelona: Paidos.
Monterde, José Enrique. 1995. "Continuismo y disidencia (1951–1962)". In *Historia del cine español*, edited by Román Gubern et al, 239–294. Madrid: Cátedra.
Palacio, Manuel. 2011. "Marcos interpretativos, Transición democrática y cine. Un prólogo y tres consideraciones". In *El cine y la Transición política en España (1975–1982)*, edited by Manuel Palacio, 20–30. Madrid: Biblioteca Nueva.
Pecourt, Juan. 2008. *Los intelectuales y la transición política. Un estudio del campo de las revistas políticas en España*. Madrid: Centro de Investigaciones Sociológicas.
Pujol Ozonas, Cristina. 2011. *Fans, Cinéfilos y Cinéfagos. Una aproximación a las culturas y los gustos cinematográficos*. Barcelona: Editoria UOC.
Riambau, Esteve 1995. "El período socialista (1982–1995)". In *Historia del cine español*, edited by Román Gubern et al., 399–454. Madrid: Cátedra.
Rubio Aróstegui, Juan Arturo, 2003. *La política cultural del estado en los gobiernos socialistas (1982–1996)*. Gijón: Trea.
Smith, Paul Julian. 1998. "Homosexuality, Regionalism and Mass Culture: Eloy de la Iglesia's Cinema of Transition". In *Modes of Representation un Spanish Cinema*, edited by, Jenaro Talens and Santos Zunzunegui, 216–251. Minneapolis: University of Minnesota Press.
Torreiro, Casimiro. 1995a. "Del tardofranquismo a la democracia (1969–1982)". In *Historia del cine español*, edited by Román Gubern. et al, 341–398. Madrid: Cátedra.
Torreiro, Casimiro. 1995b. "¿Una dictadura liberal (1962–1969)?". In *Historia del cine español*, edited by Román Gubern. et al, 295–340. Madrid: Cátedra.
Trenzado Romero, Manuel. 1999. *Cultura de masas y cambio político: el cine español de la Transición*. Madrid: Centro de Investigaciones Sociológicas & Siglo XXI.
Triana-Toribio, Núria. 2003. *Spanish National Cinema*. London and New York: Routledge
Vallés Copeiro del Villar, Antonio. 1992. *Historia de la política del fomento del cine español*. Valencia: Filmoteca de la Generalitat Valenciana.
Vernon, Kathleen M. 2011. "Cine de mujeres en la Transición: La trilogía 'feminista' de Cecilia Bartolomé, Pilar Miró y Josefina Molina." In *El cine y la transición política en España (1975– 1982)*, edited by Manuel Palacio, 145–158. Madrid: Biblioteca Nueva.
Vidal-Beneyto, José. 1981. "Hacia una fundamentación teórica de la política cultural". *Revista Española de Investigaciones Sociológicas*, 16: 123–134.
Wood, Mary P. 2007. *Contemporary European Cinema*, London: Hodder Arnold.
Zunzunegui, Santos.1987. "Informe general sobre algunas cuestiones de interés para una proyección púbIlica o el cine español en la época del socialismo". In *4 años de cine español 1983–1986*, edited by in Fancesc Llinás, 174–193. Madrid: Festival Internacional de Cine de Madrid.

Press

Contracampo. "Primer Congreso Democrático del Cine Español: Conclusiones". Abril 1979: 25–34.
Fotogramas. "Hablan los productores: El cine español está mal protegido". Diciembre 1981: 28–31.
Lara, Fernando. "Cine Español. La aventura de la producción". *Diario 16*, 8/01/1983: 25.
Lara, Fernando. "Esto es el cine español". *Fotogramas*, mayo 1983: 42–54.
Pozo Arenas, Santiago. "Política cinematográfica del PSOE. Entrevista con Salvador Clotas", *Casablanca. Papeles de cine*, diciembre 1982: 13–16.
Pozo Arenas, Santiago. "Entrevista con Pilar Miró". *Casablanca. Papeles de cine*, febrero 1983: 12–16.

ICAA reports

ICAA. 1980). "Anuario del Cine Español" Available: 1980 (culturaydeporte.gob.es) Accessed: September 29, 2022.
ICAA. 1981. "Anuario del Cine Español" Available: VOL 08 (culturaydeporte.gob.es) Accessed: September 29, 2022.
ICAA. 1982. "Anuario del Cine Español" Available: VOL 10 (culturaydeporte.gob.es) Accessed: September 29, 2022.
ICAA. 1983. "Anuario del Cine Español" Available: bolet-n-1983.pdf (culturaydeporte.gob.es) Accessed: September 29, 2022.
ICAA. 1984. "Anuario del Cine Español" Available: https://www.culturaydeporte.gob.es/dam/jcr:41901c04-e806-4d2b-adfc-8fa5a1f11ce5/bolet-n-1984.pdf Accessed: September 29, 2022.
ICAA. 1985. "Anuario del Cine Español" Available: bolet-n-1985.pdf (culturaydeporte.gob.es) Accessed: September 29, 2022.
ICAA. 1986. "Anuario del Cine Español" Available: https://www.culturaydeporte.gob.es/cultura/areas/cine/mc/anuario-cine/anuarios/ano-2006.html Accessed: September 29, 2022.
ICAA. 1987. "Anuario del Cine Español" Available: bolet-n-1987.pdf (culturaydeporte.gob.es) Accessed: September 29, 2022.
ICAA. 1988. "Anuario del Cine Español" Available: bolet-n-1988.pdf (culturaydeporte.gob.es) Accessed: September 29, 2022.
ICAA. 1989. "Anuario del Cine Español" Available: bolet-n-1989.pdf (culturaydeporte.gob.es) Accessed: September 29, 2022.

Legislation and political parties' manifestos

Programa Electoral del Partido Socialista (1979) (PSOE's manifesto of 1979)
Programa Electoral del Partido Socialista (1982) (PSOE's manifesto of 1980)
Real Decreto 3304/1983 de 28 de diciembre, sobre protección a la cinematografía.
Real Decreto 3071/1977, de 11 de noviembre, por el que se regulan determinadas actividades cinematográficas.

3 The 1990s[1]
Hoping for a Better Future

Introduction

As the previous chapter has shown, the Miró Law has been one of the most discussed pieces of legislation by Spanish scholarship. On the contrary, the R.D. 1282/1989,[2] popularly known as the Semprún Decree, has barely been analysed; this scarcity of historiography is quite surprising, since the Semprún Decree was not only designed to change the funding policies established by the Miró Law, but it also set the model for the forthcoming pieces of legislation that regulated the Spanish film industry throughout the 1990s: the R.D. 1282/1989 became the model for the Ley 17/1994, passed during the latest Socialist government (1993–1996), and for the R.D. 1039/1997, enacted by the conservative government -the PP.[3] Among the few scholars who have addressed the Semprún Decree, it is commonly agreed that its most relevant features are threefold: to correct the deficiencies of the Miró Law funding policies, particularly their subjective criterium and mechanisms which were used to award the advance subsidy (Vallés Copeiro del Villar [1992] 2000: 227); to strengthen the Spanish film industry (Riambau [1995] 2010: 406 and Monterde 2002: 99), and, finally, to rationalise state funding to avoid financial embarrassment (Jordan 2000: 2).

Valuable though they are, these studies fail to fully explain why Semprún and his collaborators undertook such a reformist film policy, because scholars who have addressed it do not frame the Decree within the wider debates that were taking place in the European Economic Community (EEC) in the late 1980s and early 1990s relating to the most suitable strategies to protect and promote the European film industries. Without situating the Semprún Decree within this wider framework, it is difficult to interpret the changes it had on the Miró Law's funding policies. Consequently, one of this chapter's main contentions is that, whereas the Miró Law was enacted following the principles of the French film policy, as it has been explained in Chapter 2, the Semprún Decree was the first piece of legislation meant to align Spanish film legislation with the European film and media policies.

DOI: 10.4324/9781003373087-4

Before addressing how these debates and subsequent initiatives informed the Semprún Decree, this chapter maps the struggles that were taking place within the field of Spanish cinema in the late 1980s and early 1990s. Like in the early 1980s when the Miró Law was passed, both the dissident film agents, who deemed cinema as a vehicle for culture, and the producers and filmmakers of popular cinema were pushing for having their demands endorsed by a new piece of legislation. The former wanted to carry on with the funding policies established by the Miró Law that had widely benefited them. The latter, marginalised by the Miró Law's funding policies and its defence of cinema as a vehicle for culture, sought to change them in order to regain access to state funding and to establish new funding policies that would lead to the production of more market-driven films. Guess who was once again missed from this discussion? As in the 1980s, the presence of women in the film industry was not a concern for the agents in the field of Spanish cinema.

In short, while the Miró Law resulted from the victory of the dissident film agents over the field of Spanish cinema, to an extent, the Semprún Decree constitutes a temporary defeat of the dissident film culture: not only because the Decree set different funding policies, thereby side-lining the demands of the dissident film agents, but also because they lost the positions of power that they had hitherto occupied within the field.

The field of Spanish cinema in the 1990s: A new decade, a new beginning

The Miró Law was widely criticised by producers and filmmakers of popular cinema, such as Jose Frade, Antonio Cuevas, Mariano Ozores and Manuel Summers, throughout the years it was in force (1984–1989). For instance, Cuevas considered that the Law was not only promoting an auteurist art-cinema at the expense of more market-driven films, but, above all, the conviction that the state, through its selective funding, was somehow controlling film production to impose its own notion of national cinema (Cuevas in *Cineinforme*, diciembre 1984: 12). This criticism was particularly relevant because Cuevas was suggesting that the government was undertaking a state-run film policy more akin to a dictatorial regime than of a democratic state. Taking into account that the cultural policy undertaken by the PSOE throughout the 1980s was particularly aimed at distancing itself from the Francoist cultural practices, the mere suggestion that the government could be imposing its own particular film culture was completely against the democratic paradigm that the PSOE's cultural policy was built upon. On the contrary, the dissident film producers, such as Alfredo Matas, Luis Megino, Andrés Vicente Gómez and Elías Querejeta, praised the Law, which had allowed them to carry out a sustained production throughout the 1980s. In Querejeta's own words, the Miró Law was the best film law that ever existed in the history of Spanish cinema (Querejeta in *Cineinforme*, noviembre 1986: 19). For Vicente Gómez, the fact that the Law favoured quality films and prestigious auteurs and that it did not support producers of popular films such as Frade were the main reasons to praise the Law (Vicente Gómez in *Diario 16*, 2/08/1986: 2–4).

The fact that Miró was replaced by Fernando Méndez Leite, a key dissident member, as Head of the ICAA, fuelled controversy. Méndez Leite made it clear from the beginning that he had no intention to change the funding policies established by the Miró Law, as he stated in an interview in 1988 (Méndez Leite in Heredero, febrero 1986:6). Thus, he wanted to keep promoting auteur art-films that encompassed cultural values, despite these films having been proven to be unsuccessful at the national box-office. On the contrary, the aforementioned producers and filmmakers of popular cinema such as Frade, Cuevas, Ozores and Summers launched a manifesto in January 1987 against the selective funding established by the Miró Law. The Manifest, signed by 108 film professionals, was published by the two main daily newspapers, the progressive *El País* (4/02/1987) and the conservative *ABC* (3/02/1987 and 6/02/1987). The supporters of the manifesto considered that for the Miró Law to be applied fairly and objectively, every project had to be entitled to the advance subsidy. The criterium to award it had to be the profitability of the films previously produced by the producer and/or production company to which the advance subsidy would be granted. Once the film was produced, then the Sub-Committee for Technical Valorisation could decide whether to further grant the film additional complementary subsidies. This extra funding should be directed towards those films considered to be of special quality and for those films budgeted at more than 55 million pesetas (*ABC*, 3/02/1987: 77), thereby maintaining the Miró Law's complementary subsidies. The supporters of the manifesto believed that by introducing such changes they would accomplish their main aim, that the projects of both auteurist filmmakers such as Carlos Saura and those by popular filmmakers such as Ozores had equal opportunities to receive state funding, because they place the criterium to award selective funding in the audiences' acceptance of the films publicly funded instead of on the quality of the projects (*ABC*, 6/02/1987: 77).

This discussion should be framed within the long-standing debate about whether the state had to protect and promote a culturally or industrially driven cinema. Producers and filmmakers of popular cinema wanted to ensure the production of popular films that appealed to national audiences by strengthening the automatic subsidy awarded a posteriori while, at the same time, introducing quantifiable criteria to award the advance subsidy, such as the potential marketability of the films. On the other hand, dissident producers and filmmakers feared that their films could not amass sufficient box-office takings to make the automatic subsidy profitable; as a result, they would no longer be able to continue the production of films. It can also be argued that underlying this discussion was also the fear of the dissident filmmakers that if Frade and his supporters managed to impose their suggested funding policies, it would lead to a return of the by then extinct subproducts. If Spanish cinema still wanted to keep its international prestige as a democratic cinema, a comeback of the "old Spanish cinema" would be a failure for the aspirations of the dissident film agents, and, to a larger extent, for their political and cultural project of a modern Spain.

In the midst of this discussion, Jorge Semprún was appointed Minister of Culture. He was put in charge of the cultural policy because Felipe González, the Spanish president, reshuffled his cabinet in 1988, having Javier Solana moved to the Ministry of Education. Semprún's appointment was initially widely celebrated among the dissident film agents due both to his unquestionable democratic background as a former militant of the Spanish Communist Party (PCE) between 1942 and 1964 and his cultural prestige as both an intellectual and writer. Semprún had lived in exile in France since 1939 because his father was a member of the Republican government; he joined the PCE in exile in 1942, fighting along with the French communist resistance, and he was subsequently deported to Buchenwald concentration camp between 1943 and 1945. After being released, he spent ten years clandestinely organising the banned PCE in Madrid, from 1952 to 1962; in particular, he was in charge of leading the intellectual sector of the party and recruiting members among university students. During these years, he forged strong bonds with key dissident agents such as Ricardo Muñoz Suay, founder of the dissident specialised film magazine *Objetivo*, Juan Antonio Bardem, Julio Diamante and Querejeta, among others. When he was expelled from the PCE in 1964 for criticising its lack of democracy, he went back to France when he became a well-regarded writer, intellectual and screenwriter of political films such as the autobiographical Alain Resnais' *La guerre est finie* (*The War is Over*, 1966), and Costa-Gavras' *Z* (1969) and *L'Aveu* (*The Confession*, 1970) (Semprún 1977).

With such a background, it was reasonable to suppose that Semprún was going to continue with Miró's funding policies, which had particularly encouraged the works of the dissident filmmakers and producers. As mentioned earlier, Miró, following Lang's film policies, believed that it was the state responsibility to guarantee the production of films, regardless of their financial viability. On the contrary, Semprún believed that in a democratic country, the state should not be the main film producer (Semprún in Jarque, 13/12/1988: n.p). Therefore, against what the dissident film agents expected, Semprún rapidly dismissed Miró's funding policies by arguing that the Miró Law did not work because it had been done by a film director to promote the work of other film directors rather than to create and consolidate a robust film industry (Semprún in Jarque, 13/12/1988: n.p). Both statements reveal an important shift in the understanding of the role that the state had to play in the management of cinema. Alongside supporting auteurist films primarily valued for their artistic merits, it was also necessary to create a self-sufficient film industry in order to reduce state intervention. To a wider extent, it can also be argued that Semprún was also reluctant to impose an official film culture. That is to say, he rejected the idea that the state was responsible for deciding which films had to be made. Consequently, it was necessary to encourage private funding in film production. Clearly, he was bearing in mind the aforementioned criticisms made by the producers and filmmakers of popular cinema, and, consequently, he wanted to distance himself from the cinephile film policies carried out by the dissident film agents. Moreover, his cultural policy was informed by the belief that, in a democratic society, the production of cultural goods had to emanate from the people rather than from the state in order to guarantee a plurality of cultural practices, as he expressed once he had left the Minister of Culture (Semprún 1993: 314).

Likewise, as it has been suggested before, in order to align Spanish film policies with the European strategies for the management of the film industry, Semprún and his collaborators realised that it was no longer sufficient to keep pouring public funds into film production, but, instead, the industry had to bring together diversified sources of funding that would include private and, above all, television capital. The first step that Semprún took to dissociate himself from the dissident film agents was to put Miguel Satrústegui, Subsecretary of the Ministry of Culture, with no links to the film industry, in charge of supervising the drafting of a new decree, instead of entrusting it to Méndez Leite, who consequently resigned as Head of the ICAA in December 1988. He was replaced by Miguel Marías, who headed the ICAA between 1988 and 1990 and drafted the new decree.

Maria's main objective, as stated in a personal interview with the author, was to establish new funding policies that would make the production sector less reliant on state subsidies and more dependent on box-office takings because he considered that the Miró Law had been a complete failure. According to Marías, the Miró Law's two most damaging effects were, first, that the Law was over-financing projects with public funds; secondly, that it was also contributing to the decapitalisation of the Film Protection Fund, since the Law was subsidising films that performed well at the box-office through a limitless automatic subsidy and the cumulative complementary subsidies. The aim of the Semprún Decree was, therefore, to fix these two negative aspects of the Miró Law. However, when asked whether there was any concern amongst policymakers about the very little presence of women in the film industry, Marías noted that there was no preoccupation about it, not even a discussion amongst film professionals whom with him negotiated the forthcoming decree. It was assumed that if women wanted to work in the film industry, they will naturally manage to do so and, therefore, no affirmative actions were needed to grant the access of women film professionals to the film industry. Furthermore, he also acknowledged that the ICAA did not make any institutional surveys to gather data on the presence of women working in the film industry. In fact, while producers and filmmakers gathered in different associations that lobbied for having their interests enshrined by the law, there was not an association that defended the women professionals' interests. Consequently, gender equality in the film industry was not a topic for discussion (Marías in Fernández Meneses, 2023). It has to be noted that while the dissident film agents and the producers and directors of commercial cinema gathered into associations -UPCE and AIPCE respectively- to lobby for having their demands consecrated by law, women did not. Therefore, they could hardly play an active role in the struggles taking part in the field of Spanish cinema during the 1980s and 1990s. This situation changed when the Women's Filmmakers and Audiovisual Professionals Association, CIMA, was born in 2006, as we will see in the next chapter.

Towards a self-sufficient industry: The Semprún Decree

When Semprún was appointed Minister of Culture, the Spanish film industry was facing another crisis. Film production had not only dropped during the years in which the Miró Law was in force from 70 featured films in 1984 to 38 in 1989, but the market share for Spanish films had also dropped from 26% in 1984 to 6% in 1989 (Vallés Copeiro del Villar [1992] 2000: 222–223). Against this background, the Decree was passed in August 1989. According to its prologue:

> In the production sector, public funding's main aim is to promote independent producers and to foster private inversion in order to reduce state interventionism and to strength the sector's financial structure
> (R.D. 1282/1989, Prólogo)[4]

To accomplish such aim, the Decree changed the state funding available, the criteria and the mechanisms to access it. Regarding the automatic, advance, and complementary subsidies for film production, the main changes are detailed in Figure 3.1.[5]

Regarding the automatic subsidy, the Decree reduced the period over which it was calculated from four to two years, thereby making it easier for the producers to recuperate their investment. The Miró Law did not set any limit for the three automatic subsidies it established, and, since they were cumulative, a film could be financed with public funds up to 65% of its box-office returns (by adding the complementary subsidies for those films considered to be of special quality and those films budgeted at more than 55 million pesetas (330,000€/£277,000), as it has been explained in Chapter 2. By establishing limits to the automatic subsidy, the Semprún Decree was trying to avoid not only over-financing projects with public funds, but also the decapitalisation of the Film Protection Fund that resulted from subsidising films that performed well at the box-office.

The advance subsidy was now paid to producers instead of to directors and it was limited to 50 million pesetas (300,000€/£258,000) per film. If the film was considered to be of extraordinary cost, the advance subsidy could reach

	Miró Law (1983)	Semprún Decree (1989)
Automatic subsidy	15% of the box-office returns during the first four years of the film's commercialisation	15% of the box office-returns during the first two years of the film's commercialisation
	Could not surpass the producer's investment, nor 50% of the film's budget	Could not surpass the producer's investment, nor 50% of the film's real cost
	No limits	Maximum of 200 million pesetas per film or 100 million if the producer had been awarded the advance subsidy
Advance subsidy	Directed towards: • Quality films • Experimental films • Films for children • Films made by new filmmakers Criteria: • Quality and artistic value of the project Limits: It could not surpass the film's budget and it could only cover up to 50% of the film's budget	Directed towards: • Films made by new filmmakers • Films of special quality Criteria: • Quality and artistic value of the project • The film's budget • The film's financing plan • The producer's financial solvency Limits: 50 million per film provided if it did not surpass the producer's own investment
Complementary subsidy	Directed towards: • Films of special quality • Films budgeted at more than 55 million pesetas These were cumulative Limits: Could not surpass the producer's investment, nor 50% of the film's budget	Two types: • 25% of the film's gross income for those films that had not been awarded the advance subsidy or received funding from elsewhere. • It could not surpass the producer's investment, nor 50% of the film's real cost • Films of special quality: ten subsidies a year of 15 million pesetas each

Figure 3.1 The Semprún Decree's main changes in the subsidies for film production
Source: The author.

200 million pesetas (1,200,000€/£1,000,000) only if the Minister of Culture approved it. The advance subsidy was now awarded by an Advisory Committee that replaced the former Sub-committee for Technical Valorisation. The committee was appointed by the Ministry of Culture among members proposed both by the film professional associations and by the Head of the ICAA (R.D.1282/1989, Capítulo II, Ayudas para la producción de largometrajes, Sección Segunda, Ayudas sobre Proyecto). The Miró Law also established limits to the advanced subsidy. However, as it has been pointed out in Chapter 2, producers tended to inflate the film's budget, and, since funding could be also found in TVE and the autonomous governments, producers could obtain benefits in the financial stage without having to release the film. Since this had been one of the most criticised aspects of the Miró Law, the Semprún Decree assured that the producer had to take financial risks in order to access to state funding by linking the advance subsidy to his investment and not to the film's budget. Another of the main criticisms made against the Miró Law was that the advance subsidy was awarded according to such an unquantifiable and subjective criterium as the quality of the films; accordingly, the Semprún Decree changed the criteria to access to it: despite recognising the importance of the quality of the projects to obtain the advance subsidy, the Decree placed the emphasis on a more quantifiable and objective criterium such as the financial viability of the film. By removing the Sub-committee for Technical Valorisation, the decree was seeking to dismiss the criticisms previously levelled against the Miró Law relating to the potential for political favouritism.

Finally, alongside both the automatic and the advance subsidy, the Semprún Decree also set two complementary subsidies aimed at fostering both market-driven films and films valued for their artistic qualities. Regarding the former, by granting 25% of gross income to those producers who had not been awarded the advance subsidy, the decree sought to promote films that had performed well at the box-office. The subsidy for those films considered to be of special quality, awarded by a jury of renowned film professionals designated annually by the Head of the ICAA, was clearly aimed at protecting those films that did not reach mainstream audiences.[6]

Barry Jordan has suggested that the Semprún Decree was the result of "the PSOE's 'neoliberal'" economic policies [which made the government adopt] a particular hard-line policy on film funding" (2000: 184–185). However, Jordan's statement can be further qualified if taking into account the following factors. Firstly, the emphasis that the Decree placed on the idea that cinema had be considered as a cultural good that had to be protected and fostered by the state (R.D.1282/1989, Prólogo) reveals that Semprún had no intention to leave Spanish cinema to the rules of the free market.[7] Secondly, by 1986 the PSOE's cultural policy had slightly changed, since the PSOE's manifesto recognised that the production and management of culture could not rely exclusively on state support, but that it was necessary instead to allow the private initiative to become part of the production of cultural goods (Apartado IV, Epígrafe 4.13).[8] Nonetheless, the PSOE still gave major importance to the role that the state had to play on the production, promotion and dissemination of cultural goods. Finally, the Decree clearly employed dual arguments in order to justify its funding policies. It is true that the Decree wanted to foster a more self-sufficient film industry and thus market criteria were put into place to allow access both to the advance subsidy and to the subsidies directed towards the distribution and exhibition sectors. However, the special protection that both the complementary subsidy and the distribution's and exhibition's subsidies provided to those films considered to be of special quality reveals that the Semprún Decree, building upon ideas proposed by the Miró Law, conceived films not as simple commodities made exclusively for entertainment, but as bearers of cultural values. Rather than pursuing the neoliberal film policy to which Jordan refers, the Semprún Decree, and, to a larger extent, the PSOE's cultural policy in the late 1980s, echoed the strategies put into place by the EEC to manage the audiovisual industry.

A European common audiovisual policy as such did not exist until the European Commission launched the "Television without Frontiers" directive (TVWF directive or 89/225/EEC) in October 3, 1989. The TVWF directive constituted the first attempt to have a common legal framework with which to regulate the European audiovisual industry (Collins 1994: 93); consequently, it is from 1989 onwards that we can speak about a European audiovisual policy, which exemplified what Richard Collins has defined as "one of the 'grand narratives' of the EEC" (Collins 1994: 91–92). Namely, the conflict between proponents of rival instruments for the realisation of Community policy goals: "between advocates of political intervention in markets to secure specific outcomes and liberals (who eschew political intervention in markets)" (Collins 1994: 91–92). This conflict, as Collin explains, embodied a number of consecutive initiatives that the EEC put into place. On the one hand, initiatives aimed at liberalising the European audiovisual market by allowing the free circulation and broadcasting of television programmes among the twelve EEC's members states - the TVWF directive. On the other hand, initiatives directed "to countervail the effects of the single market [the TVWF] had sought to create" (Collins 1994: 96); for example, the creation of pan-European funding mechanisms such as the Council of Europe's Eurimages Fund (1989) and the European Commission's MEDIA programme (1991) (Collins 1994: 93–97). Hence, while the European Commission's measures were guided by economic goals, the Council of Europe's initiatives clearly had cultural objectives. As Paul Hainsworth (1994) points out, Eurimages prioritised the cultural projects it founded because they were deemed vehicles of European identity. In fact, Eurimages' president Gaetano Adinolfi highlighted in 1991 "the eminently cultural nature of the fund, whose main objective [was] to support works which uphold the values that are part and parcel of the European identity" (quoted in Hainsworth 1994: 15).

The Semprún Decree cannot be understood outside this notion about the role that cinema had in the creation of national identities. Neither can it be framed outside the aforementioned European strategies intended to make the

European audiovisual industries more competitive so they could challenge the presence of American-produced films and television programmes in Europe. In short, the Semprún Decree has to be considered as a reflection of the tensions between the liberal and the dirigiste initiatives explained above. Hence, while is true that the Decree aimed to foster a self-sufficient film industry that would promote a competitive cinema that could compete in an increasingly globalised world, which could be regarded as a liberal initiative, the Decree itself was a dirigiste initiative, since it emphasised the need for state protection of that very same industry.

Surviving promises: New careers and unfulfilled dreams

Scholarship has highlighted the following main characteristics about the New Spanish cinema of the 1990s: firstly, its diversity and its popular appeal, often alluding to the commercial and/or critical success of such different films as *Salsa Rosa* (Manuel Gómez Pereira, 1991), *Belle Epoque* (Fernando Trueba, 1992), *Todos a la cárcel* (Luis García Berlanga, 1993), *Todo es mentira* (Álvaro Fernández Armero, 1994), *El día de la bestia* (Alex de la Iglesia, 1995), *Tesis* (Alejandro Amenábar, 1996), *Secretos del corazón* (Montxo Armendáriz, 1997), *Barrio* (Fernando León de Aranoa, 1998), *Torrente, el brazo tonto de la ley* (Santiago Segura, 1998) and *Manolito Gafotas* (Miguel Albadalejo, 1999), to name but a few. Secondly, it has been also argued that the period is characterised by the concentration of hits around very few names, Álex de la Iglesia, Fernando Trueba, Alejandro Amenábar, Santiago Segura, and the preponderance of comedy (Palacio and Vernon 2012: 481). Finally, the boom of debutant filmmakers making their first features: 158 filmmakers between 1990 and 1999, amongst whom 31 were women (Heredero 1999: 12).

As I have analysed in the previous chapter, scholars have found a direct link between the Miró Law's funding policies and the standardisation and commercial failure of the films produced throughout the 1980s, and I have already tested some of those assumptions. On the contrary, scholars have not established any connection between the legislation of the period and the films produced throughout the 1990s. That is to say, it appears to be that the renewal of the themes and visual style of Spanish films, their wider appeal for national audiences and the blooming of new filmmakers are due to a combination of the following reasons: the personal effort of the auteurs among the new generation of filmmakers to come up with different formulas that diversified the national production (Heredero 1997); the new filmmakers' rejection of previous cinematic models to return to genre formulas, primarily comedy, that had previously proven to be successful (Triana-Toribio 2003); the changes in the Spanish media landscape with the appearance of multimedia conglomerates and private television companies that started to invest in film production (Pavlovic 2009). Furthermore, when scholars have established any type of link between the state film policy and the renewal of Spanish cinema in the 1990s, they have done so by referring to the Ley 17/1994,[9] commonly known as the Alborch Law (Riambau [1995]2010, Heredero 1997, Jordan and Morgan-Tamosunas 1998, Monterde 2002, Pavlovic 2009). According to these scholars, the Alborch Law marks the moment when the state film policy adopted more aggressive market criteria, thereby contributing to the production of more marketable Spanish films. However, the Alborch Law kept in force the funding policies already established by the Semprún Decree.

Therefore, while acknowledging the reasons exposed by Carlos Heredero, Nuria Triana-Toribio and Tatjana Pavlovic mentioned above, this chapter argues that the Semprún Decree must be considered when explaining the changes in Spanish cinema of the 1990s. This is so because Semprún Decree was aimed at promoting a competitive cinema that did not rely so much on state funding as it did on private investment, television funding and box-office takings. Bearing in mind that state funding still counted for 34% of the film's cost in 1994 (Riambau [1995] 2010: 416), the modifications in the funding policies introduced by the Semprún Decree cannot be overlooked. The Semprún Decree rewarded the highest-grossing films by placing more emphasis on the automatic and complementary subsidies tied to the films' market performance rather than on the advance subsidy. Hence, it could easily be argued that these reforms played an important role in the appearance of more market-driven films, especially if one takes into account that private television networks, except Canal Plus, which established its film production branch Sogecine in 1990, did not begin to invest in film production steadily until 1999, when they were legally bound to do so by the Ley 22/1999. In short, the Semprún Decree helped to foster the diversification and popularity of Spanish films by rewarding films oriented towards the box-office. By maintaining the advance subsidy intended to new filmmakers, the Decree also contributed to the rising of debutant women filmmakers throughout the 1990s, amounting to 17% (Faulkner 2020: 65).

The presence of women in roles above-the-line (direction, scriptwriting, and production) remained low, even though it was higher than in the 1980s, as shown in Figure 3.2

- Out of 715 films produced throughout the decade, 18 were directed by women (2.52%), while in the 1990s, out of 608 films produced throughout the decade, 59 were directed by women (9.70%).
- We find only 8 films written by women (1.12%) and 51 co-written by women (7.13%) in the 1980s, while these numbers rose to 23 films written only by women (3.78%) and 118 co-written by men and women (19.41%) in the 1990s.
- Finally, we find 66 films produced by women (9.23%) in the 1980s and 142 (23.36%) in the 1990s.

WOMEN IN ABOVE THE LINE ROLES 1990-1999

YEARS	TOTAL	FILMS DIRECTED BY WOMEN		FILMS WRITTEN BY WOMEN		FILMS PRODUCED BY WOMEN	
		Nº	%	Nº	%	Nº	%
1990	41	2	4.88	5	12.20	7	17.07
1991	45	3	6.67	11	24.44	4	8.89
1992	43	2	4.65	11	25.58	7	16.28
1993	51	4	7.84	7	13.73	5	9.80
1994	52	4	7.69	14	26.92	5	9.62
1995	70	9	12.86	12	17.14	17	24.29
1996	80	8	10.00	17	21.25	22	27.50
1997	61	6	9.84	11	18.03	24	39.34
1998	99	13	13.13	32	32.32	29	29.29
1999	66	8	12.12	21	31.82	22	33.33
TOTAL	608	59	9.70	141	23.19	142	23.36

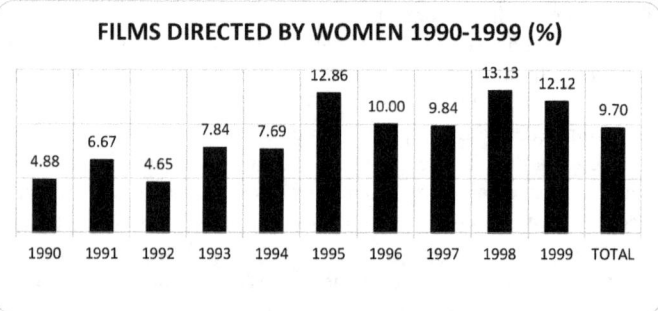

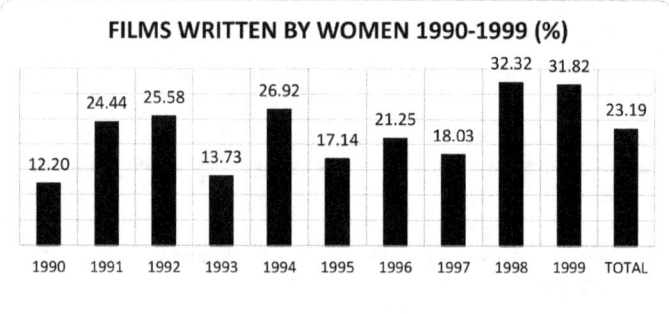

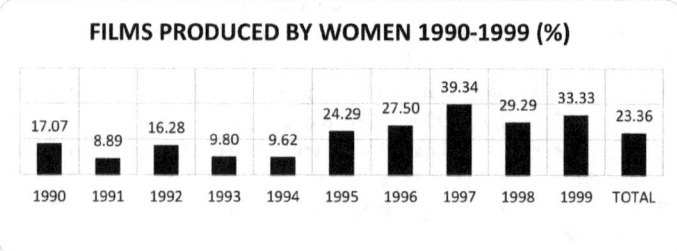

Figure 3.2 The presence of women working in the above-the-line roles in the 1990s
Source: Antonio Fernández Segura with data from ICAA and IMDB.

The 1990s saw the debut of 31 women directors: Rosa Vergés, *Boom Boom* (1990), *Souvenir* (1994) and *Tic Tac* (1997), Ana Belén, *Como ser mujer y no morir en el intento* (1991), Chus Gutiérrez, *Sublet* (1992), *Sexo oral* (1994), *Alma gitana* (1996) and *Insomnio* (1998), Gracia Querejeta, *Una estación de paso* (1992), *El ultimo viaje de Robert Raylands* (1996) and *Cuando vuelvas a mi lado* (1999), Arantxa Lazkano, *Los años oscuros* (1993), Maite Ruiz de Austri, *El regreso del viento del norte* (1993) and *¡Qué vecinos tan animales!* (1998), Cristina Esteban, *Ojalá, Val de Omar* (1994), María Miró *Los baúles del retorno* (1995), Marta Balletbò-Coll, *Costa Brava, family album* (1995) and *Cariño, he enviado a los hombres a la luna* (1998) co-directed alongside Ana Simón Cerezo, Azucena Rodríguez, *Entre rojas* (1995) and *Puede ser divertido* (1995), Icíar Bollaín, *Hola, ¿estás sola?* (1995) and *Flores de otro mundo* (1999), Mónica Laguna, *Tengo una casa* (1995), Mireia Ros, *La moños* (1996), Eva Lesmes, *Pon un hombre en tu vida* (1996), Manane Rodríguez, *Retrato de una mujer con hombre al fondo* (1996), Dunia Ayaso, *Perdona bonita, pero Lucas me quería a mí* (1996) and *El grito en el cielo* (1998), co-directed with her long-term collaborator Félix Sabroso, Yolanda García Serrano, *Amor de hombre* (1997), co-directed alongside Juan Luis Iborra, Pilar Sueioo, *Cuando el mundo se acabe te seguiré amando* (1998), María Ripoll, *Lluvia en los zapatos* (1998), Dolores Payás, *Me llamo Sara* (1998), Eugenia Kleber, *Torturado por las rosas* (1998), Nuria Villazán, *Monos como Becky* (1999), co-directed alongside Joaquim Jordá, Patricia Ferreira, *Sé quién eres* (1999), Laura Mañá, *Sexo por compasión* (1999) and Helena Tabernas, *Yoyes* (1999). In this category is worth mentioning the collaborative soft-pornographic film *El dominio de los sentidos* (1996), first feature film of its five directors Judith Collel, Isabell Gardela, Nuria Olivé-Bellés, Teresa Pelegrí and Maria Ripoll. Amongst these debutant women directors, Arantxa Lazkano, Cristina Esteban, María Miró and Ana Belén only made their debut films, leaving film direction afterwards. Ana Belén has nonetheless had a successful career as an actress since the 1960s.

The female directors from the 1970s and 1980s who continued directing films during the 1990s were Josefina Molina's with her fifth and sixth films, *Lo más natural* (1990) and *La Lola se va a los puertos* (1993) respectively, Pilar Miró with her seventh, eighth, ninth and tenth films, *Beltenebros* (1991), *El pájaro de la felicidad* (1993), *El perro del hortelano* (1996) and *Tu nombre evenena mis sueños* (1996) respectively, Isabel Coixet with her second and third feature films, *Cosas que nunca te dije* (1995) and *A los que aman* (1996) respectively, Cecilia Bartolomé with her third film *Lejos de África* (1996), Ana Díez with her second film *Todo está oscuro* (1997) and Pilar Távora with her second film, *Yerma* (1998). Consequently, from the 11 women who directed films in the 1980s, 6 managed to have a continuous career, particularly Miró who directed four films in the 1990s. The five female directors who did not directed any films in the 1990s were Isabel Mula, Lina Romay and Tana Kaleya, who directed soft pornographic films in the 1980s, Maria Luisa

Bemberg, who made career in Argentina, and Cristina Andreu, who moved into television.[10]

Regarding scriptwriting, we can find similar tendencies than in the 1980s: women directors tend to write or to co-write their own films following the auteurist mode of production -Rosa Vergés, Pilar Miró, Azucena Rodríguez, Maite Ruíz de Austri, Gracia Querejeta, Chus Gutiérrez, Arantxa Lazkano, María Miró, Icíar Bollaín, Isabel Coixet, Marta Balletbò-Coll, Mónica Laguna, Judith Collel, Isabell Gardela, Nuria Olivé-Bellés, Teresa Pelegrí, Maria Ripoll, Cecilia Bartolomé, Dunia Ayaso, Eva Lesmes, Manane Rodríguez, Mireia Ros, Ana Díez, Marisa Sistach, Eugenia Kleber, Pilar Távora, Ana Simón Cerezo, Pilar Sueiro, Dolores Payás, Nuria Villazán, Patricia Ferreira, Helena Tabernas and Laura Maná.[11]

Amongst women scriptwriters who made their debut and managed to write more than one film throughout the decade we find Carmen Rico Godoy, who wrote films for José Luís García Sánchez, Ana Belén and Enrique Urbizu; Almudena Grandes wrote the two adaptations of her own novels, *Las edades de Lulú* (Bigas Luna, 1990) and *Malena es un nombre de tango* (Gerardo Herrero, 1996); Yolanda García Serrano, who specialised in popular comedies: *El robobo de la jojoya* (Álvaro Sáenz de Heredia, 1991), *Oh, cielos* (Ricardo Franco, 1994), *¿De qué se rien las mujeres?* (Joaquin Oristell, 1996), *Amor de hombre* (Juan Luis Iborra, 1997) and all Manuel Gómez Pereira's comedies of the 1990s, including *Salsa rosa* (1991), *¿Por qué lo llaman amor cuando quieren decir sexo?* (1991), *Todos los hombres sois iguales* (1994), *El amor perjudica seriamente la salud* (1996) and *Entre las piernas* (1998); Cuca Canals, who wrote most of Bigas Luna's films of the 1990s: *Jamón, jamón* (1992), *Huevos de oro* (1993), *La teta y la luna* (1994), *La camarera del Titanic* (1997) and *Volaverunt* (1999); Ángeles González Sinde, who later came to be Ministry of Culture (2009–2011), wrote Ricardo Franco's *Lágrimas negras* (1998) and Gerardo Vera's *Segunda piel* (1999); Elvira Lindo wrote Miguel Albadalejo's films *La primera noche de mi vida* (1998), *Ataque verbal* (1999) and *Manolito Gafotas* (1999). Finally, Lola Salvador downed her screenwriting from four films in the 1980s to just two films written in the 1990s -*Tierno verano de lujurias y azoteas* (Jaime Chávarri, 1993) and *Puede ser divertido* (Azucena Rodríguez, 1995).

Lastly, regarding production, amongst the women directors who produced their own films we find Balletbò-Coll and Bartolomé; producers who started their careers in the 1980s and continued throughout the 1990s were Isabel Mula, who moved from the soft-pornographic films of the 1980s to produce dramas and international co-productions in the 1990s.[12] Ana Huete continued to back the same auteurist filmmakers as she had backed in the 1980s -Manuel Iborra, David Trueba and Emilio Martínez Lázaro[13] and she also produced the television series *Las chicas de hoy en día* (1991–1992), *Pepa y Pepe* (1995) and *Ellas son así* (1999); finally, Helena Matas carried out the production of

Tierno verano de lujurias y azoteas (Jaime Chávarri, 1993) and *Puede ser divertido* (Azucena Rodríguez, 1995). The 1990s also saw the debut of 11 women producers (I include here those who managed to produce more than one film): Rosa Romero, who backed women directors such as Rosa Vergés (*Boom, boom*, 1990), Marion Hänsel (*Entre el cielo y la tierra*, 1990), Gracia Querejeta (*El ultimo viaje de Robert Raylands*, 1996), popular filmmakers such as Félix Rotaeta (*Chatarra*, 1991) and international co-productions such as *Cambio de rumbo* (Michael Bray, 1997) and who worked alongside another debutant producer, Victoria Borrás in *Entre el cielo y lastierra* (Marion Hänsel, 1990) and *Chatarra* (Félix Rotaeta, 1991); Cristina Huete, Ana Huete's sister, who produced *Amo tu cama, rica* (Emilio Martínez Lázaro, 1991), *Two Much* (Fernando Colomo, 1995) and *La buena vida* (David Trueba, 1996); Sylvie Porchez, who acted as an executive producer of the popular franchise comedies *Makinavaja, el ultimo chorizo* (Carlos Suárez, 1992), *¡Semos peligrosos! (usease Makinavaja 2)* (Carlos Suárez, 1993) and its television spin-off *Makinavaja* (TVE, 1995–1997), as well as *Los porretas* (Carlos Suárez, 1996) and *Manolito Gafotas* (Miguel Albadalejo, 1999); Beatriz de la Gándara backed Fernando Colomo's films *Alegre ma non troppo* (1994) *El efecto mariposa* (1995), *Eso* (1997) and *Los años bárbaros* (1998), women filmmakers such as Azucena Rodríguez (*Entre rojas*, 1995), Icíar Bollaín (*Hola, ¿estás sola?*, 1995), novel directors such as Alberto Lecchi (*El dedo en la llaga*, 1996), David Menkes with his first and second features (*Más que amor, frenesí*, 1996 and *Atómica*, 1998 respectively) and Alberto Duran (*Coraje*, 1998) and Mauel Ibrora's second feature film *Pepe Guindo* (1999); Esther García, producer and production manager of Pedro and Agustín Almodóvar's production company El Deseo, who began her impressive producer career with Almodóvar's *La flor de mi secreto* (1995) and *Tengo una casa* (Mónica Laguna, 1995)[14]; Pilar Sueiro produced the independent filmmaker Juan Pinza's films *La leyenda de la doncella* (1994) and *Érase otra vez* (1999); Mariela Besuievsky backed international co-productions -*Bajo la piel* (Francisco J. Lombardi, 1996), *Don Juan, de Moliere* (Jacques Weber, 1998) and *El coronel no tiene quien le escriba* (Arturo Ripstein, 1999), Mariano Barroso's debut *Éxtasis* (1996), Gerardo Herrero's *Malena es un nombre de tango* (1996), *Territorio comanche* (1997) and *Frontera Sur* (1998); Piluca Baquero produced independent filmmakers such as Enrique Gabriel's *En la puta calle* (1996) and *Las huellas borradas* (1999), Jesús Franco's *Killer Barbys* (1996), Santiago Lorenzo's *Mamá es boba* (1998); Mate Cantero produced international coproductions -*El apartamento* (Gilles Mimouni, 1995), *La mujer del cosmonauta* (Jacques Monnet, 1997), *La vida prometida* (Regis Wargnier, 1999) and *Volaverunt* (Bigas Luna, 1999), alongside independent dramas, *El faro* (Manuel Balaguer, 1998).[15] Finally, María Dolores Barrero produced the documentaries *Mambí* (Teodoro Ríos and Santiago Ríos, 1997) and the drama *Mararía* (Antonio José Betancour, 1998).

As Figures 3.3-3.14 show, out of 608 films produced between 1990 and 1999, the number of films produced throughout the decade with women working in the different departments read as follows:

- In Film Editing, it remained below 25%, even though it raised from 14% in the 1980s to 23% in the 1990s.
- In Production Management, it increased from 12% in the 1980s to 65% in the 1990s.
- In Second Unit and Assistant Direction, it rose from 12% in the 1980s to 49% in the 1990s.
- In the Art Department, it moved from 11.5% in the 1980s to 46% in the 1990s.
- In Sound, it remained too low, from an almost insignificant 1.5% of the 1980s to 15% of the 1990s.
- In Camera and Electrical we also see very low numbers in the 1980s -11%- but they increased up to 42% in the 1990s.
- Costume and Wardrobe remained a very feminised department in the 1990s as it was in the 1980s -73% and 44% respectively.
- Makeup and Hairdressing also had bigger presence of women than men: 46% in the 1980s and 68.5% in the 1990s.
- The Editorial department saw an increase from 35% in the 1980s to 45% in the 1990s, reaffirming therefore the tendency to feminisation to this department.
- Script and Continuity had a similar pattern as the Editorial department: from 30% in the 1980s to 50% in the 1990s.
- Music improved the presence of women, from 1.8% in the 1980s to 13% in the 1990s, being excessively low numbers, nonetheless.
- Eight women worked as cinematographers throughout the whole decade.

These numbers tell us that the key trends of the 1980s did not substantially changed throughout the 1990s: despite women managed to improve their presence in those technical departments that have traditionally been a boys' club -Sound, Camera and Electrical, Music and Cinematography- Makeup and Hairdressing, Costume and Wardrobe, Editorial (assistant editors) and Script and Continuity remained highly feminised departments. Likewise, the fact that only eight women managed to work as cinematographers in the whole decade still speaks volumes about how technical departments remained a "macho" issue. Women also managed, slowly but firmly, to increase their presence in those departments that are closer to the above-the-line roles and, consequently, closer to the positions of power: Production Management and Second Unit and Assistant Direction. However, we need to be careful when appraising the major presence of women in these departments, since, as Melanie Bell has already argued, these departments have been traditionally deemed to be auxiliary

FILMS WITH WOMEN WORKING IN THE FILM EDITING DEPARTMENT			
YEARS	FILMS	Nº	%
1990	41	13	31.71
1991	45	17	37.78
1992	43	12	27.91
1993	51	12	23.53
1994	51	13	25.49
1995	70	12	17.14
1996	80	16	20.00
1997	61	12	19.67
1998	100	26	26.00
1999	66	11	16.67
TOTAL	608	144	**23.68**

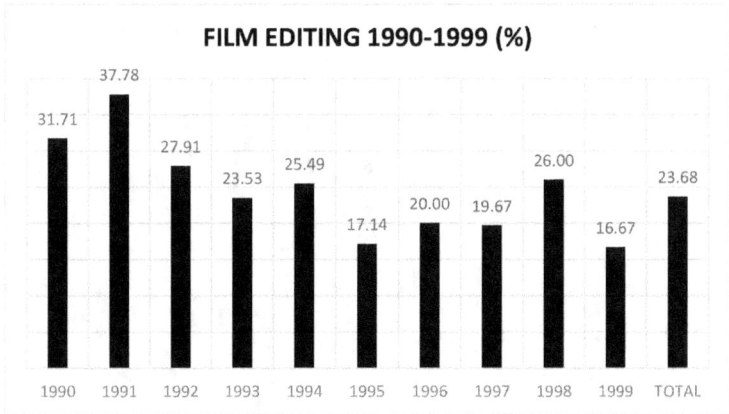

Figure 3.3 The presence of women in the Film Editing department in the 1990s
Source: Antonio Fernández Segura with data from the ICAA and IMDB.

FILMS WITH WOMEN WORKING IN THE PRODUCTION MANAGEMENT DEPARTMENT			
YEARS	FILMS	Nº	%
1990	41	8	19.51
1991	45	13	28.89
1992	43	23	53.49
1993	51	35	68.63
1994	51	34	66.67
1995	70	52	74.29
1996	80	62	77.50
1997	61	45	73.77
1998	100	75	75.00
1999	66	49	74.24
TOTAL	608	396	65.13

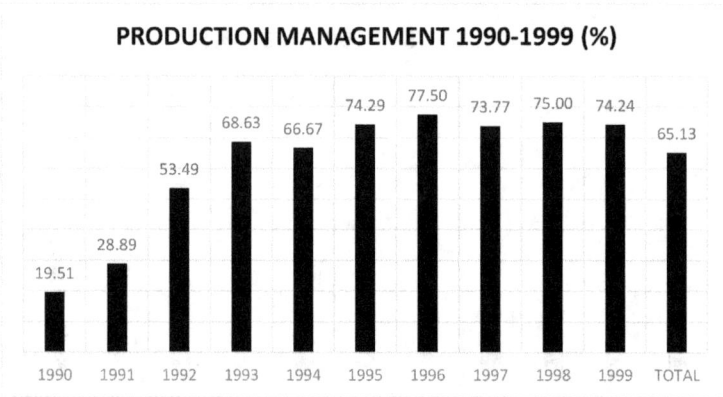

Figure 3.4 The presence of women in the Production Management department in the 1990s

Source: Antonio Fernández Segura with data from the ICAA and IMDB.

FILMS WITH WOMEN WORKING IN THE SECOND UNIT OR ASSISTANT DIRECTOR DEPARTMENT			
YEARS	FILMS	Nº	%
1990	41	11	26.83
1991	45	22	48.89
1992	43	15	34.88
1993	51	21	41.18
1994	51	23	45.10
1995	70	35	50.00
1996	80	44	55.00
1997	61	39	63.93
1998	100	42	42.00
1999	66	46	69.70
TOTAL	608	298	49.01

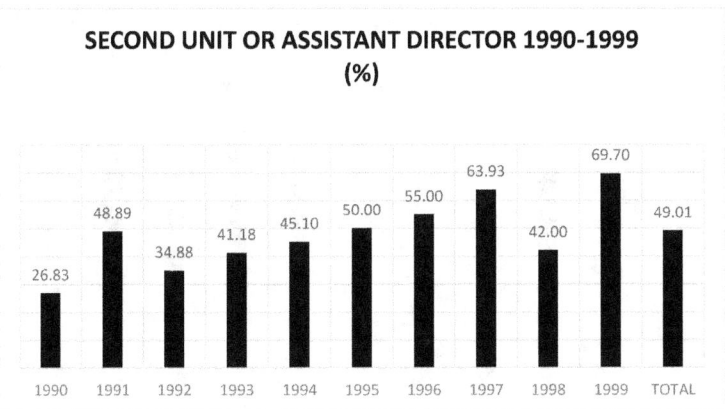

Figure 3.5 The presence of women in the Second Unit or Assistant Director department in the 1990s

Source: Antonio Fernández Segura with data from the ICAA and IMDB.

FILMS WITH WOMEN WORKING IN THE ART DEPARTMENT			
YEARS	FILMS	Nº	%
1990	41	14	34.15
1991	45	15	33.33
1992	43	20	46.51
1993	51	16	31.37
1994	51	21	41.18
1995	70	34	48.57
1996	80	39	48.75
1997	61	38	62.30
1998	100	50	50.00
1999	66	34	51.52
TOTAL	608	281	46.22

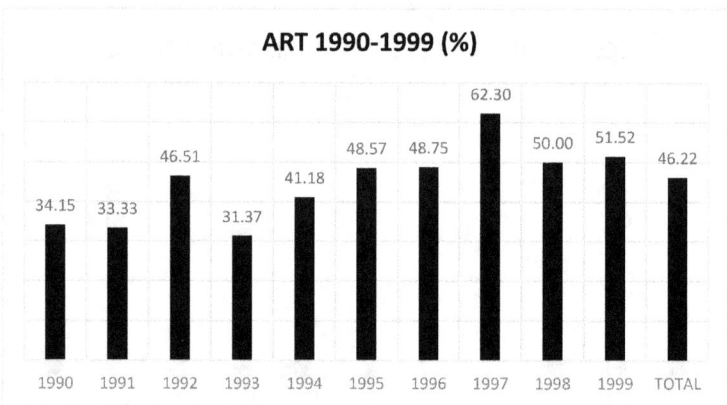

Figure 3.6 The presence of women in the Art department in the 1990s

Source: Antonio Fernández Segura with data from the ICAA and IMDB.

FILMS WITH WOMEN WORKING IN THE SOUND DEPARTMENT			
YEARS	FILMS	Nº	%
1990	41	0	0.00
1991	45	3	6.67
1992	43	3	6.98
1993	51	4	7.84
1994	51	6	11.76
1995	70	12	17.14
1996	80	15	18.75
1997	61	18	29.51
1998	100	21	21.00
1999	66	9	13.64
TOTAL	608	91	14.97

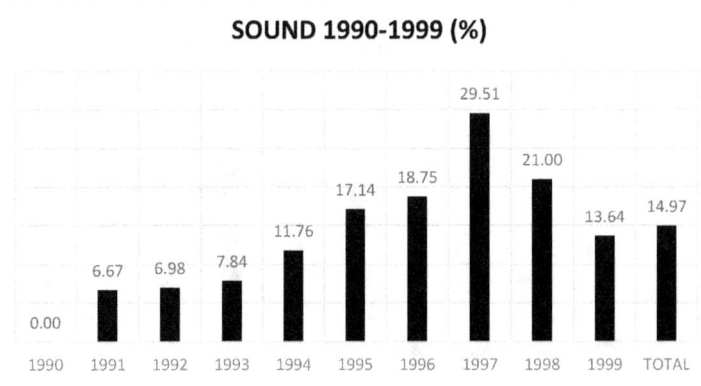

Figure 3.7 The presence of women in the Sound department in the 1990s
Source: Antonio Fernández Segura with data from the ICAA and IMDB.

80   The 1990s

FILMS WITH WOMEN WORKING IN THE CAMERA AND ELECTRICAL DEPARTMENT			
YEARS	FILMS	Nº	%
1990	41	15	36.59
1991	45	12	26.67
1992	43	12	27.91
1993	51	20	39.22
1994	51	25	49.02
1995	70	32	45.71
1996	80	36	45.00
1997	61	27	44.26
1998	100	45	45.00
1999	66	33	50.00
TOTAL	608	257	42.27

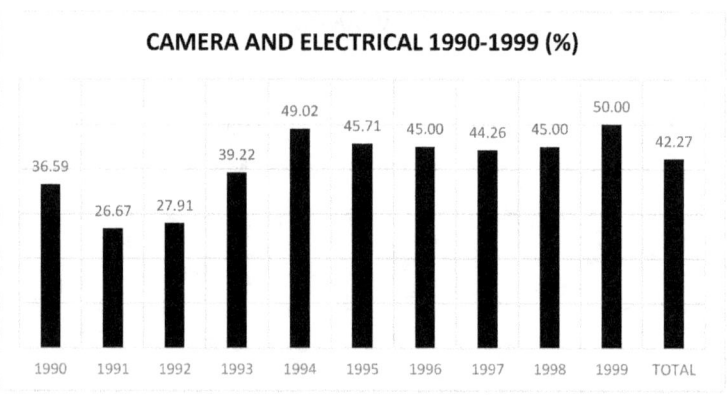

Figure 3.8 The presence of women in the Camera and Electrical department in the 1990s

Source: Antonio Fernández Segura with data from the ICAA and IMDB.

FILMS WITH WOMEN WORKING IN THE COSTUME AND WARDROBE DEPARTMENT			
YEARS	FILMS	Nº	%
1990	41	26	63.41
1991	45	29	64.44
1992	43	26	60.47
1993	51	39	76.47
1994	51	34	66.67
1995	70	58	82.86
1996	80	59	73.75
1997	61	49	80.33
1998	100	75	75.00
1999	66	53	80.30
TOTAL	608	448	73.68

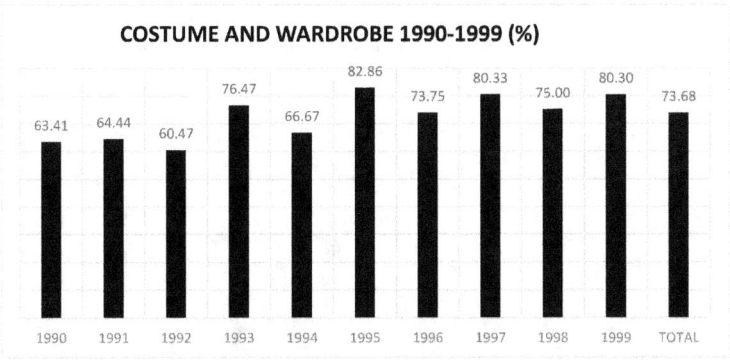

Figure 3.9 The presence of women in the Costume and Wardrobe department in the 1990s

Source: Antonio Fernández Segura with data from the ICAA and IMDB.

FILMS WITH WOMEN WORKING IN THE MAKE UP AND HAIRDRESSING DEPARTMENT			
YEARS	FILMS	Nº	%
1990	41	18	43.90
1991	45	27	60.00
1992	43	29	67.44
1993	51	31	60.78
1994	51	35	68.63
1995	70	58	82.86
1996	80	60	75.00
1997	61	43	70.49
1998	100	68	68.00
1999	66	48	72.73
TOTAL	608	417	68.59

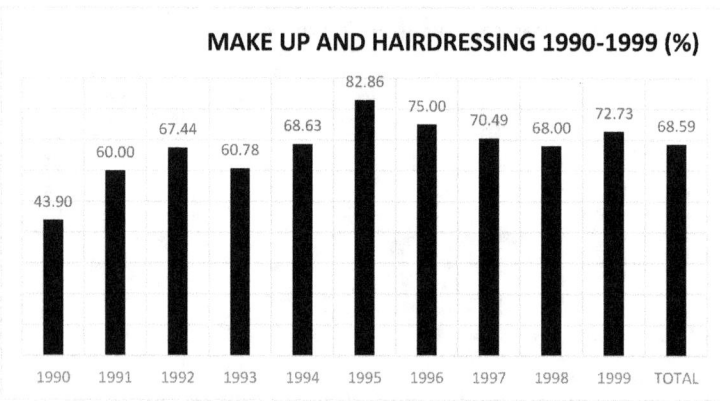

Figure 3.10 The presence of women in the Makeup and Hairdressing department in the 1990s

Source: Antonio Fernández Segura with data from the ICAA and IMDB.

FILMS WITH WOMEN WORKING IN THE EDITORIAL DEPARTMENT			
YEARS	FILMS	Nº	%
1990	41	13	31.71
1991	45	20	44.44
1992	43	21	48.84
1993	51	27	52.94
1994	51	21	41.18
1995	70	36	51.43
1996	80	33	41.25
1997	61	31	50.82
1998	100	38	38.00
1999	66	32	48.48
TOTAL	608	272	44.74

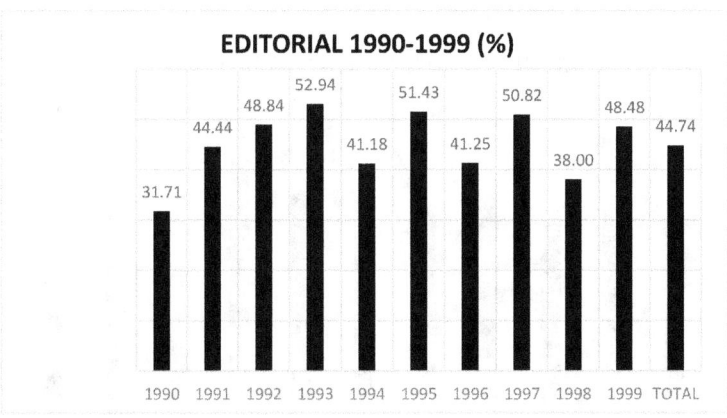

Figure 3.11 The presence of women in the Editorial department in the 1990s
Source: Antonio Fernández Segura with data from the ICAA and IMDB.

FILMS WITH WOMEN WORKING IN THE SCRIPT AND CONTINUITY DEPARTMENT			
YEARS	FILMS	Nº	%
1990	41	18	43.90
1991	45	22	48.89
1992	43	18	41.86
1993	51	29	56.86
1994	51	24	47.06
1995	70	43	61.43
1996	80	44	55.00
1997	61	35	57.38
1998	100	35	35.00
1999	66	36	54.55
TOTAL	608	304	50.00

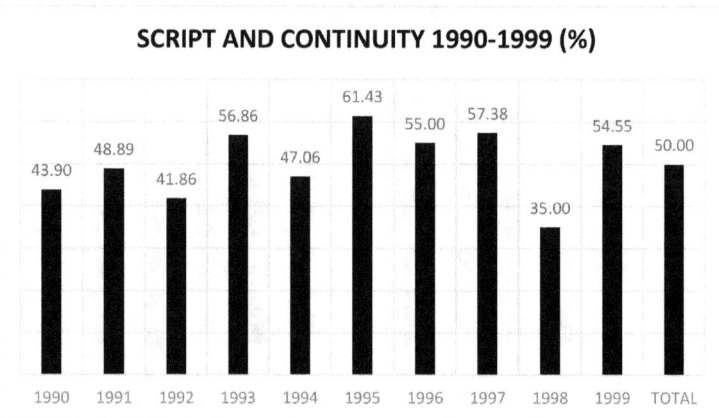

Figure 3.12 The presence of women in the Script and Continuity department in the 1990s

Source: Antonio Fernández Segura with data from the ICAA and IMDB.

FILMS WITH WOMEN WORKING IN THE MUSIC DEPARTMENT			
YEARS	FILMS	Nº	%
1990	41	3	7.32
1991	45	6	13.33
1992	43	1	2.33
1993	51	5	9.80
1994	51	4	7.84
1995	70	7	10.00
1996	80	14	17.50
1997	61	15	24.59
1998	100	13	13.00
1999	66	15	22.73
TOTAL	608	83	13.65

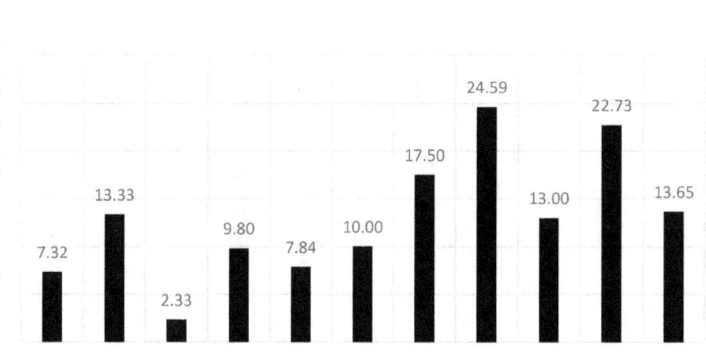

Figure 3.13 The presence of women in the Music department in the 1990s
Source: Antonio Fernández Segura with data from the ICAA and IMDB.

FILMS WITH WOMEN WORKING IN THE CINEMATOGRAPHY DEPARTMENT			
YEARS	FILMS	Nº	%
1990	41	0	0.00
1991	45	0	0.00
1992	43	0	0.00
1993	51	1	1.96
1994	51	2	3.92
1995	70	1	1.43
1996	80	1	1.25
1997	61	2	3.28
1998	100	0	0.00
1999	66	1	1.52
TOTAL	**608**	**8**	**1.32**

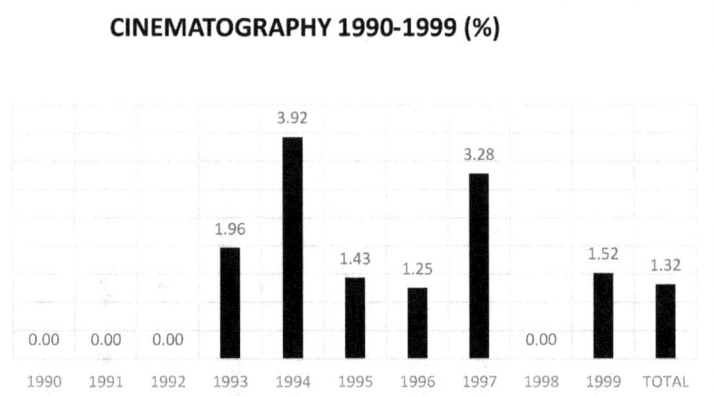

Figure 3.14 The presence of women in the Cinematography department in the 1990s
Source: Antonio Fernández Segura with data from the ICAA and IMDB.

because they support others in the workforce and, consequently, "supporting roles are rendered further inconspicuous by the misunderstanding of them—typically by men—as consisting of purely repetitive and low-skill functions" (Bell 2021, 5). Furthermore, these three departments become highly feminised, against the masculinisation of the technical departments. Consequently, despite the shift in the film policies of the 1990s, the traditional gendered division of labour in the Spanish film industry remained unchallenged.

Conclusion

This chapter has aimed to prove that the measures introduced by the Semprún Decree cannot be understood outside the European strategies of the late 1980 and early 1990s directed towards the protection and promotion of the audiovisual industries. The existing scholarship has mainly focused on the Decree itself and the reformist measures it introduced. However, valuable though they are, these studies have not acknowledged the influence that the European film and media policies had over the Decree; neither have they pointed out how Semprún and his collaborators were trying to align the Spanish film legislation with European regulations. On the contrary, the scholars who have studied the Decree have read it mainly as a reaction to the Miró Law (Vallés Copeiro del Villar [1992] 2000 and Riambau [1995] 2010). While it is true that the Semprún Decree was designed to change the funding policies established by the Miró Law, it did so because Semprún and Marías realised that, within the new EC membership context, it was no longer possible to avoid the turn that the European policymakers were making towards the idea that the film and the film and media industries had to be competitive if they wanted to survive in progressively internationalised markets. Therefore, it was necessary to guarantee the production of films that were not only financially viable in the domestic market but also that could compete in foreign markets. In order to do so, the Decree fostered private investment with the conviction that it would trigger the production of films that would appeal more to national and international audiences. Along with these strategies, the Decree also placed special protection on those films regarded to be of special quality. This not only reveals that the Semprún Decree did not entirely reject some of the ideas set by the Miró Law, but it also demonstrates the ways in which it endorsed the duality of the European strategies deployed to the protection and promotion of the film and media industries. As a result, along with measures directed towards enhancing the competitiveness of the film industry, which echoes the aims of the MEDIA programme, the Decree also encouraged the production of films that were not valued by their profitability but by their artistic merits in the same way as the Eurimages Fund did. It has to be noted that the European Audiovisual Observatory was not created until 1992 and, consequently, European films policies were not tacking gender inequality in the film industry either at the time the Semprún Decree was envisaged and passed.

The opposition that the Semprún Decree found among the dissident film agents not only brings to light debates about what kind of films were considered to be worthy enough to be funded by the state and, therefore, to constitute the canon of Spanish cinema; it also manifests deeper differences in the understanding of how the state had to manage film production in a market economy. On the one hand, the dissident film agents, staying true to its cinephile culture, considered that only art-films directed by dissident auteurs deserved state protection. Along with their cinephile understanding, their Marxist ideology made them believe that market constrains that curtail the production of any film intrinsically affects the filmmaker's freedom of expression. Since films are produced to be distributed and exhibited by companies which were meant to obtain economic profits out of them, filmmakers were always curtailed by market pressures. What logically follows from this belief is that, in a democratic society, the state had to free filmmakers from the market constraints by guaranteeing the conditions that would allow them to produce films regardless of the films' marketability. By doing so, the state would be ensuring the freedom of expression necessary in any democratic society (Diamante in *Cineinforme*, julio-agosto 1986: 47). This understanding, which guided Miró's film policies, worked throughout the years that the dissident film agents were in power (since the appointment of Miró as General Director of Cinematography in 1982 until the arrival of Semprún to the Ministry of Culture in 1988).

On the other hand, the producers and filmmakers of popular cinema believed that the state had to protect those popular films that had proven to have a wider audience appeal because they considered that cinema was an industry as well as an art form. Since the producers and filmmakers of popular cinema were not informed by a Marxist ideology, they did not believe that the market would entail any constraints to the filmmaker's freedom of expression. Considering that the Semprún Decree ultimately aligned with this later view, the dissident film agents thought that it was restraining the filmmaker's liberty by introducing market criteria in order to access state funding.

The Semprún Decree constituted a turning point in the type of film policies that were carried out since the establishment of democracy in Spain because it became the model for the forthcoming pieces of legislation up to the Ley 557/2007. In particular, the fundamental belief that Spanish cinema could not live exclusively off of state funding and had to reach the necessary competitiveness and audience appeal to live on box-office takings. From that moment on, this idea guided the practices of subsequent policymakers: from Enrique Balmaseda, when he returned as Head of the ICAA between 1994 and 1996, under Carmen Alborch's term as Ministry of Culture, to José María Otero as Head of the ICAA (1996–2004). Therefore, it could be argued that, due to the policies carried out by Semprún and his collaborators, and the decisions they made, the influence of the dissident film agents decreased significantly within the field of Spanish cinema. Their cinephile film culture was nonetheless retrieved when Fenando Lara was put in charge of the film policies in 2004 once the PSOE regained power, as next chapter will explain.

As for whether the Semprún Decree advanced the presence of women in the film industry, it clearly did not, despite the rise of women working as directors, scriptwriters, and producers in the 1990s compared to the 1980s. It could be argued, as it has also be argued regarding the Miró Law, that the advance subsidy directed to new filmmakers facilitated the debut of 31 women directors throughout the decade. However, when it comes to explain the rising numbers of women working as both scriptwriters and producers, there is not a single measure in the Semprún Decree to promote the major presence of women working in these roles; consequently, it can be argued that the major presence of women scriptwriters and producers is related to the expansion of the film industry in Spain in the 1990s rather than to the legislative changes that the Semprún Decree introduced: as Vicente Rodríguez Ortega has already argued, the emergence of new players—such as private multimedia enterprises—in the field of film production shifted the patterns of film production in the 1990s (Rodríguez Ortega 2020, 4). The same can be said about the incapacity of the Decree to assess gendered below-the-line roles: Costume and Wardrobe, Makeup and Hairdressing, Editorial and Script and Continuity remained very feminised, while the technical departments -Film Editing, Sound, Camera and Electrical, Music and Cinematography- remained very masculinised. Furthermore, the rise of women working in Production Management, Second Unit and Assistant Director and in the Art Department expanded the traditionally gendering of below-the-line roles to new positions in the 1990s.

The fact that gender inequality was not even an issue worthy of discussion for the main agents in the field of Spanish cinema during the 1990s, speaks volume about how much work was still needed in a decade that saw the consolidation of Spain as a fully modernised democratic nation. Furthermore, at a risk of stating the obvious, being able to access the film industry is only the first step for having a professional career; it is necessary to be able to sustain a continuous career: out of the 11 women who directed films in the 1980s, only 6 managed to keep directing throughout the 1990s. As for the two scriptwriters on the 1980s, only Lola Salvador kept writing films in the 1990s. Juliana San José de la Fuente left the industry. Finally, only Isabel Mula, Ana Huete and Helena Matas were able to keep their roles as producers in the 1990s. Consequently, it can be argued that the Semprún Decree's aim of creating a solid and competitive industry that could guarantee stable labour paths for the film professionals was not accomplished for the women working in the industry.

Notes

1 An older version of this chapter was published as an article in *The Hispanic Research Journal* in 2019.
2 Real Decreto 1282/1989, de 28 de agosto, de Ayudas a la Cinematografía.
3 Real Decreto 1039/1997, de 27 de junio.
4 All translations made by the author. The original quote in Spanish reads as follows: "En el sector de la producción, el esquema de ayudas públicas directas [...] se centra en el objetivo esencial de favorecer el desarrollo de empresarios independientes y de fomentar la inversión privada en la realización de películas, con la finalidad de reducir el intervencionismo estatal y fortalecer la estructura financiera del sector". (R.D. 1282/1989, Prólogo).
5 The Semprún Decree was further regulated by the R.D. 1773/1991, passed in 1991, that slightly changed the automatic subsidy established by the the Semprún Decree in order to strengthen it over the advanced subsidy. The decree established that those producers who had not been awarded the advance subsidy could choose either a complementary subsidy of 25% of the box-office returns during the two first years of the film's commercialisation or the equivalent to 33% of the producer's investment, up to a maximum of 100 million pesetas (600,000€/£518,000), providing that the film reached more than 50 millions pesetas ((300,000€/£258,000) of gross income at the box office (Real Decreto 1773/1991, de 13 de diciembre, Artículo único).
6 In order to enhance the Spanish film industry as a whole, the Semprún Decree not only focused on making funding available for film production, but they also established two lines of grants never contemplated by Spanish film legislation before to enhance the distribution and exhibition sectors.
7 The original quote in Spanish reads as follows: "el cine, como manifestación cultural y reflejo de la realidad de un país, merece y necesita ser fomentado y asistido por la sociedad en su conjunto y, en consecuencia, por la Administración del Estado" (R.D.1282/1989, Prólogo).
8 The original quote in Spanish reads as follows: "[para] facilitar el acceso de todos a la cultura [es necesario] el apoyo al desarrollo de los servicios públicos culturales y el apoyo a las iniciativas que surjan de la sociedad en un enfoque de colaboración público-privada" (Apartado IV, Epígrafe 4.13).
9 Ley 17/1994, de 8 de junio, de Protección y Fomento de la Cinematografía.
10 Amongst the female directors who co-produced with Spain and, therefore, their films count as Spanish according to the Spanish film law, we can find the French directors Marion Hänsel with her fifth and seventh films, *Entre el cielo y la tierra* (1991) and *A cielo abierto* (1998) respectively, Lisa Azuleos with her first film, co-directed alongside her husband, *Mujeres a flor de piel* (1991), Anne Fontaine with her third film, *Limpieza en seco* (1997), Daphna Kastner with her second film *Spanish Fly* (1997), Vera Belmont with her fifth film *Marquise* (1998), Charlotte de Turckheim with her debut film *¡Mamá, préstame a papá!* (1999) and Joyce Buñuel with her ninth film *¡Salsa!* (1999); the Mexican director Maria Sistach with her fifth film, *El cometa* (1998) co-directed with José Buil and the Argentinian Betty Kaplan with her second film, *Doña Bárbara* (1998).
11 Among the female directors who co-produced with Spain and wrote their own films we find the French Marion Hänsel, Daphna Kastner, Anne Fontaine, Vera Belmont, Charlotte de Turckheim, Lisa Azuleos and Joyce Buñuel and the Mexican Marisa Sistach and the Argentinian Betty Kaplan.
12 *Solo o en compañía de otros* (Santiago San Miguel, 1990), *Un soltero con mucha cuerda* (John Mark Robinson, 1993), *El cometa* (Marisa Sistach, 1998), *Marquise* (Vera Belmont, 1998).

13 *Orquesta Club Virginia* (Manuel Iborra, 1992), *La buena vida* (David Trueba, 1996), *Carreteras secundarias* (Emilio Martínez Lázaro, 1997).
14 She had been working as an assistant production manager since 1985, moving into production manager in 1987.
15 Alongside Mariela Besuievsky, she also produced Gerardo Herrero's *Territorio comanche* (1997) and *Don Juan, de Moliere* (Jacques Weber, 1998).

References

Collins, Richard. 1994. "Unity in diversity? The European single market in broadcasting and the audiovisual, 1982–1992". *Journal of Common Market Studies*, 32(1): 89–102.
Faulkner, Sally. 2020. "Middlebrow cinema by women directors in the 1990s". *Journal of Spanish Cultural Studies*, 21(1): 63–77.
Fernandez-Meneses, Jara. 2023. "Personal interview with Miguel Marias", 31st March 2023.
Hainsworth, Paul. 1994. "Politics, Culture and Cinema in the New Europe". In *Border Crossing: Film in Ireland, Britain and Europe*, edited by John, Hill, Martin McLoone and Paul Hainsworth, 8–33. The Institute of Irish Studies, The Queen's University of Belfast in association with the University of Ulster and the BFI.
Heredero, Carlos.1997. *Espejo de miradas. Entrevistas con nuevos directores del cine español de los años noventa*. Alcalá de Henares, 27o Festival de Cine de Alcalá de Henares.
Heredero, Carlos. 1999. *20 nuevos directores del cine español*. Madrid: Alianza Editorial.
Jordan, Barry 2000. "The Spanish film industry in the 1980s and 1990s". In *Contemporary Spanish Cultural Studies*, edited by Barry Jordan and Rikki Morgan-Tamosunas, 179–192. London: Arnold.
Jordan, Barry and Morgan-Tamosunas, Rikki. 1998. *Contemporary Spanish Cinema*. Manchester: Manchester University Press.
Monterde, José Enrique. 2002. "Panorama desde el siglo XXI. La industria cinematográfica de los años noventa". In *Semillas de futuro: cine español 1990–2001*, edited by Carlos F. Heredero and Antonio Santamarina, 88–127. Madrid: Sociedad Estatal Nuevo Milenio.
Palacio, Manuel and Vernon, Kathleen M. 2012. "Audiences". In *A Companion to Spanish Cinema*, Jo Labanyi and Tatjana Pavolvic, 464–486. Wiley-Blackwell.
Pavlovic, Tatjana. 2009. "Contemporary Trends (1992 to the Present)". In *100 Years of Spanish Cinema*, edited by Tatjana Pavlovic, 180–194. Oxford: Wiley-Blackwell.
Riambau, Esteve. [1995] 2010. "El período socialista (1982–1995)". In *Historia del cine español*, edited by Román Gubern et al, 399–454. Madrid: Cátedra.
Rodríguez Ortega, Vicente. 2020. "The return of genre in 1990s Spanish cinema: Industry, legislative changes and economics". *Hispanic Research Journal*, 21(1): 3–22.
Semprún, Jorge. 1977. *Autobiografía de Federico Sánchez*. Barcelona: Editorial Planeta.
Semprún, Jorge. 1993. *Federico Sánchez se despide de ustedes*. Barcelona. Tusquests.
Triana-Toribio, Nuria. 2003. *Spanish National Cinema*. London and New York: Routledge.
Vallés Copeiro del Villar, Antonio. [1992] 2000. *Historia de la política del fomento del cine español*. Valencia: Filmoteca de la Generalitat Valenciana.

Press

ABC. "Cien profesionales del cine se manifiestan contra la política de subvenciones del gobierno". 3/02/1987: 77.
ABC. "Polémica entre los profesionales sobre la política de subvenciones cinematográficas". 6/02/1987: 77.
Cineinforme. "Entrevista con Elías Querejeta". Noviembre 1986: 19.
Cuevas, Antonio. "La Ley Miró". Cineinforme. Diciembre 1984: 12.
El País. "Polémica entre los profesionales por el sistema de ayudas al cine español". 4/02/1987: n.p.
Gómez, Andrés Vicente. "El vecino del quinto". Diario 16, 2/08/1986: 2–4.
Heredero, Carlos F. "Entrevista a Fernando Méndez Leite", Imágenes de Actualidad. Febrero 1986: 6–7.
Jarque, Fietta. "Jorge Semprún acusa a Fernando Méndez Leite de amiguismo en la política de subvenciones al cine", El País, 13/12/1988: n.p.

ICAA reports

ICAA. 1990. "Anuario del Cine Español" Available: https://www.culturaydeporte.gob.es/dam/jcr:45323162-b379-4876-a138-d48a375d2758/bolet-n-1990.pdf Accessed: October 5, 2022.
ICAA. 1991. "Anuario del Cine Español" Available: https://www.culturaydeporte.gob.es/dam/jcr:4793361b-fdf1-457b-89be-c54efdd6c6fc/bolet-n-1991.pdf Accessed: October 5, 2022.
ICAA. 1992. "Anuario del Cine Español" Available: https://www.culturaydeporte.gob.es/dam/jcr:e844df1d-2ca7-4020-a986-1c9fe7345686/bolet-n-1992.pdf Accessed: October 5, 2022.
ICAA. 1993. "Anuario del Cine Español" Available: https://www.culturaydeporte.gob.es/dam/jcr:20488b31-6b94-4e17-9d2e-3f85f0692eb0/bolet-n-1993.pdf Accessed: October 5, 2022.
ICAA. 1994. "Anuario del Cine Español" Available: https://www.culturaydeporte.gob.es/dam/jcr:33a14fc1-8dd2-4414-8d6f-8e4d67841a7d/bolet-n-1994.pdf Accessed: October 5, 2022.
ICAA. 1995. "Anuario del Cine Español" Available: https://www.culturaydeporte.gob.es/dam/jcr:2ca5b093-c3bd-4905-8891-afcce5abc1f5/bolet-n-1995.pdf Accessed: October 5, 2022.
ICAA. 1996. "Anuario del Cine Español" Available: https://www.culturaydeporte.gob.es/dam/jcr:e938c352-885f-44f7-85ec-783108c3771c/boletin-1996.pdf Accessed: October 5, 2022.
ICAA. 1997. "Anuario del Cine Español" Available: https://www.culturaydeporte.gob.es/dam/jcr:e17ffac2-87f7-4884-b22f-f8af56af6ffa/boletin-1997.pdf Accessed: October 5, 2022.
ICAA. 1998. "Anuario del Cine Español" Available: https://www.culturaydeporte.gob.es/dam/jcr:7e82e667-370b-436e-97e2-65b7d1e15cd4/boletin-1998.pdf Accessed: October 5, 2022.
ICAA. 1989. "Anuario del Cine Español" Available: https://www.culturaydeporte.gob.es/dam/jcr:ce947919-c1b1-4eab-a253-6e756f4525de/boletin-1999.pdf Accessed: October 5, 2022.

Legal documents and political parties' manifestos

Council Directive 89/552/EEC of 3 October 1989 on the coordination of certain provisions laid down by law, regulation or administrative action in Member States concerning the pursuit of television broadcasting activities (Television without Frontiers Directive).

Real Decreto 1282/1989, de 28 de agosto, de Ayudas a la Cinematografía.

Real Decreto 1773/1991, de 13 de diciembre, Artículo único.

Ley 17/1994, de 8 de junio, de Protección y Fomento de la Cinematografía.

Real Decreto 1039/1997, de 27 de junio, por el que se refunde y armoniza la normativa de promoción y estímulos a la cinematografía y se dictan normas para la aplicación de 10 previsto en la disposición adicional segunda de la Ley 17/1994, de 8 de junio.

4 The 2000s
Towards a Feminist Film Law?

Introduction

As Nuria Triana-Toribio has argued, the José Luís Rodríguez Zapatero's presidency saw "the renewal of the idea that the state bears the responsibility for cultural funding because cinema is a cultural good" (2014, 66). The Law 55/2007 mainly endorsed the cultural arguments that had sustained the Miró Law (see Chapter 2). This is because Fernando Lara's appointment as Head of the ICAA brought back to the institutions the same cinephile culture that had dominated the field of Spanish cinema throughout the 1980s. As it has been explained before, Lara had been a key member of Spanish cinephile culture since the early 1970s. He had been the chief film critic alongside Diego Galán for the dissident cultural magazine *Triunfo* (1970–1978), which had opposed Francoism; in democracy, he collaborated with Fernando Méndez Leite in the film program focused on the history of Spanish cinema for Spanish National Television (TVE), *La noche del cine español*, between 1978 and 1982. Between 1984 and 2004, he headed the Valladolid International Film Festival (SEMINCI), which specialised in worldwide auteur cinema. He had also been a member of the jury in highly rated international film festivals such as Berlin and Cannes (Combarros Peláez 2005, 227). Alongside his unquestionable cinephile background, Lara believed that cinema was, above all, a vehicle for culture that had to contribute to the development of a critical consciousness among Spanish audiences (Lara 1975). Consequently, he considered that the films that deserved to be protected by the state were those auteur art-films conveying cultural values (Triana Toribio 2014).

The same understanding of what cinema – and culture, to a larger extent – should be, was shared by Carmen Calvo, as she clearly stated as early as April 2004, just one week into her new role as Minister of Culture: "we should protect culture as a universal human right, not just as a commodity" (Calvo in Ruiz Mantilla 2004, n.p.).[1] This statement should be framed within the context of the World Trade Organisation's Doha Round, launched in 2001, in which the status of the audiovisual industries was being discussed again, to which I will return in these pages. Policymakers were not the only ones pushing for this understanding of the role that cinema must play in society. To mention two striking examples: several film auteurs, scholars, critics and professionals such as Víctor Erice, Javier Maqua, and Esteve Riambau, among others, published a white paper for the defence of cultural exception in 2004 where they argued that it was necessary to protect Spanish cinema against the competition of Hollywood films because otherwise Spanish cultural identity would be jeopardised.[2] In Maqua's words:

> We believe that Spanish cinema – like other European cinemas – is going to be burnt to the ground by Hollywood cinema's occupation (of the national market) [...]. If we do not assess this issue, Spanish cultural identity will be severely damaged [...] We believe that we are facing a cultural disaster.
>
> (Maqua 2004, 13)[3]

In this context, the cinephile magazine *Cahiers du Cinéma. España*, the Spanish edition of the French magazine founded in the 1950s, was launched in May 2007. It defined itself as a "magazine that stands for an artistic and cultural conception of cinema" (mayo 2007, 74).[4] In its first editorial, the magazine stated that it was imperative to protect art-house films and independent producers against the competition of commercial films produced by the private television companies that were putting Spanish cultural diversity at its highest risk.[5]

In order to clarify the principles that guided the Law 55/2007, this chapter first explains the role that culture played for the PSOE and the ways in which the PSOE's cultural policy embraced the notion of cultural diversity fostered by European policymakers and by international organisations such as the UNESCO; it then assesses how the PSOE envisaged how gender equality could be achieved in the film industry. Secondly, it traces the struggles within the field of Spanish cinema between 2004 and 2008. The idea is to point out how these struggles affected the enactment of the Law and what arguments the Law endorsed. Finally, it examines the main innovations introduced by the Law.

Cultural diversity and gender equality: The new guiding principles for the PSOE's cultural policy

The PSOE's manifesto for the 2004 General Election was the most ambitious since 1982 as regards to its cultural policy. It also renewed the same understanding about the role that culture had to fulfil in society. Culture was defined as a "basic human right that the state should protect" (Programa Electoral del Partido Socialista 2004, 195).[6] The manifesto heavily criticised the cultural policy carried out by the conservative PP government between 1996 and 2004, which was deemed to have valued culture exclusively according

96 The 2000s

"to market criteria that have impeded both creative independence and critical cultural production that should characterise any democratic culture to flourish" (Programa Electoral del Partido Socialista 2004, 193).[7] Thus, the PSOE believed in 2004, as it had in 1982, that culture could not be measured solely by market criteria because its role was to develop a critical consciousness among Spanish citizens. Consequently, the state bore the responsibility for promoting and protecting cultural production. While acknowledging that the cultural industries were key for economic development, the manifesto also stated that cultural monopolies had been responsible for standardising cultural production, a fact that had gone against cultural diversity and freedom of creation. This cultural production, driven exclusively by market objectives, had reduced the cultural experience to a mere commodity, and citizens to simple consumers. Consequently, to fight against standardised cultural production, the state had to support independent cultural producers (Programa Electoral del Partido Socialista 2004, 193–194).

The concept that culture could not be measured by market criteria and that the state had to protect independent cultural production in order to preserve cultural diversity has to be framed within the context of the European defence of cultural diversity expressed in the Committee of Ministers' "Declaration on Cultural Diversity" (December 2000) and the Council of Europe's "Resolution of 12 February 2001 on national aid to the film and the audio-visual industries". Both directives revisited the idea that it was necessary to adopt protectionist measures towards the audiovisual industry because of its cultural importance. Consequently, European policy makers abandoned the rhetoric of the 1990s that promoted the belief that a competitive audiovisual industry was more effective in counteracting the competition of American audiovisual products. Firstly, the "Declaration on Cultural Diversity", asserted that "[c]ultural and audiovisual policies, which promote cultural diversity, are a necessary complement to trade policies" (Declaration on Cultural Diversity, 2.1, n.p.). Following the "Declaration", the aforementioned Council of Europe's "Resolution of 12 February 2001" stated both that "the audiovisual industry is a cultural industry par excellence" (2001/C 73/02, 10 (a)) and that "national aid to the film and audiovisual industries is one of the chief means of ensuring cultural diversity" (2001/C/73/02/10 (b)).

As Cristoph Beat has explained, the "Resolution" should be considered in the context of the birth of the World Trade Organisation in January 1995 (WTO henceforth), which followed the GATT's Uruguay Round (1986–1994), and which emphasised the fact that cultural goods and services were not going to be excluded from the forthcoming WTO's round of multilateral trade negotiations. Consequently, the issue of liberalising audiovisual markets would appear again, as it did in September 1999, when the WTO launched the "Millennium Round" that led to the Doha Agenda (initiated in November 2001) (Beat 2006, 555). Therefore, since the cultural exception doctrine had failed, the European policy makers came up with the term "cultural diversity" as the official policy's guideline in negotiations on the trade in audiovisual media, as stated in the European Commission's Communication to the Council and the European Parliament of 1999, "The EU Approach to the WTO Millennium Round" (COM 1991).

As Denis McQuail argues, the term cultural diversity "has been widely used in different ways to refer to many different aspects of (a changing) reality" (McQuail 2001, 83). Thus, it is not the aim of this section to propose a definition of the term, nor to participate in the debate about how the idea has shaped contemporary European cultural policies (see Shore 2001). However, the concept should be considered as indicative of the European Commission's realignment with the cultural arguments used during the Uruguay Round, which sought to guarantee that European audiovisual industries were not going to be liberalised. It follows that both the national and supranational systems of aid within the European Union were going to be maintained in the context of the Doha Agenda. This was acknowledged in the Commission's Communication as follows:

> During the forthcoming WTO negotiations, the Union will ensure, as in the Uruguay Round, that the Community and its Member States maintain the right to preserve and to develop their capacity to define and implement their cultural and audiovisual policies for the purpose of preserving their cultural diversity.
>
> (COM 1991:5)

The defence of cultural diversity was further enhanced internationally by UNESCO's "Convention on the Protection and Promotion of the Diversity of Cultural Expressions", issued in Paris on 20 October 2005 and ratified by Spain in February 2007, as the Law 55/2007 explicitly acknowledged it.[8] According to the UNESCO's convention,

> [c]ultural activities, goods and services have both an economic and a cultural nature, because they convey identities, values, and meanings, and must therefore not be treated as solely having commercial value (Introduction).

Consequently, the convention reaffirmed "the sovereign rights of states to maintain, adopt and implement policies and measures that they deem to be appropriate for the protection and promotion of the diversity of cultural expressions on their territory" (Article 1. Objectives (h). Accordingly, the Law 55/2007 specifically protected independent producers, who were considered the ones who could guarantee cultural diversity because they were not part of the cultural monopolies that had led to standardised cultural production (according to the PSOE's understanding, as stated in its manifesto).

As for gender equality, the PSOE period in government witnessed the passing of the two first pieces of legislation since the advent of democracy in 1977 that embraced gender mainstreaming (Arranz 2007, 220–221)[9]: Law 1/2004 against gender-based violence (2004)[10] and Law 3/2007 for gender equality (2007).[11] It was the latter that explicitly stated that gender equality should be guaranteed both in the private sector and in all the political, economic, work, social and cultural policies coming from the central and autonomous governments (Ley 3/2007, Artículo 1). In its articles 36 to 41, the Law assesses gender equality in the mass media: the Law stated that public media would promote an equal and non-stereotyped image of women and men in the media (Ley 3/2007, Artículo 36)[12]; as for the Spanish National Television (TVE) and the Spanish National News Agency (EFE), the Law remarks that both institutions committed not only to fostering non-sexist representations of women, but also to breaking the glass ceiling by incorporating women to directorial positions in both companies (Ley 3/2007, Artículo 37-Artículo 38). For private media, the Law voices the obligation to guarantee gender equality and to avoid any form of gender discrimination (Ley 3/2007, Artículo 39). The Law 55/2007 should be framed within these more extensive regulations aimed at achieving gender equality in all areas of Spanish society.

However, regardless of how celebrated this Law was, the film industry was still far from achieving any equality: in 2004, when the PSOE came in power, out of 130 Spanish featured films, only 20 films were directed by women and we need to bear in mind that this number includes four films co-directed alongside men plus two international co-productions: *The Holy Girl* by the Argentinian filmmaker Lucrecia Martel produced by Pedro Almodóvar's production company El Deseo, and *The Bridges of Saint Luis Rey*, directed by the Northern-Irish Mary McGuckian, which, despite having Spanish capital and being located in Spain, was shot in English, adapted a Thornton Wilder novel and was performed by American actors such as Robert De Niro. In the same fashion, out of 130 featured Spanish films in 2004, 26 films were co-scripted by women alongside men and only 6 films were scripted by women (including the co-productions *The Holy Girl* and *The Bridges of Saint Luis Rey*) (Anuario del Cine Español, ICAA, 2004). The situation did not improve between 2005 and 2007 and this is one of the reasons why the Law 55/2007 introduced affirmative action measures to achieve gender equality.

It is quite surprising that while the cultural diversity discussion was key within European institutions in the European Union, as it has been explained before, gender equality was not an issue for those very same institutions. As Paloma Arranz noted in 2007, none of the EU's legislation up to 2007 on the audiovisual industries embraced gender mainstreaming (Arranz 2007, 222–227). Actually, it was not until 2016 that the European Commission established a concrete framework for developing work towards achieving full gender equality – "The strategic engagement for gender equality 2016–2019" – which has been followed by "The Gender Equality Strategy 2020–2025".[13]

The former seeks to promote gender equality in five key areas for action: 1) equal economic independence for women and men; 2) equal pay for work of equal value; 3) equality in decision-making; 4) dignity, integrity and ending gender-based violence; and 5) promoting gender equality beyond the EU (European Commission 2016: 6). The latter pursues a dual approach of gender mainstreaming combined with targeted actions, and intersectionality as a horizontal principle for its implementation. It also focuses on seven key objectives: 1) ending gender-based violence; 2) challenging gender stereotypes; 3) closing gender gaps in the labour market; 4) achieving equal participation across different sectors of the economy; 5) addressing the gender pay and pension gaps; 6) closing the gender care gap; 7) achieving gender balance in decision-making and in politics (European Commission 2020, n.p.). However, back in 2004, this discussion was not in the table for the main European institutions. Consequently, the discussion on how to preserve cultural diversity for the Spanish film industry was in line with that which was held in the wider context of the European Union's institutions, while it seems that the debate on how to achieve gender equality in the film and audiovisual industries was particularly telling for Spanish policymakers and film professionals.

The next section will address how both discussions operated in the field of Spanish cinema between 2004 and 2008 – between the point when the PSOE came to power and the point when the Law 55/2007 was enacted.

The field of Spanish cinema (2004–2008)

When the PSOE won the general elections on 14 March 2004, there was an increase in film production, from 42 featured films in 2000 to 106 in 2003. Nevertheless, the weaknesses of the Spanish film industry remained the same: low market share for Spanish films, 16% in 2003 against 70% for American films; atomisation of the production sector (81.5% of Spanish production companies made only one film in 2003, while only ten production companies carried out 40% of the annual production); concentration of Spanish films' box-office takings across very few features per year (10 films counted for 77% of the box-office takings in 2003); and cinema attendance dropped from 140 million spectators in 2002 to 129.5 million in 2003. Television companies remained the main source for film funding, counting for 33% of the film's budget, while the producer's investment counted for 31% and state subsidies for 14%. In 2003, the total televisions' investment in film production had been 88 million euros (£76 million) (*Cineinforme*, enero 2004, 38–40).

Against this backdrop, the producers' lobby, FAPAE, launched in April 1991 and headed by Pedro Pérez, argued that in order to tackle the competition of Hollywood films it was necessary to promote quality films, which came to be identified, as in the 1980s, with high-budget films (see Chapter 2); secondly, in order to guarantee Spanish cultural diversity, the state had to protect independent producers against the competition of the private television companies (Pérez in Intxausti, 29/02/2004, n.p.). Pérez was arguably supporting the production of films such as *La gran aventura de Mortadelo y Filemón* (Javier Fresser, 2003) and *Días de fútbol* (David Serrano, 2003). The former, budgeted at 7 million euros (£6 million), was a co-production between the independent production company Películas Pendelton S.A, PRISA's production company Sogecine and the television companies Canal + and Telecinco. It grossed 22 million euros (£19 million) (ICAA). The latter, budgeted at 2 million euros (£1,700,000), was a co-production between the independent production company Telespan 2000 and Estudios Picasso (Telecinco's production company). It grossed 12 million euros (£10,500) (ICAA). Both features were the most successful Spanish films of 2003 counting for 40% of the year's total box-office takings. Taking into account both films' medium-to-high-budgets and their good market performance, it can be argued that ambitious projects came to be identified by the producers' lobby as those which were both profitable and popular with national audiences (although very few films actually were profitable). Moreover, the solid industrial grounds that would allow the production of the more ambitious films that Pérez was seeking could hardly be achieved when the success of Spanish cinema relied exclusively on two or three features a year out of so many films produced annually.

While Pérez acknowledged the key role that television funding played in film production, he also publicly supported the idea that televisions had to become a key exhibition window for the films produced by independent producers rather than producers themselves (Pérez in Sequera and Michelin, enero 2004, 32). Pérez knew that without television companies' funding it was impossible to embark upon the production of the ambitious projects he wanted since only television companies could afford to produce high-budget films. Nonetheless, he also began to push for recognition of the independent producer as a key agent in the production of films. The role that television companies had to play regarding the film industry – whether as producers, co-producers or merely promoters and exhibitors of Spanish cinema – became the main conflict between FAPAE and UTECA, the association that gathered the private television companies operating in Spain.[14] To a greater extent, it also became one of the main struggles within the field of Spanish cinema between 2004 and 2008.[15] UTECA argued that film producers did not manage to make Spanish films appealing for Spanish audiences, although film production increased in Spain yearly, and therefore they had to rely on television funding. His spokesman Alejandro Echevarría, who was also Head of Telecinco, affirmed that it made no sense to protect independent producers if they could not make Spanish cinema competitive and profitable. Consequently, independent producers had to be incorporated into major production companies (Echevarría in Sequera, enero 2007, 51).[16] UTECA made a very solid point: if Spanish films were not attracting as many spectators as they needed to become profitable at the box office, why did private television companies have to fund a loss-making cinema? Furthermore, was it necessary to produce so many films that did not perform well at the box-office? (*Cineinforme*, julio-agosto 2004, 49).[17] The overproduction of low-profit films became one of the most debated issues of the period. FAPAE, on the contrary, regretted that UTECA called for the integration of independent producers into the television production companies because it limited creative freedom as well as the fact that this statement revealed UTECA's monopolistic conception of film production that would inevitably lead to the disappearance of Spanish cinema (quoted in Sequera, enero 2007, 51).[18] The other argument that FAPAE mobilised was that of cultural imperialism. Pérez argued that, in order to avoid the abusive position that the American majors had in the Spanish market, the Spanish government had to guarantee fair competition by sanctioning by law the role of the independent producer. According to Pérez, only by recognising the independent producer's role in film production could the American majors' invasion of the national market, which would ultimately lead to the "death" of Spanish cinema, be avoided (Pérez in Martín 2005, n.p.).

The second main struggle within the field of Spanish cinema between 2004 and 2008 was that of gender equality in the film industry. In 2006 CIMA, the Women Filmmaker's and Audiovisual Professionals Association, was created.[19] According to a 2011 report from the Spanish Ministry of Culture, between 1999 and 2008, only 6'6% of feature films were directed by women; between 2000 and 2006, only 15% of the feature films were written by women and only 20% were produced by women. Likewise, the report also highlighted how the gendered division of labour had traditionally been one key characteristic of the Spanish film industry, as I have already demonstrated. Consequently, the report concluded, the role of women in the film and audiovisual industries is always downgraded to traditionally feminised roles (Ministerio de Cultura 2011, 42). CIMA was created precisely to tackle this inequality, as the association's website clearly states: its mission is to guarantee gender equality in the film and the audiovisual industries, parity of representation in the decision-making structures and a non-sexist representation of women in the media (https://cimamujerescineastas.es/que-es-cima/).

In 2006, when the Law 55/2007 was being discussed among film professionals and policymakers, CIMA's main objective was that the forthcoming Law incorporated the Article 26 of the Law 3/2007 for gender equality which stated that establishing affirmative action was necessary to promote gender equality in cultural and artistic production as well as to promote gender equality in the funding and regulating bodies for the arts (Law 3/2007, Article 26). In a personal interview with the author, Inés París – Head of CIMA between 2006 and 2012 – stated that CIMA was born out of the necessity to lobby for having women film professionals' needs consecrated by law because up to 2006 no women film professionals existed. Furthermore, París asserted that CIMA was in close dialogue with Calvo as Minister of Culture and Lara as Head of the ICAA for CIMA's demands to be heard and recognised by the new film law that was being discussed. The first issue CIMA debated was what kind of roles the Law's affirmative action measures should focus on, either on above or below-the-line roles; it was decided that the Law's affirmative action measures should focus on the former, because these positions were considered by CIMA, according to París, as the ones were the creative decisions were made[20] – one could also argue because CIMA's initial board was exclusively formed by women filmmakers and scriptwriters.[21] CIMA's aim, therefore, was to break the glass ceiling for women directors, scriptwriters and producers. According to París, the policymakers discussing the Law did not allow CIMA to have production included in the affirmative action measures due to the multiple roles production entails (from producer to executive producer, line producer, production manager, etc.), which makes more complicated to establish who should be the recipient of the positive discrimination. This is the reason why the Law only included affirmative action measures for direction and scriptwriting (París in Fernández Meneses, 2023). The idea that creative decisions can only be taken in above-the-lone toles has nonetheless been already brilliantly challenged by scholarship – see Bell (2021). Progressively, once women working in different roles started joining CIMA, the discussion on how to tackle gender inequality in roles below-the-line and the over feminisation of some roles and the over masculinisation of others began to be discussed within CIMA and with further policymakers to include gender equality measures in roles below-the-line ones. Lara also recognises that regulating the inequality that derives from having over feminised below-the-line roles against over masculinise below-the-line roles was not accomplished by the Law; it was not even discussed at that moment (Lara in Fernández Meneses, 2023).[22]

For Calvo, as expressed in a personal interview with the author, the Law 55/2007 was built over three key principles:

- What do films mean for modern societies and how do films shape social values?
- What are the best strategies to protect and promote the European film industries?
- How to advance the presence of women in the film industry and how to include a gender perspective across the Law?

According to Calvo, the latter point was achieved through two main strategies: firstly, by applying affirmative action measures that would guarantee the presence of women in the film industry; secondly, by guaranteeing by law a non-sexist representation of women in films. Furthermore, Calvo acknowledged that the presence of CIMA was paramount to achieving this ultimate objective, since it was only when CIMA began to lobby for women's interests, they began to be visible for the policymakers and other film professionals' associations alike (Calvo in Fernández Meneses, 2023).

The following section will analyse how far and in what ways both demands – those from FAPAE and CIMA – were endorsed by the Law 55/2007 and how the Law achieved its stated aims of guaranteeing gender equality.

The Law 55/2007

The Law 55/2007 began to be discussed at the end of 2005 and one year later, on 28 December 2006, Calvo and Lara presented the draft of the new Law to the public opinion. According to Lara, the draft had been agreed amongst the film professionals' associations.[23] However, two sectors opposed the Law strongly: firstly, TVE, UTECA and FORTA[24] objected the obligations the Law established for the public and private televisions to invest in film production (6% and 5% of their annual revenues respectively); secondly, FECE, the exhibitor's association, who were against the 25% screen quota for European films (Lara in Fernández Meneses, 2023).

The two main innovations the Law introduced were, firstly, the special support it provided to independent producers and its intention to tackle the market's inequalities; that is to say, its intention to fight against the predominance of Hollywood films in the national market; secondly, to introduce affirmative action measures to promote gender equality for the first time in the history of film legislation in Spain. Consequently, the Law aligned with both FAPAE's and CIMA's demands. Regarding the latter, fostering female creation by establishing gender equality as a key factor to obtain State funding for film development and film production. Regarding the former, the Law defended the figure of the independent producer as bearer and ultimate guarantor of cultural diversity against the competition of both Hollywood films and the commercial productions of private television companies. Lara put it clearly when he asserted that Spain was facing an ideological and political debate about what could happen with Spanish cinema. Either film production was left exclusively to private televisions companies, and, consequently, Spanish cinema would become a commodity made exclusively for entertainment, or the state would foster the production of an independent auteurist cinema that promoted cultural diversity and guaranteed Spain national identity (Lara in Heredero and Reviriego, mayo 2007, 71).[25]

According to París, Lara's was completely implicated in tackling gender inequality in the film industry from the moment he was appointed Head of ICAA. In a personal interview with the author, Lara explained that the first measure the ICAA took was to finance the report that CIMA had asked for to Fátima Arranz from the Complutense University of Madrid in 2006 – and published in 2007 (Arranz, 2007) – on gender inequality in the film industry, report that París considers being the birth of CIMA (París in Fernández Meneses, 2023). From there, the ICAA strengthened the position of CIMA as a key spokesperson in the talks it had with the different film professionals' organisations when discussing the drafting of the Law; consequently, most of CIMA's demands were sanctioned by the Law, as we will see briefly (Lara in Fernández Meneses, 2023).

Before addressing how the Law sanctioned the demands raised by both FAPAE and CIMA, it is necessary to clarify that the special support provided to independent producers by the Law's draft, as well as its intention to tackle market's inequalities, should also be considered as a direct consequence of the two following issues concerning production and distribution. Firstly, the importance that private television companies had acquired in film production during the early 2000s.[26] For instance, among the highest-grossing films of 2006 were *Alatriste* (Agustín Diaz Yanes), with 16 million euros (£14 million) accrued in profit, *El laberinto del fauno* (Guillermo del Toro), with 9 million euros (£7,700,000), and *Los Borgia* (Antonio Hernández), with 7 million euros (£6 million). They were mainly produced by private television companies: Estudios Picasso (Telecinco's production company) funded Yanes' and del Toro's features with 80% of the films' costs each, while Ensueño Films (Antena 3's production company) was responsible for Hernández's film. These three features had the highest budgets of the year: 22 million euros (£19 million), 15 million euros (£13 million) and 10 million euros (£8,600,000) respectively (*Cineinfome*, mayo 2007, 36). Certainly, the competitive high-budget Spanish films Pérez was arguing for, were being produced mainly by private television companies with little to no input from independent producers. Furthermore, out of the 183 production companies active in 2006, the companies that obtained the highest revenues were Estudios Picasso (10 films and 31 million euros -£27 million- in box-office takings), Ensueño Films (8 films and 9 million euros -£7,700,000) and Mediaproducción, owned by the multimedia conglomerate Mediapro, owner of La Sexta (9 films and 8 million euros -£6,800,000) (*Cineinforme*, mayo 2007, 37). Secondly, the drafting of the Law's aimed to tackle the powerful position that the subsidiaries of the American majors enjoyed in the distribution sector, which allowed them to profit highly from the distribution of Hollywood films in the national market. Despite the fact that 150 Spanish films – including co-productions – were produced in 2006, the market share for Spanish films was only 28% against 72% for non-Spanish films (mostly Hollywood films); furthermore, while Spanish films grossed 98 million euros (£85 million), non-Spanish films (again, mostly Hollywood films) grossed 538 million euros (£463 million) (*Cineinforme*, mayo 2007, 36). The highest-grossing films in the Spanish market in 2006 were the Hollywood productions *Pirates of the Caribbean: Dead Man's Chest* (Gore Verbinski), distributed by The Walt Disney Company Iberia, which grossed 28 million euros (£24 million); *The Da Vinci Code* (Ron Howard), distributed by Sony Pictures Releasing, which grossed 27 million (£23 million), and *Ice Age: The Meltdown* (Carlos Saldanha), distributed by Fox, which grossed 20 million (£17 million) (*Cineinforme*, mayo 2007, 40). This powerful position was considered to be one of the main reasons that Spanish films had such a low market share.

The Law was the first regulation to explicitly acknowledge the integration of the film industry in the wider concept of the audiovisual, which was defined as a cultural and economic strategic sector that contributed to fostering both cultural diversity and economic growth (Law 55/2007, Preámbulo). The Law's two main objectives, as stated before, were, firstly, to protect independent cultural producers against cultural monopolies in order to ensure that cultural production not driven solely by market interests and, consequently, to achieve cultural diversity; secondly, to tackle gender inequality. The Law defined independent producers, distributors, and exhibitors as those with no links to private television companies, audiovisual broadcasting companies or non-EC companies to protect both independent producers against the competition of private television companies and independent distributors against the subsidiaries of the American majors, which were considered responsible for the inequalities in the film market. Moreover, the Law was the first piece of legislation to define authors as the director, the scriptwriter, the cinematographer and the music composer (Law 55/2007, Artículo 4). It did so arguably to strengthen the role of the author as the key figure in film creation against the industrial mode of production carried out by the private television companies. In order to protect independent producers, the Law established that they were the only ones who could access advance subsidies for development and production of feature films, short films and television series (Law 55/2007, Artículo 22, Artículo 23, Artículo 25, Artículo 26, Artículo 27).[27] Likewise, only independent distributors and exhibitors could access state funding (Law 55/2007, Artículo 28, Artículo 29).[28]

The Law established concrete measures to promote gender equality in film and audiovisual creation (Law 55/2007, Artículo 19 (g)). Such measures were applied by further legislation – the Orden CUL/2834/2009 that regulated the Law – enacted in October 2009, almost two years after the Law was passed due to the controversy that it had generated among film professionals. UTECA and FECE – the Association of Cinemas – strongly opposed the Law, while CIMA, FAPAE and independent distributors such as Enrique González Macho supported it. These two years delay cost Lara his position, and he was replaced in April 2009 by Ignasi Guardans, an MEP from the European Parliament who was a specialist in European media legislation; Guardans was personally appointed by the screenwriter and film director Ángeles González-Sinde in her position as Minister of Culture (2009–2011) (García, 14/04/2009, n.p.). González-Sinde's appointment was made within the context of a wider cabinet reshuffle instigated by Rodríguez Zapatero in April 2009, which, according to the president, was aimed at fighting the effects of the economic crisis (*El País*, 08/04/2009, n.p.). The measures to promote gender equality in the film and audiovisual industries were the following:

- In the advanced grants directed towards scriptwriting of feature films, 5 points out of 100 were awarded if the script was written by a woman (Orden CUL/2834/2009, Artículo 22)
- In the advanced grants directed towards projects' development of feature films, 5 points out of 100 were awarded if the script was written by a woman or the project was directed by a woman (Orden CUL/2834/2009, Artículo 28)
- In the advanced grants directed towards the production of animated television series, 5 points out of 100 were awarded if the script was written by a woman or the project was directed by a woman (Orden CUL/2834/2009, Artículo 53)
- In the advanced grants directed towards the production of audiovisual works using new technologies, 5 points out of 100 were awarded if the script was written by a woman or the project was directed by a woman (Orden CUL/2834/2009, Artículo 99)

It has to be noted that these measures were only directed towards fostering the presence of women in directorial and scriptwriting roles, leaving aside the state's affirmative action on other key-above-the-line roles beyond production, such as editing and music composition, those very same roles that the Law 55/2007 acknowledged as being part of the film's authorship; not to mention the fact that no below-the-line-roles were considered at all by these regulations for the reasons that have been explained before.

The following trends can be drawn from these data, as Figure 4.1 shows regarding the roles above-the-line.

- The number of films produced in the 2000s almost doubled the films produced throughout the previous decade – 715 films in the 1990s and 1340 in the 2000s – growing almost steadily year by year – except in 2003 and 2004.
- The growth in production was translated into a major presence of women filmmakers. The films directed by women rose 5% – from 9,70% in the 1990s to 14,63% in the 2000s.
- The films written and co-written by women remained the same – 23% – but taking into account that the films produced in the 2000s were double, this means that the presence of women scriptwriters did not grow during the decade.
- Production saw a meaningful increase of women: out of 1340 films produced in the 2000s, 601 were produced or co-produced by women (45%), while in the 1990s out of 608 featured films 142 were produced or co-produced by women (24%). However, as we will see shortly, this major presence of women in film production was not translated into long-standing careers for women.

The 2000s 107

YEARS	TOTAL	WOMEN IN ABOVE THE LINE ROLES 2000-2009					
		FILMS DIRECTED BY WOMEN		FILMS WRITTEN BY WOMEN		FILMS PRODUCED BY WOMEN	
		Nº	%	Nº	TOTAL	Nº	TOTAL
2000	42	5	11.90	10	23.81	20	47.62
2001	106	12	11.32	26	24.53	37	34.91
2002	137	16	11.68	24	17.52	52	37.96
2003	106	18	16.98	29	27.36	53	50.00
2004	130	20	15.38	32	24.62	47	36.15
2005	139	22	15.83	32	23.02	60	43.17
2006	150	13	8.67	31	20.67	73	48.67
2007	171	23	13.45	42	24.56	88	51.46
2008	173	26	15.03	40	23.12	85	49.13
2009	186	41	22.04	52	27.96	86	46.24
TOTAL	1340	196	14.63	318	23.73	601	44.85

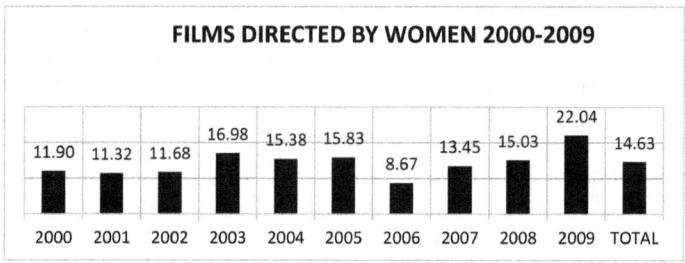

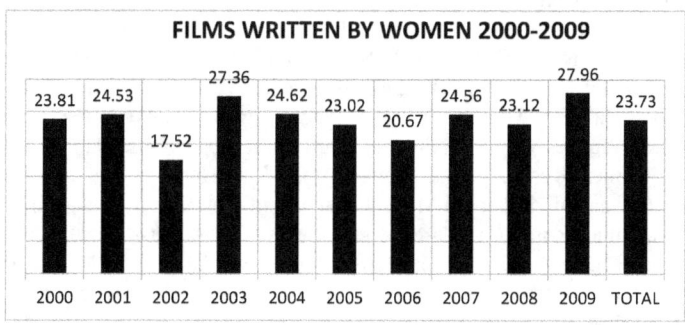

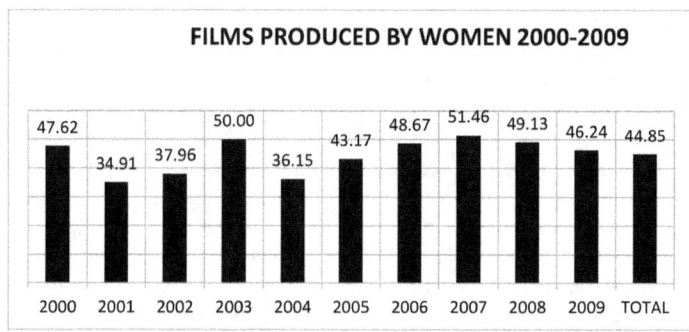

Figure 4.1 The presence of women in the above-the-line roles in the 2000s
Source: Antonio Fernández Segura with data from ICAA and IMDB

Regarding women filmmakers, we can observe the following issues:

Twenty-six women who started their directorial careers in the 1990s managed to continue directing films during the 2000s: Yolanda García Serrano,[29] Ana Díez, Mónica Laguna, Maite Ruíz Austri,[30] Eva Lesmes, Manane Rodríguez, María Ripoll, Inés París, Daniela Fejerman, Patricia Ferreira, Chus Gutiérrez, Dunia Ayaso, Helena Taberna, Isabel Coixet, Laura Mañá, Icíar Bollaín, Gracia Querejeta, Rosa Vergés, Marta Balletbò Coll,[31] Mireia Ros, Judith Colell, Azucena Rodríguez, Silvia Munt, Pilar Távora, Dolores Payás and Anna Sanmartí.

There were 30 women who made their debut in the 2000s but only directed one film: Mercedes Segovia, the producer Diana Sánchez, Natalia Díaz, Pilar García, the scriptwriter Julia Montejo, Susana Koska, Pilar Ruíz Gutiérrez, Ariadna Pujol, Elena Medina, Andrea Trigo, Lola Guerrero, Lola Barrera, Ione Hernández, Carolina del Prado, María Pilar Villalaín, Maitena Muruzabal, Natalia Díaz, Sara Gutiérrez Dewar, Gabriela Gutiérrez Dewar, the actress Mirtha Ibarra, Irena Cardona, Mercedes Fernández-Martorell, Meritxell Nicolau, Sandra Serna, Ana Rosa Fernández, Alicia Garaialde Etxebertz, Aitzpea Goneaga, Yalda Peñas, Lola Salvador and Nuria Villazán.[32]

Forty-one women debuted in the 2000s and managed to direct more than one film: Judith Colell, Teresa Pelegrí,[33] María Lidón, Lydia Zimmermann, Tania Balló, Núria Campabadal, Silvia Munt, Dominique Abel, Angéles González Sinde, Mercedes Álvarez, Silvia Quer, Ana Pérez, Marta Arribas, Elisabet Cabeza, Ana Murugarren, Nely Reguera, Lupe Pérez García, Arantxa Aguirre, Mireia Gabilondo, María Mercedes Alfonso Padrón, Libia Stella Gómez, Roser Aguilar, Estela Ilarraz, Tania Hermida, Lucinda Torre, Elena Ortega, Olivia Acosta, Mabel Lozano, Andrea Martínez, Ana Rodríguez Rosell, Lilian Rosado, Carla Subirana, Belén Macías, Susi Gozalvo, Isona Passola, Regina Álvarez, Lucía Herrera, Sonia Escolano, Anna Mª Bofarull, Mar Coll and Antonia San Juan.

Consequently, access to film direction broaden to women in the 2000s. Bearing in mind that the affirmative action measures did not begin to be implemented until the end of the decade, it can be concluded that this major access was not a consequence of the legislation of the period but of the inner dynamic of the Spanish film industry.

Regarding scriptwriters, we can see the following trends:

The auteurist mode of production – women directors who write or co-write their own films – of the 1980s and 1990s was maintained throughout the 2000s as we can see in the following cases: Beatriz Flores Silva, Mónica Laguna, María Novaro, Patricia Ferreira, Natalia Díaz, Pilar García, Eva López Sánchez, Ana Díez, Nuria Villazán, Valeria Sarmiento, Julia Montejo, Daniela Fejerman, Inés París, Mercedes Segovia, Icíar Bollaín, Chus Gutiérrez, Dunia Ayaso, Laura Mañá, Arantxa Aguirre, Silvia Munt,

Helena Taberna, Isabel Coixet, Ángeles González Sinde, Mercedes Álvarez, Gracia Querejeta, Rosa Vergés, Pilar Ruíz Gutiérrez, Susana Koska, Marta Balletbò-Coll, Marta Arribas, Ana Pérez, Elina Medina, Elisabet Cabezas, Ana Murugarren, Lola Salvador, Ariadna Pujol, Laura Mañá, Nely Reguera, Lola Barrera, Mireia Ros, Ione Hernández Sánchez, Lola Herrero, Mananae Rodríguez, Lucía Puenzo, Mercedes Alfonso, Estela Ilarraz, Tania Hermida, Lucinda Torres, Elena Ortega, Carolina del Prado, Mabel Lozano, Susi Gozalvo, Andrea Martínez Crowther, Ana Rodríguez Rosell, Carla Subirana, Maitena Muruzabal, Candela Figuera, Elena Cánovas, Sara Gutiérrez Dewar, Gabriela Gutiérrez Dewar, Mirta Ibarra, Irene Cardona, Mercedes Fernández-Martorell, Isona Passola, Marta Arribas Veloso, Ana Pérez, Regina Álvarez Lorenzo, Elisabet Cabezas, Sonia Escolano, Antonia San Juan, Paula de Luque, Dolores Payás, Anna Mª Bofarull, Aitzpea Goenaga, Anna Sanmartí, Roser Aguilar and Mar Coll.

Only eight women who debuted in the 1990s managed to keep working as scriptwriters in the 2000s: Yolanda García Serrano, Elvira Lindo, Ángeles González Sinde, Teresa Pelegrí,[34] Carmen Rico Godoy, Almudena Grandes, Cuca Canals and Katy Saavedra.

Amongst the women directors who crossover to write films for other filmmakers, we find Helena Taberna, Inés París, Nuria Villazán, Dunia Ayaso and Libia Estella González.

Women who debuted during the 2000s (those who wrote or co-wrote more than just one film) were the team formed by Dolores Falkner and Helena Mas, Lola Mayo, Verónica Fernández, Teresa Vilardell and the novelists Lucía Etxebarría and Belén Copegui. Consequently, it can be argued that while women directors tend to script their own films, the figure of the professional scriptwriter who is not also a filmmaker was still glass ceiled for women in the 2000s.

Finally, regarding women producers of the decade:

Amongst the women who debuted in production in the 1990s who continued their careers throughout the 2000s, we find Cristina Huete, who consolidated her position as the producer of the Trueba's brothers[35]; Mariela Besuievsky, with 41 films produced during the decade – acting as either producer and executive producer – ranging from high profile international coproductions such as *El hijo de la novia* (Juan José Campanella, 2001) and *Tetro* (Francis Ford Coppola, 2009), high profile Spanish projects such as *Los crímenes de Oxford* (Álex de la Iglesia, 2008) and medium budget films directed by women such as *Paisito* (Ana Díez, 2009); Esther García, who not only continued producing Pedro Almodovar's films but she was also behind *El Deseo's* production strategy,[36] backing Isabel Coixet's *Mi vida sin mi* (2002) and *La vida secreta de las palabras* (2005) and Lucrecia Martel's *La niña santa* (2004); Piluca Baquero continued producing independent and experimental filmmakers such as Gonzalo Tapia, Ramón Barea, Eugeni Bonet, Javier Rebollo and

Francisco Lombardi, Ana Huete returned to production with of Víctor García León's debut, *Más pena que Gloria* (2000) and Chus Gutiérrez's *Poniente* (2002); Beatriz de la Gándara produced the debuts of Vicente Molina Foix, *Sagitario* (2000) and Inés París and Daniela Fejerman, *A mi madre le gustan las mujeres* (2002) and she continued producing Fernando Colomo's films – *Al sur de Granada* (2002), *El próximo Oriente* (2006) and *Rivales* (2008); Mate Cantero kept producing international coproductions – Arturo Ripstein's *La virgen de la lujuria* (2001), Patrick Alessandrin *Mala leche* (2006) and Francesca's Joseph *Mallorca's Song* (2007) – and independent films – José Antonio Vitoria's *Vorvilk* (2005), Angélica Huete produced two musical documentaries – *El canto del Loco: la película* (María Pilar Villalain, 2008) and *Old Man Bebo* (Carlos Carcas, 2008) – and the comedy *Dí que sí* (Juan Calvo, 2004), finally, Sarah Halioua who kept producing international coproductions such as *El haren de Madame Osmane* (Nadir Mockneche, 2000).

Sixteen women debuted in film production in the 2000s (those who produced at least two films): Laura Imperiale and Bertha Navarro, who both specialised on international coproductions with Mexico; Rosa Bosch, who moved between high profile coproductions – *Calle 54* (Fernando Trueba, 2000) and *El espinazo del diablo* (Guillermo del Toro, 2000) – and independent productions such as *Nadar* (Carla Subirana, 2008) and *Los condenados* (Isaki Lacuesta, 2009); Beatriz Navarrete who backed independent films from Álvaro del Amo and Juan Luis Iborra, amongst others; Mariví de Villanueva, who backed low-budget genre films such as *School Killer* (Carlos Gil, 2000) and *Hot Milk* (Ricardo Bofill, 2004); Puy Oria, Montxo Armendáriz's producer; Pilar Sueiro, Juan Pinza's producer; Mercedes Gamero, who is one of the founder members of Atresmedia Cine, one of the two major Spanish film production companies and owned by the multimedia conglomerate Atresmedia: Gamero began as an associate producer in quality dramas and thrillers such as *Sin noticias de Dios* (Agustín Díaz Yanes, 2001) and *La caja 507* (Enrique Urbizu, 2001) to produce some of the most successful films of the decade such as *Fuga de cerebros* (Fernando González, 2009) and *Planet 51* (Jorge Blanco, Javier Abad, Marcos Martínez, 2009); Belén Atienza, who in 2001 started working in Telecinco Cinema, the other major film production company in Spain alongside Atresmedia and owned by the multimedia conglomerate Mediaset, producing some of the most successful films of the decade such as *El laberinto del fauno* (Guillermo del Toro, 2006) and *Alatriste* (Agustin Díaz Yanes, 2006), international coproductions such as Steven Soderbergh's *Che: El argentino* (2008) and *Che: Guerrilla* (2009), alongside novel talents such Juan Antonio Bayona, whose films have been all produced by Atienza. In 2003 she created her own production company, Apaches Entertainment; Eva Baró, who specialised in independent documentaries – *Cinemart* (Jordi Mollá, 2006) – and international coproductions, such as Peter Greenaway trilogy *Las maletas de Tulse Luper;* Isona Passola, who produced her own documentary, *Cataluña-España* (2009), Joaquin Jordá's *De niños* (2003) and the low budget horror film *Mucha sangre* (Pepe de las Heras, 2002); Patricia Roda, who produced Solomón Shang films; Beatriz Delgado, who backed low budget genre films such as *Un buen dia lo tiene cualquiera* (Santiago Lorenzo, 2007) as Chalo Loureiro also did – *Días azules* (Miguel Santemases, 2006); Eva Garrido moved between international coproductions – *Salvador Puig Antich* (Manuel Huerga, 2006) and *Vicky, Cristina, Barcelona* (Woody Allen, 2008) – and Spanish genre films such as *Va a ser que nadie es perfecto* (Joaquín Oristrell, 2006); Nahikari Ipiña, who was behind Nacho Vigalondo's *Los cronocrímenes* (2007); finally, María Zamora, who started as a production manager in 2001 in the independent production company Avalon and founded her own production company twenty years later – Elástica Films. Throughout the 2000s she was behind international coproductions such as *Las mantenidas sin sueños* (Vera Fogwill, Martin Desalvo, 2007) and independent films such as *La mujer sin piano* (Javier Rebollo, 2009).

It can be concluded that in film production, we see the same atomisation that we have also seen in film direction and scriptwriting insofar there were plenty of women who only managed to direct/write/produce one film throughout the decade; this is nonetheless a characteristic shared by their males colleagues during the 2000s and one of the main characteristics of the Spanish film industry between 1980 and 2010: the lack of strong industrial structures – beyond Atresmedia and Mediaset – that could guarantee stable jobs for the film professionals in fixed contracts.

Looking at these numbers more carefully, As for the roles-below-the line, as we can see in Figure 4.2–4.13, we find 4% of women working as cinematographers. We also see how the percentage of films with women working in below-the-line roles decreased in regards of the 1990s in all departments except Sound, that increased from 15% in the 1990s to 25% in the 2000s, and in Music, that raised from 13% in the 1990s to 20% in the 2000s:

- In Film Editing, from 23% in the 1990s to 20% in the 2000s.
- In Production Management, from 65% in the 1990s to 64% in the 2000s.
- In Second Unit and Assistant Direction, 49% in the 1990s to 43% in the 2000s.
- In Art, from 46% in the 1990s to 45% in the 2000s.
- In Camera and Electrical, from 42% in the 1990s to 37% in the 2000s.
- In Costume and Wardrobe, from 73% in the 1990s to 56% in the 2000s.
- In Make Up and Hairdressing, from 68,5% in the 1990s to 55% in the 2000s.
- In Editorial, from 45% in the 1990s to 34% in the 2000s.
- In Script and Continuity, from 50% in the 1990s to 37% in the 2000s.

Consequently, despite of the impressive rise in film produced during the 2000s – from 715 films in the 1990s to 1340 in the 2000s – the presence of women working in roles below-the-line not only did not grow accordingly,

FILMS WITH WOMEN WORKING IN THE FILM EDITING DEPARTMENT			
YEARS	FILMS	Nº	%
2000	42	12	28.57
2001	106	20	18.87
2002	137	27	19.71
2003	106	23	21.70
2004	130	20	15.38
2005	139	31	22.30
2006	150	36	24.00
2007	171	33	19.30
2008	173	26	15.03
2009	186	38	20.43
TOTAL	1340	266	19.85

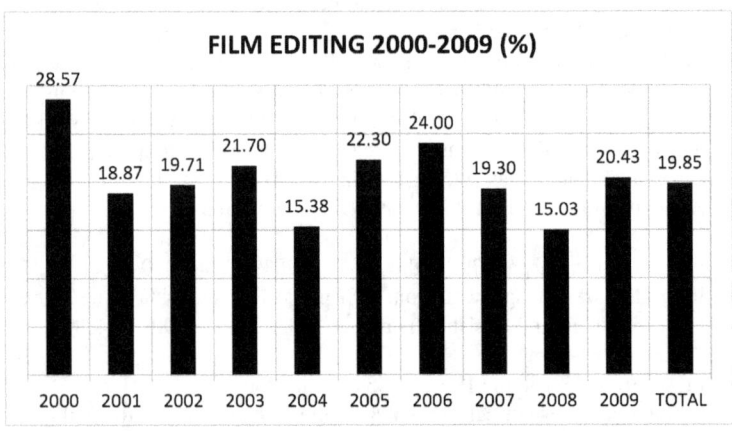

Figure 4.2 The presence of women in the Film Editing department in the 2000s
Source: Antonio Fernández Segura with data from the ICAA and IMDB.

FILMS WITH WOMEN WORKING IN THE PRODUCTION MANAGEMENT DEPARTMENT			
YEARS	FILMS	Nº	%
2000	42	23	54.76
2001	106	79	74.53
2002	137	91	66.42
2003	106	67	63.21
2004	130	85	65.38
2005	139	95	68.35
2006	150	95	63.33
2007	171	102	59.65
2008	173	104	60.12
2009	186	122	65.59
TOTAL	1340	863	64.40

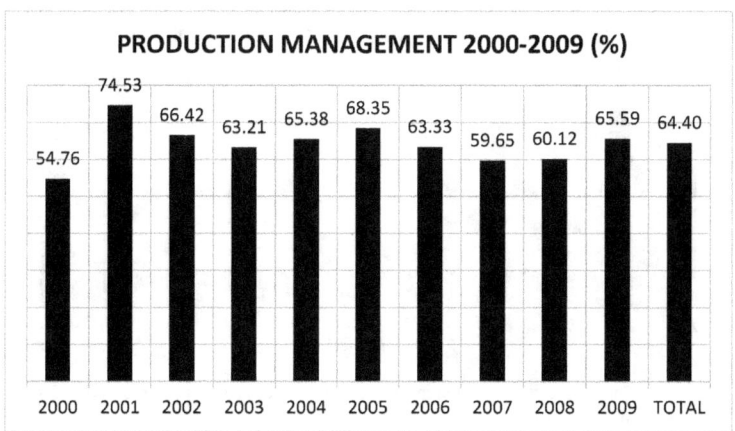

Figure 4.3 The presence of women in the Production Management department in the 2000s

Source: Antonio Fernández Segura with data from the ICAA and IMDB.

FILMS WITH WOMEN WORKING IN THE SECOND UNIT OR ASSISTANT DIRECTOR DEPARTMENT			
YEARS	FILMS	Nº	%
2000	42	20	47.62
2001	106	61	57.55
2002	137	62	45.26
2003	106	52	49.06
2004	130	60	46.15
2005	139	60	43.17
2006	150	61	40.67
2007	171	72	42.11
2008	173	68	39.31
2009	186	73	39.25
TOTAL	1340	589	43.96

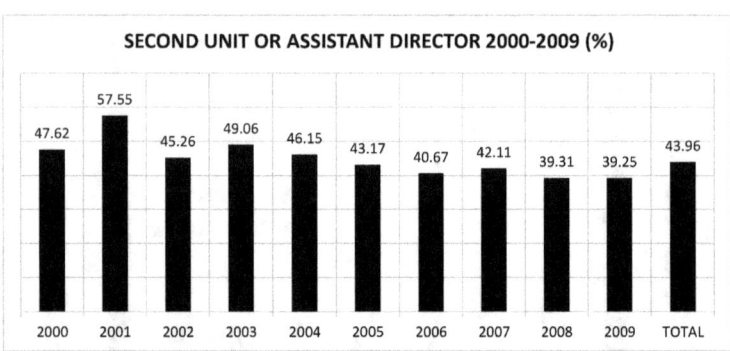

Figure 4.4 The presence of women in the Second Unit or Assistant Director department in the 2000s

Source: Antonio Fernández Segura with data from the ICAA and IMDB.

FILMS WITH WOMEN WORKING IN THE ART DEPARTMENT			
YEARS	FILMS	Nº	%
2000	42	23	54.76
2001	106	63	59.43
2002	137	64	46.72
2003	106	46	43.40
2004	130	65	50.00
2005	139	57	41.01
2006	150	67	44.67
2007	171	73	42.69
2008	173	64	36.99
2009	186	82	44.09
TOTAL	1340	604	45.07

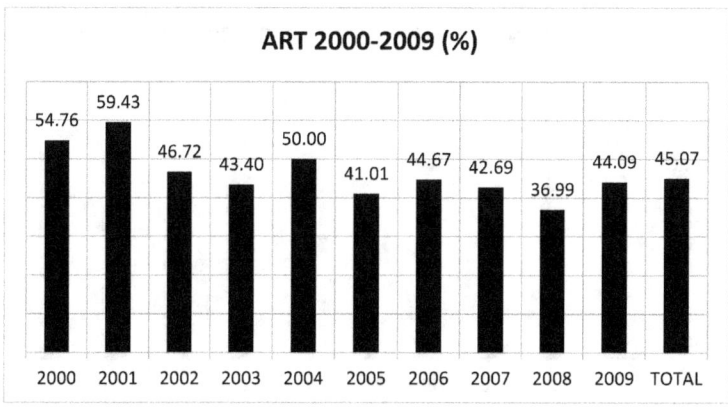

Figure 4.5 The presence of women in the Art department in the 2000s
Source: Antonio Fernández Segura with data from the ICAA and IMDB.

FILMS WITH WOMEN WORKING IN THE SOUND DEPARTMENT			
YEARS	FILMS	Nº	%
2000	42	10	23.81
2001	106	32	30.19
2002	137	36	26.28
2003	106	23	21.70
2004	130	36	27.69
2005	139	34	24.46
2006	150	44	29.33
2007	171	42	24.56
2008	173	40	23.12
2009	186	49	26.34
TOTAL	1340	346	25.82

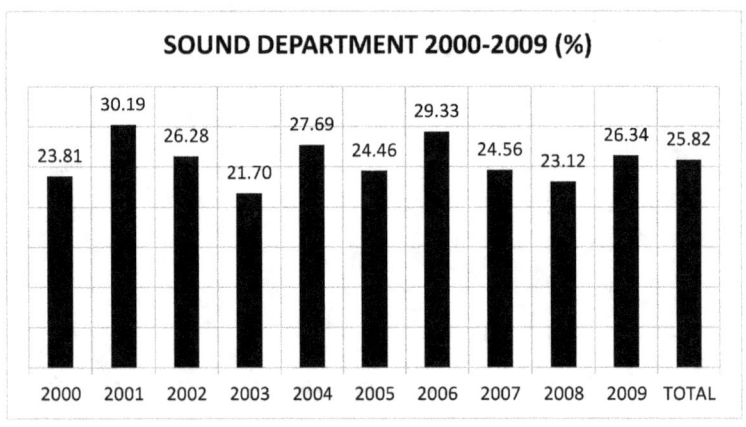

Figure 4.6 The presence of women in the Sound department in the 2000s
Source: Antonio Fernández Segura with data from the ICAA and IMDB.

FILMS WITH WOMEN WORKING IN THE CAMERA AND ELECTRICAL DEPARTMENT				
YEARS	FILMS	Nº	%
2000	42	21	50.00
2001	106	56	52.83
2002	137	47	34.31
2003	106	42	39.62
2004	130	50	38.46
2005	139	59	42.45
2006	150	49	32.67
2007	171	59	34.50
2008	173	59	34.10
2009	186	64	34.41
TOTAL	1340	506	37.76

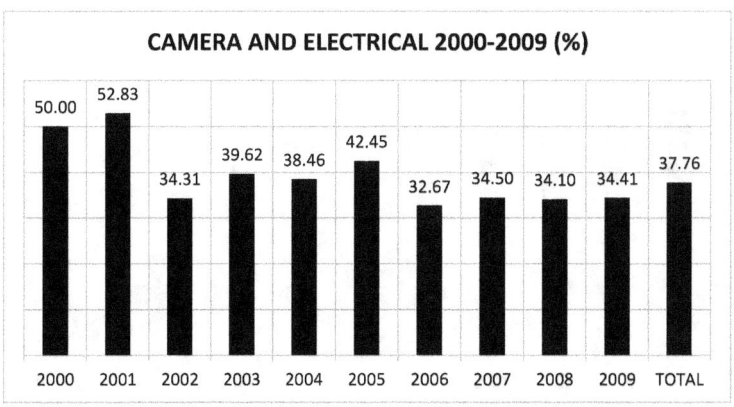

Figure 4.7 The presence of women in the Camera and Electrical department in the 2000s

Source: Antonio Fernández Segura with data from the ICAA and IMDB.

FILMS WITH WOMEN WORKING IN THE COSTUME AND WARDROBE DEPARTMENT			
YEARS	FILMS	Nº	%
2000	42	30	71.43
2001	106	76	71.70
2002	137	91	66.42
2003	106	60	56.60
2004	130	72	55.38
2005	139	82	58.99
2006	150	81	54.00
2007	171	81	47.37
2008	173	83	47.98
2009	186	97	52.15
TOTAL	1340	753	56.19

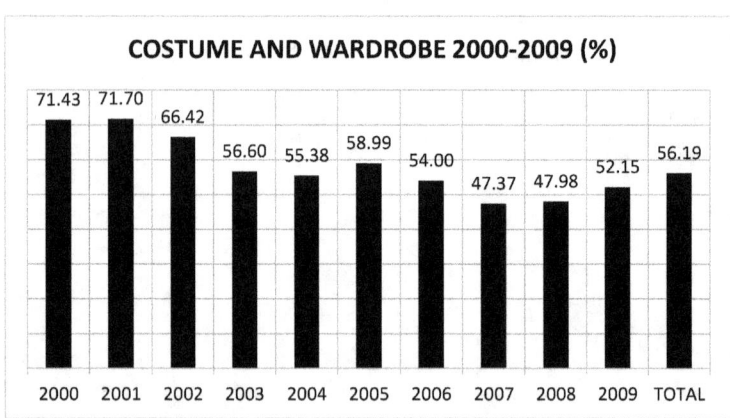

Figure 4.8 The presence of women in the Costume and Wardrobe department in the 2000s

Source: Antonio Fernández Segura with data from the ICAA and IMDB.

FILMS WITH WOMEN WORKING IN THE MAKE UP AND HAIRDRESSING DEPARTMENT			
YEARS	FILMS	Nº	%
2000	42	30	71.43
2001	106	76	71.70
2002	137	85	62.04
2003	106	61	57.55
2004	130	70	53.85
2005	139	76	54.68
2006	150	84	56.00
2007	171	87	50.88
2008	173	79	45.66
2009	186	98	52.69
TOTAL	1340	746	55.67

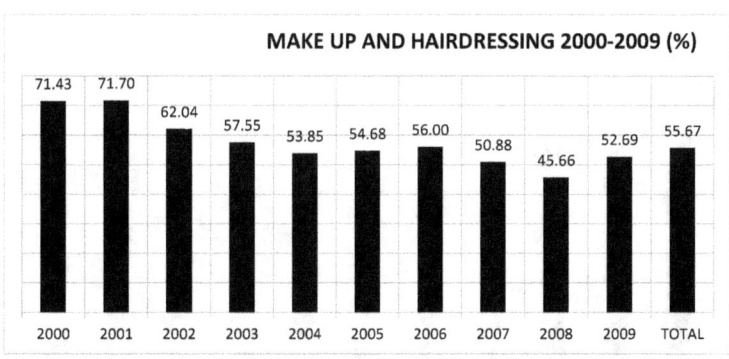

Figure 4.9 The presence of women in the Makeup and Hairdressing department in the 2000s

Source: Antonio Fernández Segura with data from the ICAA and IMDB.

The 2000s

FILMS WITH WOMEN WORKING IN THE EDITORIAL DEPARTMENT			
YEARS	FILMS	Nº	%
2000	42	22	52.38
2001	106	49	46.23
2002	137	56	40.88
2003	106	36	33.96
2004	130	43	33.08
2005	139	47	33.81
2006	150	45	30.00
2007	171	57	33.33
2008	173	50	28.90
2009	186	63	33.87
TOTAL	1340	468	34.93

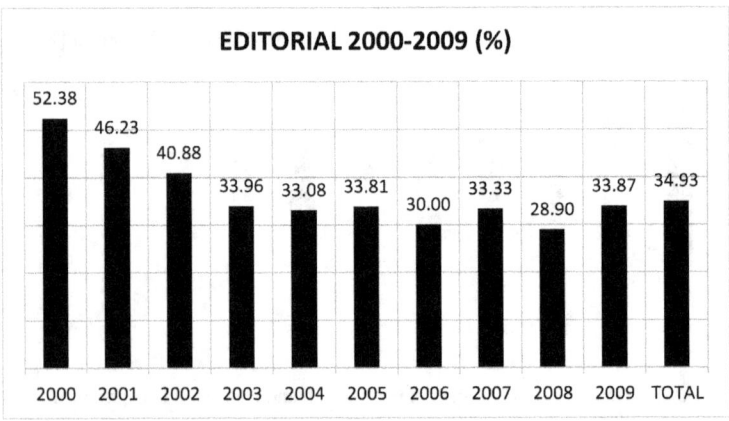

Figure 4.10 The presence of women in the Editorial department in the 2000s
Source: Antonio Fernández Segura with data from the ICAA and IMDB.

FILMS WITH WOMEN WORKING IN THE SCRIPT AND CONTINUITY DEPARTMENT			
YEARS	FILMS	Nº	%
2000	42	19	45.24
2001	106	52	49.06
2002	137	53	38.69
2003	106	41	38.68
2004	130	50	38.46
2005	139	56	40.29
2006	150	61	40.67
2007	171	62	36.26
2008	173	53	30.64
2009	186	59	31.72
TOTAL	1340	506	37.76

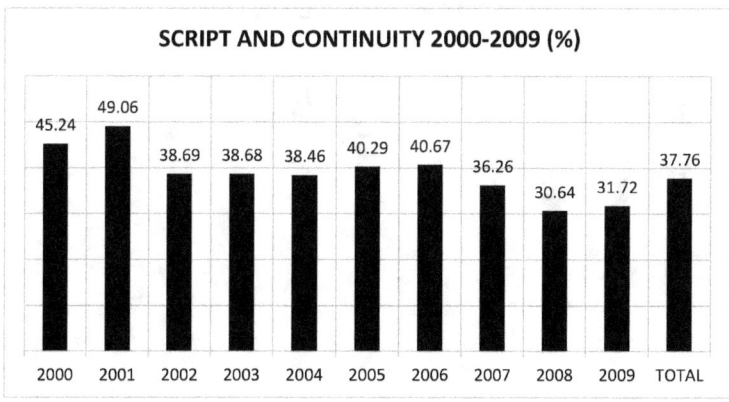

Figure 4.11 The presence of women in the Script and Continuity department in the 2000s

Source: Antonio Fernández Segura with data from the ICAA and IMDB.

FILMS WITH WOMEN WORKING IN THE MUSIC DEPARTMENT			
YEARS	FILMS	Nº	%
2000	42	11	26.19
2001	106	17	16.04
2002	137	24	17.52
2003	106	18	16.98
2004	130	21	16.15
2005	139	29	20.86
2006	150	40	26.67
2007	171	34	19.88
2008	173	31	17.92
2009	186	39	20.97
TOTAL	1340	264	19.70

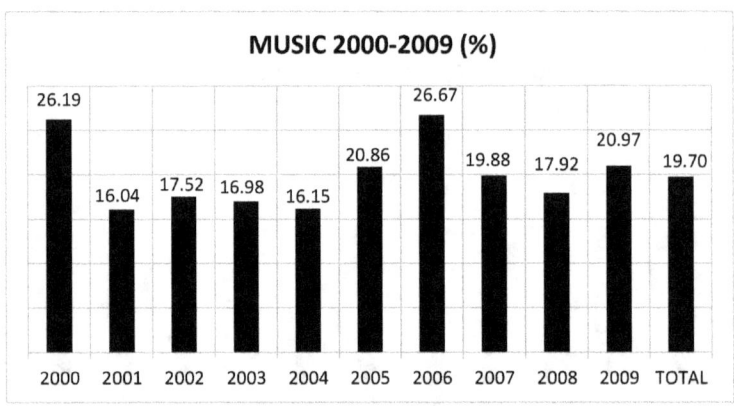

Figure 4.12 The presence of women in the Music department in the 2000s
Source: Antonio Fernández Segura with data from the ICAA and IMDB.

FILMS WITH WOMEN WORKING IN THE CINEMATOGRAPHY DEPARTMENT			
YEARS	FILMS	Nº	%
2000	42	1	2.38
2001	106	1	0.94
2002	137	4	2.92
2003	106	3	2.83
2004	130	9	6.92
2005	139	4	2.88
2006	150	7	4.67
2007	171	10	5.85
2008	173	2	1.16
2009	186	13	6.99
TOTAL	1340	54	4.03

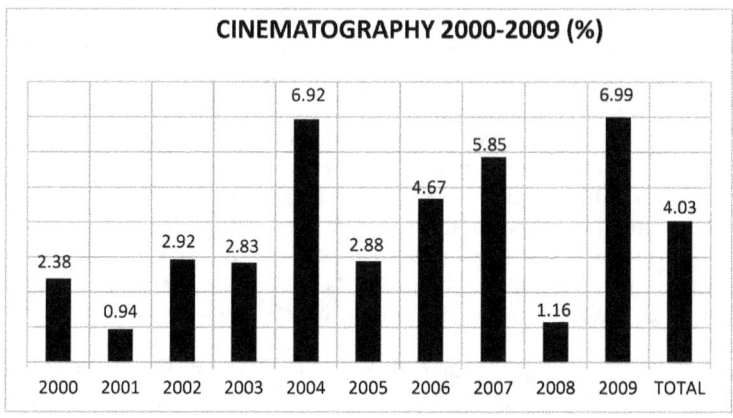

Figure 4.13 The presence of women in the Cinematography department in the 2000s
Source: Antonio Fernández Segura with data from the ICAA and IMDB.

but it decreased substantially. Similarly, the traditional over feminisation of Production Management, Second Unit and Assistant Direction, Art Department, Costume and Wardrobe, Make-Up and Hairdressing, Editorial and Script and Continuity departments was maintained. Men kept dominating the technical departments: Film Editing, Cinematography, Camera and Electrical, Sound and Music. Consequently, the gendered division of labour was still maintained.

Conclusion

How did the Law 55/2007 and the Orden CUL/2834/2009 foster the participation of female directors and screenwriters in feature films over the following five years (2010–2015) – the two categories where affirmative action measures were implemented – until a new piece of legislation was passed by the PP government once it regained power in 2011?[37]

Film production did not grow steadily between the 200 films produced in 2010 to the 255 films produced in 2015, neither the presence of women in direction nor in screen writing:

- 2010: out of 200 films produced, 12% were directed or co-directed by women and 24'5% were written or co-written by women.
- 2011: out of 199 films produced, 12% were directed or co-directed by women and 26% were written or co-written by women.
- 2012: out of 182 films produced, 14% were directed or co-directed by women and 26% were written or co-written by women.
- 2013: out of 231 films produced, 14% were directed or co-directed by women and 24% were written or co-written by women.
- 2014: out of 216 films produced, 15% were directed or co-directed by women and 30% were written or co-written by women.
- 2015: out of 255 films produced, 16% were directed or co-directed by women and 29% were written or co-written by women.

However, what can be inferred from this data is that the presence of women directors between 2010 and 2015 was very low, reaching its peak in 2014 with only 32 films directed or co-directed by women out of 216 films produced (just 15%). As for screen writing, which had better figures, the best year was 2014, which saw 65 films written or co-written by women out of 216 films produced (a mere 30%).

Having reached this point, one might wonder how effective the affirmative measures introduced by the Law 55/2007 and the Orden CUL/2834/2009 were. We may also wonder how far and in what ways the promotion of gender equality in only above-the-line roles such as direction and scriptwriting does actually solve the sexism in the film industry, since the traditional gendered division of labour in the Spanish film industry still stands: in 2020, to name a few examples, Costume and Wardrobe was still highly feminised with 88% women employed against 12% of men, while departments such as Music are still highly masculinised – 11% women as against 89% of men.[38] Consequently, we can argue that, despite its intentions, the Law 55/2007 cannot be considered a feminist film law. Moreover, the Law did not challenge the power dynamics of the field of Spanish cinema: the two main professional associations that were pushing to have their demands adopted by the Law, FAPAE and UTECA, were not only headed by men, but did have little concern to assess women inequality in the film industry. Therefore, the women film professionals had to gather in CIMA to lobby for their own interests and only then they managed to have gender inequality in the film industry acknowledged by law, regardless the fact that CIMA only focused on gender inequality the above-the-law roles such as direction, scriptwriting, and production.

The decade of the 2010s is out of the scope of this book; consequently, is left to further research to assess how far and in what ways the Law 55/2007 and further legislation has advanced the presence of women in both above and below-the-line roles: if we only focus on the above-the-line roles we will have a tinted vision of how gender inequality operates in the field of Spanish cinema.

Notes

1 "Debemos proteger la cultura como un objeto para todos, no como un objeto de consumo" (Calvo in Ruiz Mantilla 2004, n.p.) (all translations from Spanish made by the author).
2 Titled *La excepción cultural. El futuro del cine español*. Víctor Erice is one of the highest-profile Spanish film auteurs since his first release in 1973, *The Spirit of the Beehive*; Javier Maqua is a Spanish film director, novelist and screenwriter; Esteve Riambau is a film historian, lecturer at the Autonomous University of Barcelona and Head of the Catalan Cinematheque since 2010.
3 "[C]reemos que el cine español – como todos los cines europeos – va a quedar reducido a mínimos por la ocupación del estadounidense [...] De modo que, si no lo remediamos [...] nuestra identidad cultural nacional quedará dañada [...] Creemos que estamos ante un desastre cultural" (Maqua 2004: 13).
4 "Una revista de opinión comprometida con una concepción artística y cultural del cine" (*Cahiers du Cinema. España*, mayo 2007:74).
5 Titled *Diez objetivos para el cine español*.
6 "Una necesidad básica, un derecho de la ciudadanía que se tiene el deber de cuidar" (Programa Electoral del Partido Socialista 2004, 195).
7 "Una lógica de mercado que [niega] tanto la independencia creadora como el espíritu crítico que ha de caracterizar la democracia" (Programa Electoral del Partido Socialista 2004, 193).
8 Prior to the Convention, the UNESCO had issued the non-binding "Universal Declaration of Cultural Diversity" in November 2001.
9 According to the European Institute for Gender Equality, gender mainstreaming "involves the integration of a gender perspective into the preparation, design, implementation, monitoring and evaluation of policies, regulatory measures and spending programmes, with a view to promoting equality between women and men, and combating discrimination" (EIGE, n.p.)

10 Ley Orgánica 1/2004, de 28 de diciembre, de Medidas de Protección Integral contra la Violencia de Género.
11 Ley Orgánica 3/2007/de 22 de marzo, para la Igualdad Efectiva de Mujeres y Hombres.
12 It should be noted that in Spain, beyond the Spanish National Television, there are public television channels in all of 17 the autonomous governments to which these measures also apply.
13 Prior to that, the European Commission had launched the "Strategy for equality between women and men 2010–2015 (COM (2010) 491)" to achieve the objectives of Europe 2020, even though gender equality is legally recognized as early as in the Treaty of Rome's Article 8 (1958). For further information, see https://ec.europa.eu/info/policies/justice-and-fundamental-rights/gender-equality/gender-equality-strategy_en
14 Telecinco, Antena 3 and Sogecable gathered in UTECA in 1998 to defend their interests as private television companies. Cuatro and La Sexta joined UTECA in 2005 and 2006 respectively (Yáñez 2009, 39).
15 This struggle was the result of the Law 22/1999 that legally bounded private and public television companies to invest 5% and 6% of their year revenues respectively in film production.
16 "La solución del cine español no pasa por seguir protegiendo al productor independiente, como si éste fuera el único capaz de reflotar una industria que languidece y no el mayor causante de sus males, sino, muy al contrario, por defender estructuras fuertes e integrar en ellas a ese mal llamado productor independiente" (Echevarría in Sequera, enero 2007, 51).
17 According to the data provided by the ICAA, between 2000 and 2004 film production in Spain grow steadily: 42 featured films in 2000, 106 in 2001, 137 in 2002, 106 in 2003 and 130 in 2004.
18 "Lamentamos que UTECA pida textualmente la integración de los productores en las estructuras televisivas, por lo que supone de desprecio a la libertad de creación y producción […] Lamentamos la concepción monopolística de producir cine sólo bajo su paraguas, lo que, como todo el mundo intuye, conllevaría a la desaparición del cine español en un futuro cercano" (Pérez quoted in Sequera, enero 2007, 51).
19 CIMA: Asociación de Mujeres Cineastas y de Medios Audiovisuales: https://cimamujerescineastas.es/
20 TACE is the union that gathers the film professionals working in below-the-line roles in Spain and they negotiate their working conditions alone. This is another reason that can explain why CIMA did not push for equality measures in the roles below-the-line, whose struggles were being tackled by TACE.
21 Cristina Andreu, Icíar Bollaín, Isabel Coixet, Judith Collel, Ana Díez, Chus Gutiérrez, Daniela Féjerman, Patricia Ferreira, Eva Lesmes, Laura Mañá, Josefina Molina, Cayetana Mulero, Inés París, Dolores Payás, Helena Taberna, María Ripoll, Manane Rodríguez, Mireia Ros and Teresa Pelegrí.
22 It has to be noted that it was not until 2020 through the Orden CUD/582/2020, that affirmative action measures were introduced to tackle inequality in below-the-line roles and to assess the over feminization of some below-the-line roles against the over masculinization of some below-the-line roles. The Orden CUD/582/2020 did so by granting more points to get access to the funding directed towards the production of feature and short films to those projects that had only women working in the different departments (Orden CUD/582/2020, Artículo 18, Artículo 23, Artículo 26, Artículo 33).
23 FAPAE, FEDICINE, the Association of Film Distributors, CIMA and ADICINE, the Associaton of Independent Distributors (Sequera in *Cineinforme*, enero 2007, 48).
24 The Association of Public Regional Televisions created in 1989.

25 "Yo creo que estamos, en realidad, ante un debate ideológico y político sobre lo que supone el cine español. O bien se hace sólo un cine con los criterios impulsados por las televisiones, o bien se hace también un cine español independiente, que promueva la diversidad cultural, que responda a lo que conocemos como cine de autor en sus vertientes más variadas. O el cine es solamente una industria de entretenimiento, o es un medio de cultura que pone en juego toda la identidad de un país [...] Son dos modelos contrapuestos, pero creo que se pueden y se deben reconciliar. Ahora bien, por pura dinámica capitalista, si no ponemos una serie de mecanismos, ese modelo de cine de diversión acabará por comerse al cine independiente, de autor, cultural" (Lara in Heredero and Reviriego, mayo 2007, 71).
26 As Casimiro Torreiro notes, the highest grossing films between 2004 and 2008 were produced by private television companies (See Torreiro [1995] 2010, 497–498 for a complete list).
27 Artículo 22. Ayudas para la creación de guiones y al desarrollo de proyectos; Artículo 23. Ayudas a proyectos culturales y de formación no reglada; Artículo 25. Ayudas selectivas para la producción de largometrajes sobre Proyecto; Artículo 26. Ayudas generales para la producción de largometrajes sobre proyecto; Artículo 27. Ayudas para la producción de cortometrajes
28 Artículo 28. Ayudas para la distribución de películas; Artículo 29. Ayudas para las salas de exhibición cinematográfica.
29 Who had written popular comedies in the 1990s for directors such as Manuel López Pereira.
30 Who specialised in animation films.
31 Who made her last film in 2004.
32 Who had codirected *Monos como Becky* in 1999 alongside Joaquim Jordá.
33 Both Judith Collel and Teresa Pelegrí had directed the collaborative soft pornographic film *El imperio de los sentidos* in 1996, so they debuted in directing their solo feature films.
34 Who kept working as a scriptwriter despite having debuted in film direction.
35 She backed Fernando Trueba's *Calle 54* (2000), *El embrujo de Shanghai* (2002), *El milagro de Candeal* (2004) and *El baile de la victoria* (2009) and David Trueba's *Obra maestra* (2000), *Soldados de Salamina* (2003) and *Bienvenido a casa* (2006).
36 *El Deseo* is Pedro Almodóvar and his brother Agustín Almodóvar production company.
37 The Real Decreto Ley 6/2015, del 14 de mayo. The reason to focus exclusively on the presence of female directors and screen writers in feature films is because there is no data on the presence of women in the production of animated series and audiovisual works. The ICAA only complies the feature films produced by year, signalling their directors. The data on the films produced written by women has been obtained by looking at each film produced yearly between 2010 and 2015 at IMDB.
38 According to the report published by CIMA. The categories considered in the report are the following: Executive Production, Direction, Screenwriting, Music Composition, Production Management, Cinematography, Editing, Set Design, Costume Design, Makeup and Hairdressing, Sound Design and Special Effects.

References

Arranz, Fatima. 2007. *Mujeres y hombres en el cine español: una investigación empírica*. Madrid: UCM.
Beat Graber, Christoph. 2006. "The New Unesco Convention on Cultural Diversity: a Counterbalance to the WTO?". *Journal of International Economic Law*, 9(3): 553–574.

Bell, Melanie. 2021. *Movie Workers. The Women Who Made British Cinema*. Illinois: University of Illinois Press.
Combarros Peláez, César. 2005. *50 años Semana Internacional de cine de Valladolid. 1956–2005*. Valladolid: Semana Internacional de cine de Valladolid.
Cuenca, Sara 2020. *CIMA 2020. La representatividad de las mujeres en el sector cinematográfico del largometraje español*. CIMA e ICAA.
Fernández Meneses, Jara. 2023. "Personal interview with Inés París", 1st of March.
Fernández Meneses, Jara. 2023. "Personal interview with Fernando Lara", 30th of March.
Fernández Meneses, Jara. 2023. "Personal inteview with Carmen Calvo", 20th of April.
Jordan, Barry. 2011. "Audiences, Film Culture, Public Subsidies: The End of Spanish Cinema?". In *Spain on screen. Developments in contemporary Spanish Cinema*, edited by Anne Davies, 19–40. London: Palgrave Macmillan
Lara, Fernando. 1975. "El cine español ante una alternativa democrática". In *7 trabajos de base sobre el cine español*, edited by Fernando Lara *et.al*, 219–244. Valencia: Fernando Torres Editor.
Maqua, Javier (coord.). 2004. *La excepción cultural. El futuro del cine español*. Madrid: ADIRCE.
McQuail, Denis. 2001. "The Consequences of European Media Policies and Organisational Structures for Cultural Diversity". In *Differing Diversities: Transversal Study of the Theme of Cultural Policy and Cultural Diversity*, edited by, Tony Bennett, 73–92. Strasbourg: Council of Europe Publishing.
Paris, Inés. 2011. "La situación de las mujeres españolas en el mundo del cine". In *Mujeres y cultura: políticas de igualdad*, 41–49. Madrid: Ministerio de Cultura.
Shore, Cris. 2001. "The Cultural Policies of the European Union and Cultural Diversity". In *Differing Diversities: Transversal Study of the Theme of Cultural Policy and Cultural Diversity*, edited by in Tony Bennett, 107–122. Strasbourg: Council of Europe Publishing.
Torreiro, Casimiro. [1995c] 2010. "Epílogo provisional (2005–2008)". *Historia del cine español*, edited by Román Gubern. *et al*, 497–512. Madrid: Cátedra.
Triana-Toribio, Nuria. 2014. 'Residual film cultures: Real and imagined futures of Spanish cinema'. *Bulletin of Hispanic Studies*, 91(1): 65–68.
Yáñez, Jara. 2010. *La artimética de la creación. Entrevistas con productores del cine español contemporáneo*. 39 Festival de Cine de Alcalá de Henares-Comunidad de Madrid: Alcalá de Henares.

Press

Cahiers du Cinema. España. "Diez objetivos para el cine español". Mayo 2007: 74–75.
Cineinforme. "Autofinanciación y coproducciones, prioridades de la FAPAE". Mayo 1995: 63.
Cineinforme. "Panorama". Enero 2004: 38–40.
Cineinforme. "Se aprueba el reglamento sobre la financiación obligatoria de los operadores de televisión de cine europeo y español". Julio-agosto 2004: 48–49.
Cineinforme. "Mercado cinematográfico mundial". Septiembre 2007: 56–62.
Cineinforme. "Mercado cinematográfico español". Mayo 2007: 34–43.
El País. "Zapatero acomete su cambio de Gobierno más profundo para vencer a las crisis", 8/5/2009: n.p.

García, Rocío. "El sector del cine espera aliviado la llegada de Guardans". *El País*, 14/4/2009: n.p.

Heredero, Carlos y Reviriego, Carlos. "Entrevista con Fernando Lara". *Cahiers du Cinéma. España*. Mayo 2007: 71–73.

Intxausti, Aurora. "La apuesta por el cine español". *El País*, 29/2/2004: n.p.

Martín, Javier. "Los productores quieren una delimitación legal de sus funciones". *El País*, 26/3/2005: n.p.

Ruiz Mantilla, Jesús. "Arranca la batalla por la excepción cultural". *El País*, 25/4/2004: n.p. Available: https://elpais.com/diario/2004/04/25/cultura/1082844001_850215.html Accessed: February 23, 2022.

Sequera, David y Michelin, Gerardo. "Pedro Pérez: queremos traer nuevos inversores al cine con la creación de sociedades de capital riesgo y fondos de inversión para películas". *Cineinforme*. Enero 2004: 32–35.

Sequera, David. "Las bases de la nueva Ley del Cine ya están en la mesa de los diferentes agentes del sector Audiovisual". *Cineinforme*. Enero 2007: 48–50.

ICAA reports

ICAA. 2000. "Anuario del Cine Español" Available: https://www.culturaydeporte.gob.es/dam/jcr:018a7593-b1c8-4a50-86a9-541e8017f57ba/boletin-2000.pdf Accessed: February 24, 2022.

ICAA. 2001. "Anuario del Cine Español" Available: https://www.culturaydeporte.gob.es/dam/jcr:d5b427a5-2303-4e0c-a979-2a3350866545/bolet-n-2001.pdf Accessed: February 24, 2022.

ICAA. 2002. "Anuario del Cine Español" Available: https://www.culturaydeporte.gob.es/cultura/areas/cine/mc/anuario-cine/anuarios/ano-2002.html Accessed: February 24, 2022.

ICAA. 2003. "Anuario del Cine Español" Available: https://www.culturaydeporte.gob.es/cultura/areas/cine/mc/anuario-cine/anuarios/ano-2003.html Accessed: February 24, 2022.

ICAA. 2004. "Anuario del Cine Español" Available: https://www.culturaydeporte.gob.es/cultura/areas/cine/mc/anuario-cine/anuarios/ano-2004/produccion-espanola.html Accessed: February 23, 2022.

ICAA. 2005. "Anuario del Cine Español" Available: https://www.culturaydeporte.gob.es/cultura/areas/cine/mc/anuario-cine/anuarios/ano-2005.html Accessed: February 24, 2022.

ICAA. 2006. "Anuario del Cine Español" Available: https://www.culturaydeporte.gob.es/cultura/areas/cine/mc/anuario-cine/anuarios/ano-2006.html Accessed: February 25, 2022.

ICAA. 2010. "Anuario del Cine Español" Available: https://www.culturaydeporte.gob.es/cultura/areas/cine/mc/anuario-cine/anuarios/ano-2010.html Accessed: March 2, 2022.

ICAA. 2011. "Anuario del Cine Español" Available: https://www.culturaydeporte.gob.es/cultura/areas/cine/mc/anuario-cine/anuarios/ano-2011.html Accessed: March 2, 2022.

ICAA. 2012. "Anuario del Cine Español" Available: https://www.culturaydeporte.gob.es/cultura/areas/cine/mc/anuario-cine/anuarios/ano-2012.html Accessed: March 2, 2022.

ICAA. 2013. "Anuario del Cine Español" Available: https://www.culturaydeporte.gob.es/cultura/areas/cine/mc/anuario-cine/anuarios/ano-2013.html Accessed: March 2, 2022.
ICAA. 2014. "Anuario del Cine Español" Available: https://www.culturaydeporte.gob.es/cultura/areas/cine/mc/anuario-cine/anuarios/ano-2014.html Accessed: March 2, 2022.
ICAA. 2015. "Anuario del Cine Español" Available: https://www.culturaydeporte.gob.es/cultura/areas/cine/mc/anuario-cine/anuarios/ano-2015.html Accessed: March 2, 2022.

Legal documents and political parties' manifestos

Council of Europe. 2000. "Declaration on Cultural Diversity".
Council of Europe. 2001. "Resolution of 12 February 2001 national aid to the film and audiovisual industries" (2001/C 73/02).
European Institute for Gender Equality: "What is Gender Mainstreaming". Accessible: What is Gender mainstreaming | EIGE (europa.eu). Accessed: February 24, 2022.
Decreto 2062/2008, de 12 de diciembre, por el que se desarrolla la Ley 55/2007, de 28 de diciembre, del Cine.
European Commission. 1999. "Communication to the Council and the European Parliament: The EU Approach to the WTO Millennium Round".
European Commission. 2010. "Strategy for equality between women and men 2010–2015" (COM (2010) 491)
European Commission. 2016. "Strategic Engagement for Gender Equality 2016–2019". Luxembourg: Publications Office of the European Union.
European Commission. 2020. "Gender Equality Strategy". Available: https://ec.europa.eu/info/policies/justice-and-fundamental-rights/gender-equality/gender-equality-strategy_en#gender-equality-strategy-2020-2025. Accessed: February 24, 2022.
Ley 22/1999, de 7 de junio.
Ley Orgánica 1/2004, de 28 de diciembre, de Medidas de Protección Integral contra la Violencia de Género.
Ley Orgánica 3/2007, de 22 de marzo, para la Igualdad Efectiva de Mujeres y Hombres.
Ley 55/2007, de 28 de diciembre, de Cine.
Ministerio de Cultura. 2011. *Mujeres y cultura: políticas de igualdad*.
Orden CUL/2834/2009, de 19 de octubre, por la que se dictan normas de aplicación del Real, Decreto 2062/2008, de 12 de diciembre.
Orden CUD/582/2020, de 26 de junio, por la que se establecen las bases reguladoras de las ayudas estatales para la producción de largometrajes y de cortometrajes y regula la estructura del Registro Administrativo de Empresas Cinematográficas y Audiovisuales.
Programa Electoral del Partido Socialista (2004).
Real Decreto Ley 6/2015, del 14 de mayo.
UNESCO. 2001. "Universal Declaration of Cultural Diversity".
UNESCO. 2005. "Convention on the Protection and Promotion of the Diversity of Cultural Expressions".

Conclusion

Unchallenged structural gender inequalities

After having analysed the film policies carried out by the Spanish state between 1980 and 2010 and how far and in what ways they have contributed to tackle gender inequality in the film industry, the obvious conclusion is that Spanish film policies have not managed to break the patterns we might expect to see in any male-dominated industry as the Spanish film industry is: there is both vertical segregation by gender – male dominance of high-status work – and horizontal segregation by gender – where a number of occupations within the industry are sorted by traditional gender roles (Jones and Pringle 2015, 39). Applied to the Spanish film industry, this means that men dominate the above-the-line roles (vertical segregation), and that there are gendered below-the-line roles: the technical departments such as Film Editing, Camera and Electrical, Cinematography, Music and Sound are dominated by men while the departments of Art Direction, Production Management, Costume and Wardrobe, Make Up and Hairdressing, Editorial and Script and Continuity remain highly feminised (horizontal segregation). And both the vertical and horizontal segregation by gender has remained throughout three decades regardless of the film policies that have regulated each decade.

In the 1980s, the field of Spanish cinema was dominated by the dissident film agents' cinephile culture. These agents managed to have their defence of cinema as a vehicle for culture consecrated by law because Pilar Miró, a key dissident film agent, was in charge of the ICAA – at that time called General Direction of Cinematography (1982–1985), and therefore, in charge of enacting the R.D.3304/1983, popularly known as the Miró Law that regulated the Spanish film industry between 1983 and 1989. It is quite surprising that a law that emerged from a socialist party and from those left-wing agents who had been actively engaged in fighting the patriarchal fascist dictatorship of Francisco Franco did not consider that the new democratic cinema they were trying to build had to guarantee gender equality for the film professionals working in the national film industry. We have also seen how Miró's habitus as a film auteur and key member of the dissident film agents shaped her film policies and

DOI: 10.4324/9781003373087-6

her defence of quality cinema that she understood as films that conveyed cultural values that would contribute to develop a critical consciousness amongst Spanish audiences. However, she was not concerned about gender inequality in the Spanish film industry. The presence of women working both in above and below-the-line roles remained extremely low in the 1980s – with not a single department having at least 50% of female workforce throughout the decade. And even with these low numbers, the traditional gendered division in the below-the-line roles was maintained: women's presence was major in the departments of Makeup and Hairdressing, Costume and Wardrobe, Editorial and Script and Continuity; men dominated the technical departments such as Film Editing, Sound, Camera and Electrical, Cinematography and Music.

The understanding of what type of film policies were most suitable to protect and promote the Spanish film industry changed in the 1990s when Jorge Semprún arrived at the Ministry of Culture (1988–1991) and Miguel Marías at the ICAA (1988–1990) and the R.D. 1282/1989, popularly known as the Semprún Decree, was enacted. From supporting a quality cinema, Semprún and Marías wanted to have a competitive cinema that could be profitable both in the national market and abroad in a progressively globalised industry. For so doing, the emphasis sifted from advance subsidies directed towards quality projects to automatic subsidies that would benefit those films that performed well at the box office. The Decree succeeded in creating more appealing films that accrued better revenues at the box office. However, as happened in the 1980s, gender inequality was not an issue for discussion. Once again, it is quite surprising that a policymaker such as Semprún, former member of the Spanish Communist Party and active fighter against the patriarchal fascist dictatorship of Francisco Franco was not concerned by how gender inequality dominated the Spanish film industry. As I have explained in Chapter 1, following Joan Acker, I consider the Spanish film industry as a "gender regime" insofar gender is one of the key principles that structures the Spanish film industry (Ackers 2006a, 8). One of the key characteristics of "gender regimes" as "inequality regimes" (Ackers 2006b, 444) is the "invisibility of the inequalities" (Ackers 2006b, 552). This is to say, "the degree of awareness of inequalities" that exist in any given gender regime (Ackers 2006b, 552). I argue that this invisibility translates into the field of Spanish cinema in the very fact that throughout the 1980s and the 1990s gender inequality in the film industry was so invisible that it was not even discussed amongst the film professionals and the policymakers when discussing the best policies to protect and promote the Spanish film industry. This invisibility derived in the fact that the Semprún Decree, as the Miró Law, did not introduce any affirmative action that could tackle the structural gender inequality of the Spanish film industry. Despite the fact that 31 women debuted in film direction throughout the 1990s, the presence of women in roles above-the-line (direction, scriptwriting, and production) remained relatively low, even though it was higher than in the 1980s: out of 608 films produced throughout the decade, 59 were directed by women (9.70%), 23 films written only by women (3.78%), 118 co-written by men and women (19.41%) and 142 (23.36%) films were produced by women. When it comes to roles below-the-line, the situation fluctuated between departments: Makeup and Hairdressing, Costume and Wardrobe, Editorial and Script and Continuity remained very feminised departments; Film Editing, Sound, Camera and Electrical, Music and Cinematography stayed highly masculinised; finally, Production Management, Second Unit and Assistant Direction and the Art Department saw an impressive rise in the number of films produced that had women working in these departments: from overall 12% in the three departments in the 1980s to 65%, 49% and 46%, respectively, in the 1990s. The rise of female workforce in these departments is a double-edged sword because they are three departments that are, as Makeup and Hairdressing, Costume and Wardrobe, Editorial and Script and Continuity, traditionally deemed to be fit for women's due to the stereotypes that are associated to women work. As Melanie Bell has already argued "women are commonly assumed to be naturally patient and meticulous, with an aptitude for detail work, and to have highly developed skills in communication and empathy" (Bell 2021, 5). These assumptions explain women's overrepresentation in Production Management, Second Unit and Assistant Direction, the Art Department, Makeup and Hairdressing, Costume and Wardrobe, Editorial and Script and Continuity. These roles are also deemed to be auxiliary, and, consequently, lower skilled than the technical departments such as Film Editing, Sound, Camera and Electrical, Music and Cinematography. As Melanie Bell also argues, these auxiliary roles are considered to "support others in the workforce (predominantly but not exclusively men) and free them to concentrate on tasks ascribed greater value" (Bell 2021, 4).

Gender inequality in the film industry did not become a topic for discussion amongst film professionals and policymakers until CIMA, the Women's Filmmakers and Audiovisual Professionals Association, was born in 2006 and it gained enough power within the field of Spanish cinema to be able to push for women film professionals' demands. Because of this new redistribution of power within the field of Spanish cinema – not only because CIMA started fighting for women's rights, but also because Carmen Calvo became Minister of Culture (2004–2007) and Fernando Lara Head of the ICAA (2004–2009) and they were both willing to include CIMA's demands in the new film law – the first affirmative action film law, the Law 55/2007, came into being. However, we need to bear into mind that affirmative action measures were implemented only to advance directorial and scriptwriting roles: the Law came into force from 2008 on and we can see fluctuation of women directors from 15% in 2008, 12% in 2010 and 2011 to 16% in 2015 (these five years coincide with the period when Spain was hit harder by the 2008 global financial crisis. In 2015, a new piece of legislation was introduced by the PP's conservative government that regained power in 2011). Regarding female scriptwriters, we see that the numbers also oscillated between 23% in 2008 and 29% in 2015, reaching its peak in 2014 with 30%. Consequently, it can be said that the Law 55/2007 did not solve the structural gender inequality of the Spanish film industry.

As I finish typing this book, a new film law is being discussed in the Spanish parliament.[1] If approved, this would be the first law to be enacted to include affirmative action measures to tackle gender, race and ableism inequality in the film industry by establishing quotas directed towards the inclusion of women, racialised people and people with disabilities in the film industry. Regarding gender inequality, the Law explicitly states that the quota should be at least 30% (Articulo 16. Disposiciones generales). We need to bear in mind that the concrete measures to foster the presence of minorities in the film industry are not detailed in the laws (which just establish the general legal framework) but in the consequents decrees and orders that regulate the Spanish laws, so the Law's draft is not enough material to fairly assess how these measures are going to be concretely implemented. However, the initiatives directed to tackle gender inequality are, once again, aimed at promoting directors and scriptwriters, but both producers and the roles below-the-law are not protected by affirmative action. Consequently, one might wonder what Spanish policymakers have learnt from the past, and, particularly for the effects that the first affirmative action film law, the Law 55/2007, has had over the Spanish film industry.

In this book, I have assessed how far and in what ways Spanish film legislation has tackled the structural gender inequality of the Spanish film industry by looking at two key issues: the access and presence of female professionals working in above and below-the-line roles and whether women in direction, scriptwriting and production have managed to have continuous careers in the film industry. However, gender inequality in the film industry is also manifested in a myriad of different facts such as that women do not get an equal share of the available funds, they usually have lower budgets or that they have to leave the film industry in order to take caring duties up, amongst many others. Consequently, there is plenty of research to be done on the diverse ways gender inequality still operates in the Spanish film industry, as well as on the multiple, intersecting and complex patterns of inequalities that cross class, race, sexuality, ableism, age and other differences. I hope this book serves to set the ground for further lines of research.

Note

1 Proyecto de Ley del Cine y de la Cultura Audiovisual

References

Acker, Joan. 2006a. "The gender regime of Swedish banks". *Scandinavian Journal of Management*, 22: 195–209 (first published SJM, 1994, 10: 117–130).

Acker, Joan. 2006b. "Inequality regimes: Gender, class, and race in organizations". *Gender & Society*, 20(4): 441–464.

Bell, Melanie. 2021. *Movie Workers. The Women Who Made British Cinema*. Champaign, IL, USA: University of Illinois Press.
Jones, Deborah and Pringle, Judith K. 2015. "Unmanageable inequalities: Sexism in the film industry". In "Gender and Creative Labour", edited by in Bridget Conor, Rosalind Gill and Stephanie Taylor, 37–49. *Sociological Review Monograph Series*, 63: S1.
Liddy, Susan. (ed.). 2020. *Women in the International Film Industry. Policy, Practice and Power*. London: Palgrave Macmillan.

Index

Note: *Italicized* and **bold** page numbers refer to figures and tables, respectively; and page numbers followed by "n" refer to notes.

ABC 4, 61
Abel, Dominique 108
above-the-line roles, presence of women in: 1980s *40*; 1990s *70*; 2000s *107*
A cielo abierto (1998) 90n11
Acker, Joan 19–20, 21n4, 132
A contratiempo (1981) 55n18
Acosta, Olivia 108
Adinolfi, Gaetano 67
Aguilar, Roser 108, 109
Aguirre, Arantxa 108
Aguirre, Esperanza 15
AIPCE 17, 34, 64
Alatriste (2006) 104, 110
Albadalejo, Miguel 72
Alborch, Carmen 15, 88
Alborch Law 69
Alegre ma non troppo (1994) 73
Alessandrin, Patrick 110
Alfonso, Mercedes 109
Alma gitana (1996) 71
Almodóvar, Agustín 30–31, 73, 98; *La ley del deseo* 30; *Matador* 30
Almodóvar, Pedro 109
A los que aman (1996) 71
Al sur de Granada (2002) 110
Álvarez, Marta 13
Álvarez, Mercedes 108, 109
Álvarez, Regina 108
Amenábar, Alejandro 68
A mi madre le gustan las mujeres (2002) 110
Amor de hombre (1997) 71, 72
Amo tu cama, rica (1991) 73
Ander eta Yul (1988) 39, 53

Andreu, Cristina 39, 53, 72
androcentric bias 2, 10–11
androcentrism 2
Atienza, Belén 110
Apache Kid (Bianco Apache) (1986) 54n16
Apaches Entertainment 110
Apocalipsis caníbal (1980) 54n16
Aragón, Manuel Gutiérrez 34
Armendáriz, Montxo 110
Arranz, Fátima 103; *Cine y género en España. Una investigación empírica* 20n1
Arranz, Paloma 98
Arribas, Marta 108, 109
Art department, presence of women in: 1980s *45*; 1990s *78*; 2000s *115*
Así como habían sido (1986) 54–55n16
Association of Cinemas 105
Ataque verbal (1999) 72
Atómica (1998) 73
Atresmedia Cine 110, 111
Austin, Guy 33
Austri, Maite Ruiz de 71, 72, 108
avances sur recettes system 28, 35
Ayaso, Dunia 71, 72, 108, 109
Azuleos, Lisa 90n11, 90n12

Baecque, Antoine de: "La cinéphilie ou l'invention d'une culture" 27, 54n3
Bajo la piel (1996) 73
Baker, Sarah 8n1
Balanza, Teresa Vera 13
Balio, Tino 32
Balletbò-Coll, Marta 71, 72, 108, 109
Balló, Tania 108

Balmaseda, Enrique 16
Bandera negra 30, 31, 54n10
Baquero, Piluca 73, 109
Bardem, Juan Antonio 34, 54n12, 62
Barea, Ramón 109
Baró, Eva 110
Barrera, Lola 108, 109
Barrio (1998) 68
Barrios altos (1987) 41, 55n19
Barroso, Mariano 73
Bartolomé, Cecilia 36, 39, 41, 71, 72
Bayona, Juan Antonio 110
Bearn, o la sala de muñecas (1983) 39, 55n19
Beat, Christoph 96
Belén, Ana 71, 72
Bell, Melanie 13, 19, 41, 74, 102, 133
Belle Epoque (1992) 68
Belmont, Vera 90n11, 90n12
Beltenebros (1991) 71
Bemberg, Maria Luisa 39, 53, 71–72
Bennet, Tony 18
Berlanga, Luis García 34
Besuievsky, Mariela 73, 91n16, 109
Bofarull, Anna Maria 108, 109
Bollaín, Icíar 71–73, 108
Bonet, Eugeni 109
Boom, boom (1990) 71, 73
Borau, José Luis 34, 36
Borrás, Victoria 73
Bosch, Rosa 110
Bourdieu, Pierre: *Distinction. A Social Critique of the Judgements of Taste* 10, 14; on habitus 14; *Rules of Art, The* 10, 14; theory of cultural production 17, 21n2; theory of field 3, 10, 13–15, 17, 20n2, 26
Bridges of Saint Luis Rey, The 98
British Association of Cine-Technicians 5
Brumal (1988) 39
Buil, José 90n11
Buñuel, Joyce 90n11, 90n12

Cabal, Fermín 41
Cabezas, Elisabet 108, 109
Cahiers du Cinéma 4, 27, 36, 95
Calle 54 (2000) 110
Calvo, Carmen 5, 7, 15, 94, 101–103, 133
Cambio de rumbo (1997) 73
Camera and Electrical department, presence of women in: 1980s *47*; 1990s *80*; 2000s *117*

Camila (1984) 39, 53
Camí-Vela, María 13
Campabadal, Núria 108
Campoy, Eduardo 17
Camus, Mario 36
Canal Plus 69
Canals, Cuca 72, 109
Cánovas, Elena 109
Cantero, Mate 73, 110
Capítulo II 66
Cardona, Irena 108
Cariño, he enviado a los hombres a la luna (1998) 71
Carreteras secundarias (1997) 91n14
Casas, Fernando Vizcaíno 54n12
Cataluña-España (2009) 110
CCI *see* cultural and creative industries (CCI)
Cela, Camilo José 33
censorship 27, 35, 37
Cerezo, Ana Simón 71, 72
Chatarra (1991) 73
Che: El argentino (2008) 110
Che: Guerrilla (2009) 110
CIMA *see* Spanish Women's Filmmakers and Audiovisual Professionals Association (CIMA)
cine-club movement 26
Cinéfilos y Cinéfagos. Una aproximación a las culturas y los gustos cinematográficos (Pujol Ozonas) 21n2
Cineinforme 4
Cinemanía 4
Cinemart (2006) 110
Cinematography department, presence of women in: 1990s *86*; 2000s *123*
Cine y género en España. Una investigación empírica (Arranz) 20n1
Civil War 30
Clarín, Leopoldo Alas 33
Clotas, Salvador 33
Cobb, Shelley 3–4, 19
Coixet, Isabel 3, 39, 53, 71, 72, 108, 109
Colell, Judith 71, 72, 108
Coll, Mar 108, 109
Collins, Richard 67
Colomo, Fernando 41, 73, 110
Committee of Ministers: "Declaration on Cultural Diversity" 96
Como ser mujer y no morir en el intento (1991) 71

Contemporary European Cinema (Wood) 33
Copegui, Belén 109
Coraje (1998) 73
Cosas que nunca te dije (1995) 71
Costa Brava, family album (1995) 71
Costa-Gavras 62
Costume and Wardrobe department, presence of women in: 1980s *48*; 1990s *81*; 2000s *118*
Council of Europe: Eurimages Fund 67; "Resolution of 12 February 2001" 96
Craik, Jennifer 18
Crimen en familia (1985) 54n16
Crowther, Andrea Martínez 109
Cuando el mundo se acabe te seguiré amando (1998) 71
Cuando vuelvas a mi lado (1999) 71
Cuentos eróticos (1980) 39
Cuevas, Antonio 60, 61
cultural and creative industries (CCI) 19
cultural capital 34
cultural diversity 95–99
cultural imperialism 101
cultural mode of production 27
cultural policy studies, definition of 18
Cunillés, Jose Maria 39
Cunningham, Stuart 18

Da Vinci Code, The (2006) 104
Decree of 1977 35
de la Fuente, Juliana San José (aka Jackie Kelly) 41, 89
de la Gándara, Beatriz 73, 110
de la Iglesia, Álex 68
del Amo, Álvaro 110
del Castillo, Pilar 15
Delgado, Beatriz 111
Delibes, Miguel 30, 33
Delirios de amor (1984) 39, 53
del Prado, Carolina 108, 109
del Toro, Guillermo 104
de Luque, Paula 109
Demasiado viejo para morir joven (1988) 39, 53
De niños (2003) 110
De Niro, Robert 98
Depravación (1982) 39
¿De qué se rien las mujeres? (1996) 72
Después de... (1981) 39, 41
Dewar, Gabriela Gutiérrez 108, 109
Dewar, Sara Gutiérrez 108, 109

Diamante, Julio 62
Días azules (2006) 111
Días de fútbol (2003) 100
Díaz, Natalia 108
Díez, Ana 39, 53, 71, 72, 108
Di que sí (2004) 110
Dirigido Por 4
Distinction. A Social Critique of the Judgements of Taste (Bourdieu) 10, 14
Dolores, María 73
Domínguez, Trinidad Núñez 13
Doña Bárbara (1998) 90n11
Don Juan, de Moliere (1998) 73, 91n16
Duran, Alberto 73

Echevarría, Alejandro 100
Editorial department, presence of women in: 1980s *50*; 1990s *83*; 2000s *120*
EEC *see* European Economic Community (EEC)
EFE *see* Spanish National News Agency (EFE)
EIGE *see* European Institute for Gender Equality (EIGE)
El amor perjudica seriamente la salud (1996) 72
El apartamento (1995) 73
Elástica Films 111
El baile del pato (1989) 55n18
El caballero del dragón (1985) 29–31, 54n10, 55n18
El canto del loco: la película (2008) 110
El carnaval de las bestias (1980) 55n17
El caso Almería (1984) 54n16
El cometa (1998) 90n11, 90n13
El coronel no tiene quien le escriba (1999) 73
El dedo en la llaga (1996) 73
El Deseo 73, 98, 109
El día de la bestia (1995) 68
El dominio de los sentidos (1996) 71
El efecto mariposa (1995) 73
El espinazo del diablo (2000) 110
El faro (1998) 73
El grito en el cielo (1998) 71
El haren de Madame Osmane (2000) 110
El hijo de la novia (2001) 109
El jardín secreto (1984) 41
El laberinto del fauno (2006) 104, 110
Ellas son así (1999) 72

El Lute: camina o revienta 30, 31, 54n10, 55n16
El Lute II, mañana seré libre (1988) 55n16
El Mundo 4
El País 4, 61, 105
El pájaro de la felicidad (1993) 71
El pecador impecable 30, 31, 54n10
El perro del hortelano (1996) 33, 71
El próximo Oriente (2006) 110
El regreso del viento del norte (1993) 71
El retorno del hombre lobo (1981) 55n17
El robobo de la jojoya (1991) 72
Elsaesser, Thomas 27, 54n4
El ultimo kamikaze (1984) 55n17
El ultimo viaje de Robert Raylands (1996) 71, 73
En la puta calle (1996) 73
Ensueño Films 104
Entre el cielo y la tierra (1990) 73, 90n11
Entre las piernas (1998) 72
Entre rojas (1995) 71, 73
EOC 36, 37
Érase otra vez (1999) 73
Erice, Víctor 34, 36, 95, 125n2
Escolano, Sonia 108, 109
Escudero, José María García 36, 54n12
Eso (1997) 73
España 4
Esquilache (1988) 39
Esteban, Cristina 71
Estoy en crisis (1982) 55n18
Estudios Picasso 104
Etxebarría, Lucía 109
Etxebertz, Alicia Garaialde 108
EU *see* European Union (EU)
Eurimages Fund 67
European Audiovisual Observatory 87
European Commission: MEDIA programme 67, 87; "Strategy for equality between women and men 2010–2015 (COM (2010) 491)" 126n13; "Television without Frontiers" directive (TVWF directive or 89/225/EEC) 67; "The EU Approach to the WTO Millennium Round" 97
European cultural policy 13
European Economic Community (EEC) 11, 32, 59, 67

European Institute for Gender Equality (EIGE) 125n9
European Union (EU) 11, 97, 98
Éxtasis (1996) 73

Falkner, Dolores 109
FAPAE 17, 99–101, 103–105, 125, 126n23
Faulkner, Sally 37
FECE 103, 105
Fejerman, Daniela 108, 110
feminism 10; first wave 17; second wave 17
feminist policy analysis 11, 20
Fernández, Ana Rosa 108
Fernández, Verónica 109
Fernández-Martorell, Mercedes 108, 109
Ferreira, Patricia 71, 72, 108
Figuera, Candela 109
Film Editing department, presence of women in: 1980s *42*; 1990s *75*; 2000s *112*
Film Policy. International, National and Regional Perspectives (Moran) 18–19
Film Protection Fund 29, 63
First Democratic Conference on Spanish Cinema of 1978 34
First World War 11
Flores de otro mundo (1999) 71
Foix, Vicente Molina 110
Fontaine, Anne 90n11, 90n12
Forbes, Jill 27
FORTA 103
Fotogramas 4
Fox 104
Frade, José 34, 60, 61
Franco, Francisco 132
Franco, Jesús 34, 35, 39, 72, 73
Frémaux, Thierry: "La cinéphilie ou l'invention d'une culture" 27, 54n3
Frontera Sur (1998) 73
Fuga de cerebros (2009) 110
Función de noche (1981) 39

Gabilondo, Mireia 108
Gabriel, Enrique 73
Galán, Diego 34, 36, 94
Galdós, Benito Pérez 33
Gamero, Mercedes 110
García, Esther 73, 109

García, Lupe Pérez 108
García, Pilar 108
García-López, Sonia 13
Gardela, Isabell 71, 72
Garrido, Eva 111
Gary Cooper que estás en los cielos (1989) 37, 39
GATT's Uruguay Round (1986–1994) 96
gender-based violence 98, 99
gendered division of labour 41, 53, 87, 101, 124
gender equality 2, 4, 8, 10–13, 20, 95–99, 101–103, 105, 106, 124, 126n13, 131
gender inequality 1–2, 4–6, 8, 13, 20, 21n4, 39, 89, 102, 103, 105, 125; structural 11, 19, 131–134
gender mainstreaming 125n9
gender regime 19–20, 21n4, 132
gender stereotypes 42
Gill, Rosalind 19, 21n3
Godoy, Carmen Rico 72, 109
Goenaga, Aitzpea 108, 109
Gómez, Libia Stella 108
González, Felipe 35, 62
González, Libia Estella 109
González-Sinde, Ángeles 15, 72, 105, 108, 109
Gozalvo, Susi 108, 109
Grandes, Almudena 109; *Las edades de Lulú* 72; *Malena es un nombre de tango* 72
Greenaway, Peter 110
Guardans, Ignasi 16, 105
Guardia Civil 35
Guerrero, Lola 108
Gutiérrez, Chus 71, 72, 108, 110
Gutiérrez, Pilar Ruíz 108, 109

habitus 16; definition of 14
Hablamos esta noche (1982) 37, 39
Hainsworth, Paul 67
Halioua, Sarah 110
Hänsel, Marion 73, 90n11, 90n12
Heredero, Carlos 37, 52
Hermida, Alicia 39
Hermida, Tania 108, 109
Hernández, Antonio 104
Hernández, Ione 108
Herrera, Lucía 108
Herrero, Gerardo 17, 73, 91n16

Herrero, Lola 109
Hesmondhalgh, David 8n1
Higson, Andrew 32–33
Historia de la política de fomento del cine español (Vallés Copeiro del Villar) 12
Hola, ¿estás sola? (1995) 71, 73
Holy Girl, The 99
Hombres que rugen (1984) 41
Hopewell, John 37, 52, 54n2
Hot Milk (2004) 110
Howard, Ron 104
Huete, Ana 41, 72, 89, 110
Huete, Cristina 73
Huevos de oro (1993) 72
Huida al sur: la desbandada (1981) 54n16
Hunter, Ian 18

Ibarra, Herminia 6
Ibarra, Mirtha 108, 109
Iberia 104
Iborra, Juan Luis 71, 110
Iborra, Manuel 14, 72, 73
ICAA *see* Spanish Film Institute (ICAA, General Direction of Cinematography)
Ice Age: The Meltdown (2006) 104
ICPS *see* Institute for Cultural Policy Studies (ICPS)
"*l'état culturel*" (the cultural State) 31
Ilarraz, Estela 108, 109
IMDB *see* International Movie Data Base (IMDB)
Imperiale, Laura 110
Insomnio (1998) 71
Institute for Cultural Policy Studies (ICPS) 18
International Movie Data Base (IMDB) 3, 5
intersectionality 6, 99
Ipiña, Nahikari 111
Iquino, Ignacio F. 41

Jamón, jamón (1992) 72
Jones, Deborah 21n4
Jordá, Joaquin 71, 110–111
Jordan, Barry 66

Kaleya, Tania 39, 71
Kaplan, Betty 90n11, 90n12

Kastner, Daphna 90n11, 90n12
Kendrigan, Mary Lou 11
Killer Barbys (1996) 73
Kleber, Eugenia 71, 72
Koska, Susana 108, 109

La bestia y la espada mágica (1983) 55n17
La buena vida (1996) 73, 91n14
La caja 507 (2001) 110
La camarera del Titanic (1997) 72
"La cinéphilie ou l'invention d'une culture" (de Baecque and Frémaux) 27, 54n3
La desnuda chica del relax (1981) 41
Ladoire, Oscar 41
La excepción cultural. El futuro del cine español 125n2
La flor de mi secreto (1995) 73
La gran aventura de Mortadelo y Filemón (2003) 100
Lágrimas negras (1998) 72
La guerre est finie (*The War is Over*, 1966) 62
Laguna, Mónica 71, 72, 108
La industria del cine en España: legislación y aspectos económicos 1896–1970 (Pozo Arenas) 12
La ley del deseo (Almodóvar) 30
La leyenda de la doncella (1994) 73
La línea del cielo (1983) 55n18
La Lola se va a los puertos (1993) 71
Lamet, Juan Miguel 16, 34–36, 38
La moños (1996) 71
La mujer del cosmonauta (1997) 73
La mujer sin piano (2009) 111
La niña santa (2004) 109
La noche del cine español (1978–1982) 94
La primera noche de mi vida (1998) 72
Lara, Fernando 5, 7, 16, 34–36, 89, 94, 101, 103, 133
Las aventuras de Enrique y Ana (1981) 55n19
Las bicicletas son para el verano (1984) 39, 41, 55n19
Las chicas de hoy en día (1991–1992) 72
Las chicas del tanga (1983) 39
Las edades de Lulú (Grandes) 72
Las huellas borradas (1999) 73
Las mantenidas sin sueños (2007) 111
La teta y la luna (1994) 72

Latidos de pánico (1983) 55n17
L'Aveu (*The Confession*, 1970) 62
La vida alegre (1987) 55n18
La vida prometida (1999) 73
La vida secreta de las palabras (2005) 109
La vieja música 30, 31, 54n10
La virgen de la lujuria (2001) 110
Law 1/2004 98
Law 55/2007 2, 7, 11, 94, 97, 98, 101, 103–125, 133, 134; Artículo 4 105; Artículo 19 (g) 105; Artículo 22 105; Artículo 23 105; Artículo 25 105; Artículo 26 105; Artículo 28 105; Artículo 29 105
Lazaga, Pedro 54n6
Lázaro, Emilio Martínez 72
Lázaro-Reboll, Antonio: *Spanish Horror Film* 20n2; *Spanish Popular Cinema* 20n2
Lazkano, Arantxa 71, 72
Lecchi, Alberto 73
Lejos de África (1996) 71
León, Victor García 110
Lesmes, Eva 71, 72, 108
Ley 3/2007: Artículo 1 98; Artículo 26 101; Artículo 36 98; Artículo 36–41 98; Artículo 37–38 98; Artículo 39 98
Ley 6/2015 127n37
Ley 17/1994 59, 69
Ley 557/2007 88
Liddy, Susan: *Women in the International Film Industry: Policy, Practice, Power* 19
Lidón, María 108
Limpieza en seco (1997) 90n11
Lindo, Elvira 72, 109
Lluvia en los zapatos (1998) 71
Lo más natural (1990) 71
Lombardi, Francisco 110
Lorenzo, Regina Álvarez 109
Lorenzo, Santiago 73
Los años bárbaros (1998) 73
Los años oscuros (1993) 71
Los baúles del retorno (1995) 71
Los Borgia (2006) 104
Los condenados (2009) 110
Los crímenes de Oxford 109
Los cronocrímenes (2007) 111
Losilla, Carlos 53
Los nuevos curanderos (1986) 39, 53

Index

Los porretas (1996) 73
Los santos inocentes 30
Loureiro, Chalo 111
Lozano, Mabel 108, 109
Luna, Bigas 72

Macho, Enrique González 105
Macías, Belén 108
Makeup and Hairdressing department, presence of women in: 1980s *49*; 1990s *82*; 2000s *119*
Makinavaja (1995–1997) 73
Makinavaja, el ultimo chorizo (1992) 73
Mala leche (2006) 110
Malena es un nombre de tango (Grandes) (1996) 72, 73
Mallorca's Song (2007) 110
¡Mamá, préstame a papa! (1999) 90n11
Mamá es boba (1998) 73
Mambí (1997) 73
Mañá, Laura 71, 72, 108, 109
Manifest, The 61
Manolito Gafotas (1999) 68, 72, 73
Maqua, Javier 95, 125n2
Mararía (1998) 73
Marías, Miguel 5, 7, 12, 63, 132
Marquise (1998) 90n11, 90n13
Martel, Lucrecia 98, 109
Martínez, Andrea 108
Martín-Márquez, Susan 13
Mas, Helena 109
Más pena que Gloria (2000) 110
Más que amor, frenesí (1996) 73
Matador (Almodóvar) 30
Matas, Alfredo 34, 39, 41, 60
Matas, Helena 72–73, 89
Mayo, Lola 109
McGuckian, Mary 98
McPhail, Beverly A. 10, 20
McQuail, Denis 97
Mediapro 104
Mediaproducción 104
MEDIA programme 67, 87
Mediaset 110, 111
Medina, Elena 108, 109
Megino, Luis 34, 36, 60
Me llamo Sara (1998) 71
Méndez Leite, Fernando 5, 11–12, 16, 39, 61, 63, 94
Menkes, David 73
Mercer, Colin 18
methodological issues 3–6

Miller, Toby 18
Ministry of Culture 15, 31–32, 63, 66, 72, 101, 132
Ministry of Education 15, 62
Ministry of Sports 15
Miró, María 71, 72
Miró, Pilar 3, 5, 15, 35, 36, 71, 131; and classic cinephilia 36–38
Miró Law 26–36, 53, 54n7, 59–68, 87, 89, 94, 95, 102, 132; changes in subtitles **65**; effects on film industry 38–53, *40, 42–52*
Mi vida sin mí (2002) 109
Molina, César Antonio 15, 37, 39
Molina, Josefina 3, 71
Monos como Becky (1999) 71
Montejo, Julia 108
Monterde, José Enrique 16, 52
Moran, Albert: *Film Policy. International, National and Regional Perspectives* 18–19
movie workers 13
Mucha sangre (2002) 111
Mujeres (1983) 39
Mujeres a flor de piel (1991) 90n11
Mula, Isabel 39, 41, 53, 71, 72, 89
Mundo Joven 37
Munt, Silvia 108
Murugarren, Ana 108, 109
Muruzabal, Maitena 108, 109
Music department, presence of women in: 1980s *52*; 1990s *85*; 2000s *122*

Nacional III (1982) 55n19
Nadar (2008) 110
Nanas de espinas (1984) 39
Naschy, Paul 41
Navarrete, Beatriz 110
Navarro, Bertha 110
NCE *see* New Spanish Cinema (NCE)
new democratic cinema, making 26–55
New Spanish Cinema (NCE) 36–38, 53
Nicolau, Meritxell 108
No desearás al vecino del quinto 34
Novaro, María 108

Oakley, Ann 3
Objetivo 62
Oh, cielos (1994) 72
Ojalá, Val de Omar (1994) 71
Old Man Bebo (2008) 110
Olea, Pedro 36
Olivé-Bellés, Nuria 71, 72

Operación mantis (1984) 55n17
Opera prima (1980) 55n18
oppression 4, 18, 20, 36
Orden CUD/582/2020 126n22
Orden CUL/2834/2009 105, 124; Artículo 22 106; Artículo 28 106; Artículo 53 106; Artículo 99 106
O'Regan, Tom 18
Oria, Puy 110
Orquesta Club Virginia (1992) 91n14
Ortega, Elena 108, 109
Ortega, Josefa María Silva 13
Ortega, Vicente Rodríguez 89
Otero, José María 16, 88
Ozores, Mariano 54n6, 60, 61

Padrón, María Mercedes Alfonso 108
Paisito (2009)
Palacio, Manuel 26, 37
París, Inés 5, 101–103, 108–110
Passola, Isona 108–110
Patino, Basilio Martín 34, 36, 54n12
Pavlovic, Tatjana 69
Payás, Dolores 71, 72, 108, 109
PCE *see* Spanish Communist Party (PCE)
Pecourt, Juan 34
Pelegrí, Teresa 71, 72, 108, 109
Películas Pendelton S.A 100
Peñas, Yalda 108
Pepa y Pepe (1995) 72
Pepe Guindo (1999) 73
Perdona bonita, pero Lucas me quería a mí (1996) 71
Pereira, Manuel Gómez 72
Pérez, Ana 108, 109
Pérez, Pedro 17, 99–101
Petro, Patrice 2, 3
Picazo, Miguel 36
Pinza, Juan 73, 110
Pirates of the Caribbean: Dead Man's Chest (2006) 104
Planet 51 (2009) 110
political economy of film 18, 19
Poniente (2002) 110
Pon un hombre en tu vida (1996) 71
Popular Party (PP) 15, 16, 133
Porchez, Sylvie 73
¿Por qué lo llaman amor cuando quieren decir sexo? (1991) 72
Pozo Arenas, Santiago: *La industria del cine en España: legislación y aspectos económicos 1896–1970* 12

PP *see* Popular Party (PP)
Pringle, Judith K. 21n4
PRISA 100
Production Management department, presence of women in: 1980s *43*; 1990s *76*; 2000s *113*
PSOE *see* Socialist Party (PSOE)
Puede ser divertido (1995) 71, 72, 73
Puenzo, Lucía 109
Pujol, Ariadna 108, 109
Pujol Ozonas, Cristina 27, 37; *Cinéfilos y Cinéfagos. Una aproximación a las culturas y los gustos cinematográficos* 21n2

qualitative methods 4
quantitative methods 4, 8n3
Quer, Silvia 108
Querejeta, Elías 29, 34, 38, 60, 62, 72, 73
Querejeta, Gracia 71, 108, 109
¡Qué vecinos tan animales! (1998) 71
¡Que vienen los socialistas! 54n6

Rajoy, Mariano 15
Real Decreto 1039/1997 59, 90n3
Real Decreto 1282/1989 *see* Semprún Decree
Real Decreto 1773/1991 90n5
Real Decreto 3304/1983 131
Rebollo, Javier 109
Regueiro, Francisco 36
Reguera, Nely 108, 109
Resnais, Alain 62
Retrato de una mujer con hombre al fondo (1996) 71
Riambau, Esteve 52, 95, 125n2
Ripoll, María 71, 72, 108
Ripstein, Arturo 110
Rivales (2008) 110
Roda, Patricia 111
Rodríguez, Azucena 71–73, 108
Rodríguez, Mananae 71, 72, 108, 109
Romay, Lina 39, 71
Romero, Manuel Trenzado 31
Romero, Rosa 73
Ros, Mireia 71, 72, 108, 109
Rosado, Lilian 108
Rosell, Ana Rodríguez 108, 109
Rotaeta, Félix 73
Rules of Art, The (Bourdieu) 10, 14

Saavedra, Katy 109
Sabroso, Félix 71

Sagitario (2000) 110
Saldanha, Carlos 104
¡Salsa! (1999); 90n11
Salsa Rosa (1991) 68, 72
Salvador, Lola 39, 72, 89, 108, 109
Salvador Puig Antich (2006) 111
Saly, Julia 41
Sánchez, Diana 108
Sánchez, Domingo 39
Sánchez, Eva López 108
Sánchez, Ione Hernández 109
Sánchez, José Luís García 72
San Juan, Antonia 108, 109
Sanmartí, Anna 108, 109
Sarmiento, Valeria 108
Saura, Carlos 34, 61
Scholz, Annette 13
School Killer (2000) 110
Schwarzenegger, Arnold 32
Scott, Jacqueline 4
Script and Continuity department, presence of women in: 1980s *51*; 1990s *84*; 2000s *121*
Second Unit or Assistant Director department, presence of women in: 1980s *44*; 1990s *77*; 2000s *114*
Secretos del corazón (1997) 68
Secta siniestra (1982) 41
Segovia, Mercedes 108
Segunda piel (1999) 72
Segura, Santiago 68
Se infiel y no mires con quién 30, 31, 54n10
¡Semos peligrosos! (usease Makinavaja 2) (1993) 73
Semprún, Jorge 5, 7, 15, 62
Semprún Decree 7, 59, 60, 63–69, 88, 89, 90n2, 90n5, 90n6, 132; changes in the subsidies **65**
Sé quién eres (1999) 71
Serna, Sandra 108
Serrano, Yolanda García 71, 72, 108, 109
sexism: definition of 21n3
Sexo oral (1994) 71
Sexo por compasión (1999) 71
Shang, Solomón 111
Silva, Beatriz Flores 108
Sin noticias de Dios (2001) 110
Sistach, Marisa 72, 90n11, 90n12
Smith, Paul Julian 20n2
Socialist Party (PSOE) 11, 15, 16, 26, 27, 31–35, 53, 60, 66–67, 89; cultural policy 95–99

Soderbergh, Steven 110
Solana, Javier 15, 62
Solo o en compañía de otros (1990) 90n13
Sony Pictures Releasing 104
Sound department, presence of women in: 1980s *46*; 1990s *79*; 2000s *116*
Souvenir (1994) 71
Spanish Communist Party (PCE) 54n12, 62
Spanish film industry 14–17; methodological issues 3–6; weak nature of 1; *see also individual entries*
Spanish Film Institute (ICAA, General Direction of Cinematography) 3–5, 8n4, 15, 16, 38, 39, 63, 100, 101, 103, 127n37, 131, 132
Spanish Fly (1997) 90n11
Spanish Horror Film (Lázaro-Reboll) 20n2
Spanish National News Agency (EFE) 98
Spanish National Television (TVE) 29, 36, 54n8, 66, 94, 98, 103
Spanish Popular Cinema (Lázaro-Reboll and Willis) 20n2
Spanish Women's Filmmakers and Audiovisual Professionals Association (CIMA) 5, 8n4, 64, 101–105, 125, 126n20, 127n37, 133
Spirit of the Beehive, The (1973) 125n2
S-rated production 28, 54n6
Stallone, Sylvester 32
Street, Sarah 27
structural discrimination 11
Suay, Ricardo Muñoz 54n12, 62
Sub-committee for Technical Valorisation 30, 61, 66
Subirana, Carla 108, 109
Sublet (1992) 71
Sueiro, Pilar 71–73, 110
Summers, Manuel 60, 61
Sweden 11–12

Tabernas, Helena 71, 72, 108, 109
TACE 126n20
Tapia, Gonzalo 109
Tasio 29, 31, 54n10
Távora, Pilar 39, 71, 72, 108
Tejedor, María Concepción Martínez 13
Telecinco Cinema 110
"Television without Frontiers" directive (TVWF directive or 89/225/EEC) 67

Tengo una casa (1995) 71, 73
Territorio comanche (1997) 73, 91n16
Tesis (1996) 68
Tetro (2009) 109
theory of cultural production 17, 21n2
theory of field 3, 10, 13–15, 17, 20n2, 26
Thornham, Sue 17–18
Tic Tac (1997) 71
Tierno verano de lujurias y azoteas (1993) 72, 73
Todo es mentira (1994) 68
Todo está oscuro (1997) 71
Todos a la cárcel (1993) 68
Todos los hombres sois iguales (1994) 72
Torre, Lucinda 108
Torreiro, Casimiro 36, 54n6
Torrente, el brazo tonto de la ley (1998) 68
Torres, Lucinda 109
Torturado por las rosas (1998) 71
Treaty of Rome (1958): Article 8 126n13
Triana-Toribio, Nuria 26, 28, 30, 32, 69, 94
Trigo, Andrea 108
Triunfo 34, 94
Trueba, David 72
Trueba, Fernando 41, 68
Tu nombre evenena mis sueños (1996) 71
Tu novia está loca 30, 31, 54n10
Tura, Jordi Solé 15
Turckheim, Charlotte de 90n11, 90n12
TVE *see* Spanish National Television (TVE)
Two Much (1995) 73

Una estación de paso (1992) 71
Un buen dia lo tiene cualquiera (2007) 111
UNESCO 95; "Convention on the Protection and Promotion of the Diversity of Cultural Expressions" 97
Un soltero con mucha cuerda (1993) 90n13
UPCE 17, 34, 35, 64
Urbizu, Enrique 72
UTECA 17, 100, 101, 103, 105, 125

Va a ser que nadie es perfecto (2006) 111
Vallé-Inclán, Ramón del 33

Vallés Copeiro del Villar, Antonio: *Historia de la política de fomento del cine español* 12
Vega, Lope de 33
Veloso,. Marta Arribas 109
Vera, Gerardo 72
Verbinski, Gore 104
Vergés, Rosa 71–73, 108, 109
Vicente Gómez, Andrés 60–61
Vicky, Cristina, Barcelona (2008) 111
Vidal-Beneyto, José 31
Vigalondo, Nacho 111
Vilardell, Teresa 109
Villalaín, María Pilar 108
Villanueva, Mariví de 110
Villazán, Nuria 71, 72, 108, 109
Virino, Concepción Cascajosa 13
Vitoria, José Antonio 110
Volaverunt (1999) 72, 73
Vorvilk (2005) 110

Wasko, Janet 18
Whelehan, Imelda 17
Werther (1986) 39, 41
Wilder, Thornton 98
Williams, Linda Ruth 19
Willis, Andrew: *Spanish Popular Cinema* 20n2
Women and Film 18
Women in the International Film Industry: Policy, Practice, Power (Liddy) 19
Wood, Mary P.: *Contemporary European Cinema* 33
World Trade Organisation (WTO) 94; Doha Agenda 97; "Millennium Round" 96
Wreyford, Natalie 3–4, 19
WTO *see* World Trade Organisation (WTO)

X-rated production 28

Yanes, Agustín Diaz 104
Yerma (1998) 71
Yo amo la danza (1984) 41
Yoyes (1999) 71

Z (1969) 62
Zamora, María 111
Zapatero, José Luís Rodríguez 94
Zapatero, Rodríguez 105
Zecchi, Barbara 13
Zimmermann, Lydia 108
Zunzunegui, Santos 52

For Product Safety Concerns and Information please contact our EU representative GPSR@taylorandfrancis.com
Taylor & Francis Verlag GmbH, Kaufingerstraße 24, 80331 München, Germany

www.ingramcontent.com/pod-product-compliance
Lightning Source LLC
Chambersburg PA
CBHW051749230426
43670CB00012B/2216